INTERNATIONAL ORGANIZATIONS AND SMALL STATES

Participation, Legitimacy and Vulnerability

Jack Corbett, Xu Yi-chong and Patrick Weller

I0134959

B BRISTOL
UNIVERSITY
PRESS

First published in Great Britain in 2023 by

Bristol University Press
University of Bristol
1-9 Old Park Hill
Bristol
BS2 8BB
UK
t: +44 (0)117 374 6645
e: bup-info@bristol.ac.uk

Details of international sales and distribution partners are available at bristoluniversitypress.co.uk

© Bristol University Press 2023

British Library Cataloguing in Publication Data
A catalogue record for this book is available from the British Library

ISBN 978-1-5292-0768-2 hardcover
ISBN 978-1-5292-0769-9 paperback
ISBN 978-1-5292-0772-9 ePub
ISBN 978-1-5292-0771-2 ePdf

Cover design: Andrew Corbett
Front cover image: Bigstock/zhudifeng

Contents

List of Tables

List of Acronyms

ACP	African, Caribbean, and Pacific Group of States
ADB	Asian Development Bank
AOSIS	Alliance of Small Islands States
BINGOs	Business Interest Non-Governmental Organizations
BRICS	Brazil, Russia, India, China, and South Africa
C20	Committee of Twenty
CARICOM	Caribbean Community and Common Market
CO_2	Carbon Dioxide
CoCo	Coordination Committee
ComSec	Commonwealth Secretariat
COP	Conference of the Parties
COP21	2015 United Nations Climate Change Conference
CTD	Committee on Trade and Development
DFAT	Australian Department of Foreign Affairs and Trade
DG	Director General
DICs	Developing Island Countries
EB	Executive Board
EC	European Commission
ECOSOC	United Nations Economic and Social Council
EDs	Executive Directors
EOs	External Offices
EU	European Union
FAO	Food and Agriculture Organization
FfD	Financing for Development
FOC	Flag of Convenience
FOSS	Forum of Small States
FY	Fiscal Year
GATT	General Agreement on Tariffs and Trade
GDP	Gross Domestic Product
GHG	Greenhouse Gas
GNI	Gross National Income
GVCs	Global Value Chains

HAC	High Ambition Coalition
HIPCs	Heavily Indebted Poor Countries
HIV	Human Immunodeficiency Virus
HQs	Head Quarters
IAEA	International Atomic Energy Agency
IAPH	International Association of Ports and Harbours
IBRD	International Bank for Reconstruction and Development
ICHCA	International Cargo Handling Coordination Association
ICS	International Civil Servant
IDA	International Development Association
IEG	Independent Evaluation Group
IEO	Evaluation Office of the International Monetary Fund
ILO	International Labour Organization
IMF	International Monetary Fund
IMFC	Monetary and Financial Committee
IMO	International Maritime Organization
INC	Intergovernmental Negotiating Committee
IOs	International Organizations
IP	Intellectual Property
IPCC	Intergovernmental Panel on Climate Change
IR	International Relations
IRI	International Registries Inc.
ISWG-GHG	Intersessional Working Group on Reduction of GHG Emissions
IUU	Illegal, Unreported, or Unregulated
LDC	Least Developed Country
LIO	Liberal International Order
MCST	Micronesian Center for Sustainable Transport
MDGs	Millennium Development Goals
MDRI	Multilateral Debt Relief Initiatives
MEPC	Marine Environment Protection Committee
MGSS	Ministerial Group on Small States
MIRAB	Migration, Remittances, Aid, and Bureaucracy
NAMA	Non-Agricultural Market Access
NCDs	Non-Communicable Diseases
NGOs	Non-Governmental Organizations
NIEO	New International Economic Order
NY	New York
OAS	Organization of American States
ODA	Official Development Assistance
OECD	Organisation of Economic Co-operation and Development

OECS	Organization of Eastern Caribbean States
OHCHR	Office of the United Nations High Commissioner for Human Rights
OPCS	Operations Policy and Country Services
PACER	Pacific Agreement on Closer Economic Relations
PAHO	Pan American Health Organization
PETAC	Pacific Financial Technical Assistance
PIDF	Pacific Islands Development Forum
PIFS	Pacific Islands Forum Secretariat
PINGOs	Pastoralists Indigenous Non-Governmental Organizations
PM	Prime Minister
PNG	Papua New Guinea
PR	Permanent Representative
PROFIT	People, Resource Management, Overseas Engagement, Finances, and Transportation
PSIDS	Pacific Small Island Developing States
QUAD	Quadrilateral Security Dialogue
RMI	The Republic of the Marshall Islands
S&DT	Special and Differential Treatment
SAMOA Pathway	SIDS Accelerated Modalities of Action
SHAC	Shipping High Ambition Coalition
SIDS	Small Island Developing States
SIEs	Small Island Economies
SITE	Small Island Tourist Economy
SNIJs	Small Non-Sovereign Jurisdictions
SPS	Sanitary and Phytosanitary
SVEs	Small and Vulnerable Economies
TBT	Technical Barriers to Trade
TOURAB	Tourism, Remittances, Aid, and Bureaucracy
TRIPs	Trade-Related Aspects of Intellectual Property Rights
UCL	University College London
UK	United Kingdom
UN	United Nations
UNCTAD	United Nations Conference on Trade and Development
UNDESA	United Nations Department of Economic and Social Affairs
UNDP	United Nations Development Programme
UNESCO	United Nations Educational, Scientific and Cultural Organization
UNFCCC	United Nations Framework Convention on Climate Change
UNGA	United Nations General Assembly

UNHRC	United Nations Human Rights Council
UN-OHRLLS	United Nations Office of the High Representative for the Least Developed Countries, Landlocked Developing Countries and Small Island Developing States
UNSC	United Nations Security Council
UNSIDS	United Nations Conference on Small Island Developing States
UPU	United Postal Union
US	United States
USP	University of the South Pacific
VPs	Vice President
WB	World Bank
WBG	World Bank Group
WHA	World Health Assembly
WHO	World Health Organization
WIPO	World Intellectual Property Organization
WTO	World Trade Organization

Acknowledgements

This book would not have been possible without generous assistance from others. Most obviously we owe a substantial debt to our interviewees and informants who have educated us on the interaction between international organizations (IOs) and small states. Special thanks go to those who facilitated our access to key meetings at the United Nations (UN) General Assembly, International Maritime Organization (IMO), and United Nations Human Rights Council (UNHRC). We have taken these stories and experiences and identified patterns and trends relevant to the academic literature. We hope that in the process we have retained a sense of the practical urgency and importance of the issues we discuss for those who live them each day.

Our efforts have been greatly assisted by three research assistants: Nienke Van de Maat, Melodie Ruwet, and Diana Leon-Espinoza. Chapter 4 in particular includes sections that have been drawn from an article we published with Melodie: Corbett, J, et al (2020) 'Climate governance, policy entrepreneurs and small states: explaining policy change at the International Maritime Organisation', *Environmental Politics*, 29(5): 825–44. We thank Melodie for her permission to include those sections here.

This book has also benefitted from discussions with numerous colleagues at our respective institutions: the University of Southampton and Griffith University. Jack in particular benefitted from comments received during visits and talks at the Islands and Small States Institute at the University of Malta and would like to thank Godfrey Baldacchino, Stefano Moncada, and Lino Briguglio for making those trips possible. We received helpful comments from participants at the AGORA V workshop at the University of Warwick in 2014 and the Pacific Islands Political Science Association conference at the Université de la Nouvelle-Calédonie in 2019. We are also indebted to colleagues and collaborators far and wide with whom we have discussed this book and its findings. Particular thanks go to: Baldur Thorhallsson, Anders Wivel, Wouter Veenendaal, John Connell, Jessica Byron, Matt Bishop, Külli Sarapuu, Tennyson Joseph, Wendy Grenade, Stephanie Lawson, Tom Long, Jason Sharman, and George Carter.

Sections of this book have been published previously as journal articles. In addition to the article on the IMO, we are grateful for permission to use material from:

- Corbett, J., Xu, Y.-C., and Weller, P. (2018) 'Climate change and the active participation of small states in international organisations', *The Round Table*, 107(1): 103–5.
- Corbett, J., Xu, Y.-C., and Weller, P. (2018) 'Small states and the "throughput" legitimacy of international organizations', *Cambridge Review of International Affairs*, 31(2): 183–202.
- Corbett, J., Xu, Y.-C., and Weller, P. (2019) 'Norm entrepreneurship and diffusion "from below" in international organisations: How the competent performance of vulnerability generates benefits for small states', *Review of International Studies*, 45(4): 647–68.

We are indebted to reviewers at each of these journals for their comments and criticisms that have helped us refine our arguments.

Our specific gratitude to the team at BUP, including Stephen Wenham for his patience, and Caroline Astley, Helen Flitton, and their team for handling the production process so smoothly.

Finally, we would like to thank the Australian Research Council (grant number DP160100897) for providing the funding to make this research possible.

1

Introduction

On 11 July 2018 the United Nations Security Council (UNSC) met to debate the nexus between climate change and security. In total, 19 countries participated in the discussion.[1] In addition to the president (Sweden) and the permanent members, statements were invited from countries for whom climate change is already having a significant impact, including regional representatives from Africa, Central America, the Middle East, the Caribbean, and the Pacific. A statement was also delivered by the Maldives on behalf of the Alliance of Small Islands States (AOSIS). Egypt was invited to make a statement as chair of the G77 but declined at the last minute. No nation explicitly dissented to the discussion taking place. This was not the first time the UNSC had debated the nexus between climate change and security, having previously discussed the issue in 2007 and 2011. At the 2007 meeting more than 50 countries participated. In 2011 that number grew to over 60. On both occasions, views were essentially split with EU countries and some climate-affected small states on one side, and the G77 plus China on the other. This latter group were opposed to the UNSC, rather than the United Nations Framework Convention on Climate Change (UNFCCC) or the Second Committee, being used as the forum for these discussions.

The difference between 2007 and 2011, and 2018, raises important questions. First, why did climate change get placed on the UNSC agenda in 2007 and 2011, and again in 2018, despite initial opposition from large and powerful states in the G77 plus China grouping? Second, why is there such a difference in the number of countries speaking on this issue and their views, as evidenced by the strong statement of the G77 against using the UNSC as a venue to debate climate change in 2007 and 2011, and their silence in 2018? The short answer is the increased level of coordinated engagement of the smallest members of the international system – Small Island Developing

States (SIDS) and those from the Pacific (PSIDS) in particular – who learnt from the experience of 2011 and adapted their strategy for 2018.

The PSIDS bloc backed Sweden's bid for a temporary seat on the UNSC in return for their support on two issues: Oceans (the UN had held an Oceans Conference in 2017 and appointed the former permanent representative for Fiji, and former president of the United Nations General Assembly (UNGA), as UN Envoy for the Ocean) and a debate on climate change and security in the UNSC. Arguing that climate change was intensifying security threats in the Lake Chad region, Somalia, West Africa, and the Sahel, Sweden delivered on the promise to the PSIDS when they took over the presidency in mid-2018.

Historically, the G77 approach to climate negotiations has been that no developing country should be bound by an emissions deal. This resulted in a schism between large states such as China, India, Brazil, and others, and members of AOSIS who are neither big polluters or among the very poorest states in the world (Bishop and Payne, 2012: 1542). On this basis, the 2018 UNSC debate was likely to follow 2007 and 2011, with Russia, China, and the G77 the key dissenting voices. Reflecting this earlier position, when the G77 Chair, Egypt, circulated their draft statement it echoed the wording of the 2007 and 2011 debates:

> The Group of 77 and China underlines the importance of the General Assembly, the Security Council and the ECOSOC to work within their respective mandates as set out in the United Nations Charter. The Group underscores that the primary responsibility of the United Nations Security Council is the maintenance of international peace and security, as stipulated in the relevant articles of the Charter of the United Nations ... we reiterate our expectation that the initiative of the Security Council to hold this debate does not create a precedent that undermines the mandate of UN principal organs, relevant bodies, processes and instruments that address this issue in all its complexities.

The eight PSIDS members of the G77 were not satisfied:

> '[The] G77 ... basically ignored us ... Nauru [chair of the PSIDS] came and was like "G77 is still inscribed on the speakers list". They were like "please, other countries, can you also object". Then we started texting, like "I've just sent this to G77" and "I've just sent that to G77". "Okay, let's expect that there will be a meeting tomorrow" ... at six o'clock in the morning the email is out, "it's going to be in Room One at nine o'clock, everybody come".' (Interview with PSIDS diplomat)

Egypt called a last-minute meeting on the morning of the debate in an attempt to resolve the differences between the PSIDS and the rest of the G77. Representatives from all eight of the PSIDS attended. They sat together as a group. The Permanent Representative (PR) for Fiji, as president of Conference of the Parties (COP), and Nauru, as chair of the PSIDS, spoke on their behalf. Fiji's PR was the most senior diplomat in the room. He argued that PSIDS were 'frontline states' from a security perspective and were therefore adamant that this issue needed to be debated in the UNSC. The chair asked whether there were any amendments that could be made to the draft statement that the PSIDS would endorse. Nauru then spoke and emphasized the importance of solidarity, arguing that while the UNSC's mandate was to deal with war and conflict, climate change was the security issue of the day and should be treated the same as HIV, Ebola, and other non-traditional threats that have been addressed by the UNSC.

In the ensuing discussion Argentina, Algeria, Ethiopia, China, Venezuela, India, Kuwait, South Africa, and Saudi Arabia opposed the PSIDS and spoke in support of the draft statement. Aside from other Pacific states, like Papua New Guinea (PNG), the only voice who supported the PSIDS was Costa Rica who argued that given the lack of consensus the G77 should decline to give a statement. In the end the Chair agreed with Costa Rica on the grounds that there was not enough time to reach a consensus and therefore the G77 would decline Sweden's invitation to speak on this issue. The PSIDS would have preferred that they had given a supportive statement but overall were pleased:

> 'It's taken a long time to tone back hostility within G77. It's a number of countries, including some of the bigger ones, that are very hostile. But we've over the years gained a little more ground and a little more ground and a little more ground.' (Interview with PSIDS diplomat)

A key reason for this has been the effects of climate change itself, as this SIDS diplomat reflected:

> 'More countries have realized that climate change is becoming a security issue to their countries … the African countries [in particular] have realised that the climate change has security implications. So that's why a lot of the focus in the Security Council now are on the Lake Chad Basin, Somalia and the other resolutions that have come out that makes the clear [links between] climate change [and] insecurity.' (Interview with SIDS diplomat)

But the effects do not put themselves on the agenda; countries have to lobby for them to be there and that is where the PSIDS have been crucial:

> 'But at the end of the day G77 is only what the members tell them. One thing that you could see if you compare what happened in the G77 to statements by members of the G77 made on public record, things were very different ...
>
> China in G77 they were like "no, we have to express that it's the wrong place". Today (in the UNSC), not a peep about that. Arab group, very outspoken in G77 [but] a very different message in public.
>
> ... I think if you did a count, in G77 you would probably have more on our side than on the side of Argentina, Brazil, India, maybe Algeria and China, or Cuba and Venezuela. But then ... they [Latin Americans] have that feeling maybe the Americans are going to pull something on them. For the Chinese, they are afraid that the Security Council could dispatch green helmets that are shutting down their factories. It's completely ridiculous.' (Interview with PSIDS diplomat)

The important point is that despite hostility from large and powerful states, the ensuing UNSC debate was weighted in favour of the SIDS. Nauru's Head of State represented the PSIDS, but the council also heard from Maldives as Chair of AOSIS, Trinidad and Tobago as Chair of the Caribbean Community and Common Market (CARICOM), and the Prime Minister of Curaçao, who spoke on behalf of the Kingdom of the Netherlands. Their view was supported by a number of African nations. The statements by China, Russia, and the Arab Group were muted in comparison with 2011.

Our contribution: a tale of two dilemmas

The headline story of this vignette is the ability of even the smallest members to shape the agenda of international organizations (IOs). SIDS thus serve as emblematic examples of the wider community of small states within IOs. We posit that because these island states are both small and developing, any influence they have, and any strategies from within IOs that succeed in involving them, are likely to also be effective when cohorts of slightly larger and wealthier states are considered. In which case, the vignette reveals two dilemmas that are inherent to the interactions between IOs and small member states, both at the UN but also across the multilateral system. The main contribution of this book is to bring these perspectives – IOs and small states – into conversation and to explain how they interact.

The IOs' dilemma is that to be effective as multilateral actors, they must be inclusive and member driven. But the increasing participation of more and more active members makes consensus harder to obtain and gridlock more likely. Consequently, IOs win themselves legitimacy on one hand by increasing participation but then lose it on the other due to growing concerns about effectiveness. The small states' dilemma is that while they depend on a permissive liberal order for their survival and prosperity as states (Wivel and Crandall, 2019), the costs of participating in that order are disproportionately high for the smallest (Panke, 2013; Corbett and Connell, 2015). Representation in New York is expensive and most have very small missions. A large foreign service and global network of diplomats is well beyond their reach. The perpetual question for policymakers in small states is whether the price of participation is worth it.

Our focus on the interaction between these dilemmas contributes to the literature on IOs by drawing attention to hitherto neglected actors – small states – across multiple institutions. We use SIDS as a proxy for small states more generally. We ask: why do both large states and secretariats encourage and facilitate the participation of SIDS? We argue they do so in order to enhance the 'throughput' legitimacy of IOs as global actors. There are a lot of small states and different IOs have different definitions of who they are. SIDS in particular are among the key clients of IOs. But regardless of which definition they adopt, small states are a large component of IOs membership. Ignoring them undermines key norms of IOs: the sovereign equality of member states and the right to development. To be legitimate global actors IOs need to be seen as assisting all members, including small states, both in word and in deed. The problem, as we have seen, is that including them is difficult, in no small part because they rarely have the capacity for sustained engagement across multiple IOs. The perpetual concern is that the imperative to include states who do not have the capacity to engage will complicate decision-making and undermine effectiveness. To balance this dilemma IOs manage inputs and outputs by way of throughputs: they assist small states to participate effectively in their everyday processes and practices. They are not always successful. Indeed, many of their efforts are symbolic rather than substantive. But they are nevertheless significant because the complete absence of small states would undermine IOs' claim to being legitimate global actors. Our book thus extends accounts of pluralism at IOs, which has thus far focused heavily on the role of international non-governmental organizations (NGOs) and the secretariat, by adding the experience of hitherto neglected small states and SIDS in particular.

We also contribute to the literature on small states in international relations (IR), which has thus far been dominated by work on European states. We ask: why are small states active and effective participants on some issues in some IOs? We argue that their common dilemma explains variation. We refer to their attempts to balance this dilemma as the 'competent performance of vulnerability'. That is, in pursuing their interests, small states have won attention and assistance by prosecuting arguments about why they deserve special and differential treatment (S&DT), both in relation to climate change and economic and social issues. Small states have not acted alone and they have certainly not had it all their own way. Their successes have been noteworthy but circumscribed. Capacity constraints remain a major impediment to their effectiveness. And, like all states, they face opposition from other states with different interests and agendas. But they do act and these actions are consequential, at least some of the time. The book thus extends arguments about how European small states achieve influence in the multilateral sphere by showing that the factors deemed significant in those cases – rhetorical action, collaboration, and active participation – are important for small states in other regions, too.

These two dilemmas interact and the interaction between them can help us explain the previous vignette about climate change and the UNSC, as well as many other similar instances across very different IOs. Each instance is contingent. But there are patterns across IOs that stem from the common dilemmas that we identify. By moving back and forth between these everyday practices and processes, and the dilemmas that underpin them, we are able to tell a story about how IOs are changing and the consequences of those changes for all states, large and small. At this historical juncture, in which the relevance and legitimacy of global governance is said to be under threat from renewed nationalism (see contributions to Lake et al, 2021 for discussion), describing and explaining these shift takes on added significance for all those who care about the future of the liberal international order (LIO).

The IOs dilemma: the legitimacy imperative

Former Director General of the World Intellectual Property Organization (WIPO), Francis Gurry, argued in 2013 that:

> The great advantages of universal multilateralism are inclusiveness and legitimacy. Those advantages are costly in terms of process ... So there is a balance to be achieved between process expense and efficiency, with inclusiveness, legitimacy and effectiveness, the consequences of choice. Democracy is not necessarily adopted for its efficiency. The risk of exclusion is related to the risk of unequal strength. Arguably the weakest are most protected in the multilateral world. (Gurry, 2013)

Gurry's quote captures the dilemma that all IOs grapple with. The legitimacy of IOs is said to derive from a combination of inputs and outputs (for example, Buchanan and Keohane, 2006; Uhlin, 2010; Agné et al, 2015; Zürn, 2018). 'Input' legitimacy stems from the principle of sovereign equality – the idea that IOs are responsive to all member states, regardless of their size. 'Output' legitimacy is a product of what IOs do and how these actions benefit their members, including developing countries. The complicating factor is that while participation has changed fundamentally, IOs still operate with the formal structures and rules that were adopted over six decades ago. The decisions of IOs, rightly or wrongly, were often regarded as a consequence of unequal participation. Yet, as Gurry notes, more participation has the potential to exacerbate a cycle in which the problems of IOs are blamed on unequal participation (inputs). But more participation exacerbates ineffectiveness (outputs). Despite considerable changes to the IO system in recent decades, both unequal participation and the perception of ineffectiveness sharpens questions about their legitimacy (for example, Dahl et al, 1999; Goodhart, 2007; Goodhart and Taninchev, 2011; Kuyper, 2014).

One means by which IOs have sought to generate greater 'input' legitimacy is by taking the principle of sovereign equality – one state, one vote – seriously. IOs have always been under pressure from their member states to 'promote a formal display of equality among nations that are in reality profoundly unequal' (Niezen and Sapignoli, 2017: 12). This imperative was created when new states sought recognition from the recently created UN as a means of affirming their sovereign status (for example, Vital, 1967, 1971; Reid, 1974). But the common consensus for much of the twentieth century was that a 'club model' of decision-making prevailed nonetheless (Keohane and Nye, 2001). In this view, IOs were created by the initiatives of a few large and rich states that negotiated the rules of the game (see, classically, Waltz, 1979). The majority of members were either non-participants or passive participants (for example, Hey, 2003; Drezner, 2008).

This is no longer true (Chong and Maass, 2010). A decade ago, Keohane and Nye concluded that the old club model in which a small number of rich countries controlled the agenda had been undercut by 'greater participation' of a diverse number of states and 'their increased assertiveness' (Keohane and Nye, 2001: 269, 271; see also Lyne et al, 2009). This shift was caused by the proliferation of membership of IOs (Lake and O'Mahony, 2004; Mansfield and Pevehouse, 2006; vanGrasstek, 2013; Tallberg et al, 2013), the impact of emerging powers, demands that 'democratic norms [be] applied to international institutions' (Keohane and Nye, 2001: 281), the willingness of IOs to help their smaller members build their multilateral capacities (International Monetary Fund [IMF], 2013), the membership of the World Trade Organization (WTO) more than doubling between 1995 and 2010 (Laker, 2014), and some small states' determination to 'to play an effective role' in IOs (Cooper and Shaw, 2009: 11). Together these developments have changed the IOs' world – the environment within which they work and the practices they adopt. This renewed emphasis on the 'input' legitimacy of IOs via increased responsiveness has, in turn, seen the world's smaller states, individually or collectively, assume a more prominent role (Baldacchino, 2009: 29). The LIO is not just permissive of their participation; it is conducive of it (Long, 2022).

To be clear, we do not contend that all states, and especially the smallest, have the same influence or the same interests in IOs. Nor do we overlook the fact that the participation of the smallest states is often influenced by powerful patrons (Veenendaal, 2017) with whom they seek 'shelter' (Thorhallsson, 2011; Bailes and Thorhallsson, 2013; Panke, 2017) and gain other functional benefits derived from conformity to institutionalized global norms (Sharman, 2015). IOs' engagement in small states has to be balanced against the competing demands made by large countries (Mountford, 2008: 5). Our more qualified claim is that a combination of factors point to a change in their participation (Sharman, 2017), including that IOs themselves have encouraged and assisted smaller members through training and technical assistance programmes (World Bank, 2000; IMF, 2013); large and/or rich states have consciously assisted the smallest states in developing their capacity at IOs via bilateral or multilateral initiatives (for example, the Commonwealth Office in New York and Geneva); a growing number of small states have made conscious decisions to be active in IOs, committing more resources (Cooper and Shaw, 2009) while others participate through regional or other types of groupings, to aggregate their numbers and thus their influence; and the expanded IO agenda, especially on various aspects of development, offers more opportunities for all states to participate (Bexell et al, 2010; Kleine, 2013).

One consequence of the increasing participation of more and more members is that IO operations have become more complicated (Porter et al, 2001), bringing renewed focus on their inability to reach consensus on key issues (Goldin, 2013: 3) and the collapse of multilateral negotiations (Vlcek, 2008; see also Harbinson, 2015). Concern that increased participation will complicate decision-making is not new – for some, the smallest members have always been 'irritants' (Lewis, 2009: vii) – but this concern has increased, in part because, despite the rules and procedures enshrining equality, it is increasingly clear that not all states have the capacity to participate on all issues all of the time (Wallis, 2010; Bishop, 2012; Corbett and Connell, 2015). The practice of consensus decision-making, regardless of the formal rules, only exaggerates the paralysis in some IOs, as seen in the prolonged

Doha round of trade negotiations at the WTO, the divided membership in the leadership elections in the Food and Agriculture Organization (FAO) or International Labour Organization (ILO) in 2012, or the way H1N1, Ebola, or COVID pandemics were managed at the World Health Organization (WHO).

Sometimes IOs appear to be trapped in a perpetual cycle in which they win themselves input legitimacy via the active participation of more states while perceptions of ineffectiveness and an inability to satisfy all members means they lose output legitimacy (Agné et al, 2015). All IOs face this dilemma to varying degrees. As Gurry illustrates, IOs themselves are well aware of the need to grapple with this dilemma. They cannot solve the problem by returning to the old club model. Reforming yesterday's formal rules and institutions is too difficult given the interests involved. Instead, much innovation consists of attempting to change the informal practices and processes by which IOs make decisions.

We borrow and adapt the term 'throughput' from the work of Vivian Schmidt (2006, 2013) to describes these attempts. The term draws attention to the way IOs use institutional processes and practices to promote inclusion. By ensuring that as many members are involved in decision-making as possible, IOs believe that outcomes for developing countries in particular are likely to be improved because their nationals are shaping the design of projects and programmes. If they fail then responsibility is shared also. Our contention is that balancing 'inputs' and 'outputs' by way of 'throughputs' has become the new imperative of IOs. We identify three features of the way IOs seek to generate throughput legitimacy:

1. **Promoting Norms and Principles**: the twin norms of sovereign equality and the right to development are bedrock assumptions upon which IOs operate. These norms and principles create an imperative for IOs to pay attention to even their smallest members, to champion programmes and projects that will benefit their development, and to support their participation wherever possible regardless of the impact on their effectiveness.

2. **Upholding Rules and Traditions**: there is a great diversity of rules and traditions between IOs. The preference for consensus across the multilateral system typically favours the smallest by nominally providing them with veto power, particularly when they act as a bloc. But while the rules and traditions of some IOs, like the UNGA, are especially amenable to the creation of categories like SIDS because they allow every state to represent themselves, others like the World Bank (WB) and WHO are structured around regional representation, which makes it much harder for small states to work together.

3. *Facilitating Mutual Assistance and Cooperation*: mutual assistance and cooperation is the *raison d'être* of multilateralism. When leaders of IOs seek election, secretariats seek clients, and NGOs seek to draw attention to their agenda at IOs, small states are useful allies. The presence of friends and allies can help us to explain why SIDS have been able to overcome capacity constraints on certain issues and in certain IOs. It can also explain why some IOs have been more receptive to SIDS on different issues and at different times.

These features of IOs' attempts to win throughput legitimacy are not necessary and sufficient conditions. They are a heuristic device that provides analytic clarity to what are otherwise a series of contingent interactions. But taken together, they have theoretical and empirical implications for the study of IOs. Specifically, we provide further support to the growing body of evidence that IOs operate on the basis of plurality and consensus, rather than the old club model. This body of work has highlighted that two sets of actors are shaping the agenda at multilateral institutions: NGOs and the secretariat of IOs. When combined with the economic rise of the BRICS (Brazil, Russia, India, China, and South Africa), the old hegemony of the US and Western Europe in particular is said to have waned, signalling the strengthening of the rules-based LIO. We add SIDS, as a proxy for small states, to this list and in doing so argue that this move is significant because it reveals the consequences of a rules-based order. SIDS may not gain the S&DT that they desire but the fact that they are able to succeed on some issues some of the time is symbolically significant.

The symbolic importance of small states belies their neglect by mainstream studies of IOs. The obvious pantomime villain here is realist IR but in truth most constructivist studies of IOs outside the EU are guilty of overlooking them too. While more recent studies on IOs, including some that we cover here, include a wide range of topics and perspectives, they seldom systematically consider the role played by small states (for example, Barnett and Finnemore, 2004; Hawkins et al, 2006). The field typically follows Waltz (1979) and his call to study 'a few big and important things' remains because it would be 'ridiculous to construct a theory of international politics based on Malaysia and Costa Rica'. This approach is hopelessly Eurocentric (Acharya, 2014) and flouts mainstream principles of social scientific case selection – representativeness and variation – because it only accounts for the exceptions: large states (Veenendaal and Corbett, 2015).

This book addresses both gaps. We provide a more nuanced and sophisticated explanation of the long-standing assumptions that small states are either free-riders or spoilers in IOs, and that power and wealth are the only determinants of influence in multilateral cooperation. We support the claim that the *authority* of IOs to 'create issues, set agendas, establish and implement rules or programs, and evaluate and/or adjudicate outcomes' is 'due to its representation of different constituencies' (Avant et al, 2010: 2, 20). In doing so we show that a key temperature test for the LIO is how inclusive it is of its smallest members.

The small states' dilemma: the disproportionate costs of statehood

The countries we have come to call SIDS are among the most recent members of the sovereignty club. The UN had 51 members in 1945. Today it has 193. Despite the world population having doubled in this same period, the trend towards smaller states means that the average size of the state has shrunk (Lake and O'Mahoney, 2004). Many of these new states have small populations. More than 100 have populations of less than 10 million; 39 have populations of less than 1 million. One consequence of this trend is that regardless of the definition used, the number of states that can be thought of as 'small' has grown steadily in recent decades. They have also become increasingly active participants in the multilateral system.

The growing number of very small states seeking membership of IOs attracted a boutique literature at the height of the decolonization period (for example, Benedict, 1967; Vital, 1967, 1971; Reid, 1974). These studies emphasized the capacity deficits of small states, their propensity to complicate decision-making, and their ability to shape outcomes only when 'America's crusading spirit presented small allies with bargaining influence' (Keohane, 1971: 163) or when large states allowed them 'to act collectively to help shape developing international attitudes, dogmas, and codes of proper behaviour' (Keohane, 1969: 297). From there, small states largely disappeared from the study of IOs (for discussion, see Baldacchino, 2009; Bishop, 2012).

Since the turn of the millennium there has been a renewed interest in small states among IR scholars in particular (for review, see Long, 2017a and b; Thorhallsson, 2018b). In relation to IOs, much of this work has focused on European small states and their participation in the EU (for example, Arter, 2000; Thorhallsson, 2000, 2012, 2018a; Ingebritsen, 2002; Kronsell, 2002; Browning, 2006; Wivel and Thorhallsson, 2006; Panke, 2010; Grøn and Wivel, 2011; Bailes and Thorhallsson, 2013; Smed and Wivel, 2017; Crandell and Sulg, 2020) and the role of Pacific and Caribbean states in climate negotiations (for example, Ashe et al, 1999; Chasek, 2005; Betzold, 2010; Benwell, 2011; Betzold et al, 2012; Panke, 2012a; de Águeda Corneloup and Mol, 2014; Jaschik, 2014; Carter, 2015, 2020a; Manoa, 2015; Ourbak and Magnan, 2018; Petzold and Magnan, 2019). These scholars have focused on how small states overcome structural weaknesses – financial and human resources – via 'smart' strategies, including agenda setting, forum shopping, issue prioritization, and coalition building (Panke, 2012b; 2013). Taken together, these works posit that small states should be treated as 'objects, not subjects' (Neumann and Gstöhl, 2006: 19) of international politics. There is, of course, a body of scholarship on small states outside Europe and climate negotiations. But it tends to either: (1) focus on specific IOs like the UNGA (for example, Panke, 2013); (2) describe their foreign policy generally rather than participation in IOs specifically (for example, edited collections by Dommen and Hein, 1985 and Cooper and Shaw, 2009; Braveboy-Wagner, 2007 on the Caribbean or Fry, 2019; Fry and Tarte, 2015 on the Pacific); or (3) capture the engagement of individual countries on certain issues (for example, Bueger and Wivel, 2018 on Seychelles; Baxter et al, 2018 on Qatar; Jackson, 2012 on Antigua and the WTO; Wallis, 2010 on Tonga and the WTO; and assorted publications on Bhutan's campaign for Gross National Happiness – for example, Theys and Rietig, 2020). This book is unique because it examines interactions between SIDS and multiple IOs.

European small states are 'most likely' cases for the argument that size-related constraints can be overcome in IOs because they are all high-income countries. Many have much larger populations than those discussed here: Iceland aside, the Scandinavian countries that dominate this literature are all substantially bigger than the small islands of the Caribbean and Pacific. SIDS therefore represent a much more significant test case for arguments about the potential influence of small countries on IOs. A key reason is that for the countries we now call SIDS the costs of statehood are disproportionately high. At the extremes, a least developed country (LDC) like Tuvalu, which has a population of around 10,000, is highly dependent on foreign aid for the maintenance of basic services. As a consequence, while the Tuvaluan government has a very small foreign service and minimal overseas representation, the costs of maintaining even these limited features of modern statehood is prohibitively high. We might therefore expect that a state like Tuvalu would focus on the minimum level of interaction with IOs to ensure sovereign recognition and secure survival. And that they would do so by adopting 'the typical features of a sovereign state, despite radical diseconomies of scale, largely on symbolic grounds, which may provide incidental benefits' (Sharman, 2015). It requires a more significant departure from the orthodox assumptions that underpin IR scholarship to claim Tuvalu could be a 'smart' state. And yet in 2009 Tuvalu brought COP15 to a standstill in a bid to achieve deeper emissions cuts and despite opposition from larger countries, including China and India.

The claim that SIDS like Tuvalu seek conformity to promote legitimacy can explain why small states exist. It also aligns with arguments about how European small states seek influence in IOs primarily as a means of increasing their 'status' (de Carvalho and Neumann, 2015) in a hierarchy in which large is stronger than small. It runs into problems, however, when countries like Tuvalu, confronted with the existential threat of climate change (Vaha, 2015), see their very existence as intimately intertwined with the norms and practices of global governance. As a result, rather than seeking conformity to promote legitimacy, SIDS have instead sought to *draw attention to their vulnerability and smallness* to secure survival.[2] By drawing attention to the existential threat they face, SIDS have used their vulnerability to carve out a space for themselves in the multilateral world, succeeded in placing their concerns on IO agendas, and 'generated international interest in their conditions' (Baldacchino, 2009). Rather than being exclusively dependent on large states, we show that active and creative small states have used the SIDS label and the metaphor of smallness to realize specific goals. Our central argument is that SIDS were not given the label or a place in IOs, they *fought* for them by drawing attention to their unique condition. The fact that we call them SIDS and can refer to an identifiable SIDS agenda in IOs is evidence of their influence and ability to construct a constitutive norm – it creates new actors, interests, or categories of action (Finnemore and Sikkink, 1998) – based on the idea of differentiated development.

This competent performance of vulnerability involves three interrelated strategies:

1. ***Rhetorical action*** (Schimmelfennig, 2001; Browning, 2006) of the type identified by scholars working on the agency of African states in the international system (Jourde, 2007; Lee, 2013; Laker, 2014), that invokes existing norms in multilateral forums to highlight the unique economic and environmental circumstances of SIDS (and in WTO the Small, Vulnerable Economies or SVEs) and posits that they cannot be overcome by conventional development strategies.
2. ***Collaboration*** or coalition building between SIDS to take advantage of the principle of sovereign equality and the preference for consensus within IOs. Both allow SIDS to nominally act as veto players on key decisions and as participants in leadership selections with a swag of votes to cast. By threatening vetoes or promising votes, SIDS have been able to demonstrate that they can act as a grouping that maximizes the use of its own label/grouping in IOs.
3. ***Active participation*** (Panke, 2013) in the processes and everyday practices of IOs, including proposing initiatives or motions; holding leadership positions; taking up positions on boards and other decision-making bodies; coordinating positions; drafting text; holding press conferences and issuing press releases; briefing ministerial groups, delegations, and taskforces; and attending workshops, meetings, and conferences. The

reason participation in the processes and practices of IOs is important to our explanation is that the presence of SIDS in IO decision-making cannot be assumed due to well-known capacity deficits; whereas large states can have missions and delegations for most if not all IOs, SIDS are often defined by their absence. A focus on the smallest and most peripheral members reveals, therefore, that norm diffusion is always contingent on *presence*.

In addition to extending the literature on the strategies of European small states, our argument that a dry and essentially static concept like vulnerability has been used by a group of states typically associated with structural weakness (Wivel and Oest, 2010: 434) to advance their interests in multilateral forums is significant because it contributes to theoretical debates about the relationship between norms and hierarchies in the international system. Specifically, we build on Towns's work on norm diffusion 'from below' (Towns 2010; 2012). Towns's intervention critiques the existing norms literature for assuming that diffusion always spreads from the core to the periphery, making large states, IOs, and other transnational advocacy coalitions the primary norm diffusers. In Towns's account, which was employed to explain the rise of policies that sought to incorporate women into the state, diffusion was more dynamic. Indeed, she argues that countries on the periphery, who have a low rank in the hierarchical order, can increase their standing by initiating and adhering to norms.

The idea that states would seek to dispense with or reinvent a hierarchical order 'from below' is consistent with Towns. The crucial point, and one on which our argument turns, is that 'development' is only one hierarchy in which SIDS are situated; the perception of state size is related to economic size but in the international sphere it is also a distinct hierarchy. Thus, while it initially implies a reduced rank, the competent performance of vulnerability and the constitutive norm of differentiated development that SIDS seek to promote, once accepted, would eventually result in SIDS increasing their rank on development indices (or at least that is the aim). But acquiring S&DT (that is, trade concessions at the WTO) that could enable this to occur would be contingent on continued acceptance of their vulnerability and thus a lowly rank in the related hierarchy, defined by size, in which large is stronger than small. Consequently, rather than seeking to increase their standing via conformity, SIDS are attempting to stress their weakness to increase their development and, in cases like Tuvalu, secure survival.

The important caveat here is that while SIDS in the Caribbean, Pacific, and Indian Ocean regions have pursued this strategy, European small states, which tend to be wealthier, have historically preferred the more conventional route of seeking to act *as if* they were a large state to promote their 'status' (de Carvalho and Neumann, 2015; Baxter et al, 2018). Interestingly, however, as we will discuss further in relation to the WHO (Chapter 6), the norm of differentiated development is spreading and so even countries that are no longer considered as SIDS (for example Malta) nevertheless adopt similar discursive strategies on issues like health. Whether this will prove beneficial remains to be seen. Similarly, while we are at pains to show that the SIDS have already generated assistance, it is important to note that one of the main benefits they hope to achieve, that as yet remains unrealized, is compensation for the adverse consequences of climate change, also referred to as 'loss and damage' (Benwell, 2011; Calliari, 2016; Ourbak and Magnan, 2018). Again, whether they will be successful in this pursuit is an open question. However, SIDS could not prosecute the case without the label and associated identity which are synonymous with acute vulnerability. Indeed, it may be that SIDS are unsuccessful in pursuing 'loss and damage' compensation but the constitutive norm 'differentiated development' remains.

Approach, cases, data, and analysis

This book is about how IOs and small states interact. There are a number of ways to study actors and their relationships within institutions. In political science and international relations, the most popular is a version institutionalism (see Lowndes and Roberts, 2013 for review). The key assumption that underpins this and related approaches is that institutions create incentives and constrain behaviour, and actors seek to work within these rules to maximize their objectives. As will be clear by now, while we see institutional rules and traditions as an important part of this story, we do not start our narrative account with them. Rather, following the interpretive tradition, we start with the actors themselves, how they see the world, how their understandings create dilemmas, and how these dilemmas shape their actions. This interpretive account of how actors and their dilemmas cause actions within an institutional context is a departure from mainstream studies and so requires some clarification.

Approach: explaining how these two dilemmas interact

At the empirical core of this book is an attempt to explain why IOs encourage the participation of small states and why small states participate in IOs. To answers these questions, we focus specifically on how the label and category small island developing states (SIDS), and variants like the small, vulnerable economies (SVEs), have become a constitutive norm in IOs over the last three decades. We argue that the rise of these labels is the outcome of the interaction between the two dilemmas outlined previously. Dilemmas arise because beliefs, cultures, or traditions are never seamless accounts of the world actors inhabit. They have fault lines, and contain tensions, contradictions, and unsolved mysteries. These can be revealed when actors confront different belief systems to their own (Bevir and Rhodes, 2010). But they are also made visible by political disputes within a largely self-contained community (Boswell et al, 2019). Scholars such as Krasner (1999) argue that the presence of internal contradictions reveal the hidden hand of the logic of consequences lurking beneath logics of appropriateness. Our starting assumption is that this is incorrect: it is logics of appropriateness all the way down because, as Max Weber (2012 [1904]) argued a century ago, actors have ideas about their interests. The job of scholars is to uncover these ideas and the intersubjective traditions they constitute, reveal the contradictions or dilemmas inherent to them, and show how actors act to balance or resolve them.

Our approach thus assumes that multilateralism is social, constituted by inter-subjective knowledge, meaningful practices, and relations. And this relational view of identity allows for differentiation between states by rendering them 'distinctly recognisable' (Towns, 2010). Identities are not fixed; they change and this change is important for how we explain why, for example, some states would come to see themselves as a distinctly recognizable group called SIDS. In this sense our account has affinities with constructivist international relations (see Lynch, 2013; Bevir, Daddow, and Hall 2013). For example, we affirm the early English School's position that relations between states, and by extension the institutions that constitute them, are 'contingent mental constructs, socially-generated and sustained, reflecting the beliefs of engaged agents about their rules, usefulness and propriety' (Bevir and Hall, 2020: 164). We depart from mainstream forms of constructivism in important ways. First, we question Wendt's (2004) assumption that states can be treated as actors. Rather, we decentre the state into the constituent meanings and beliefs of situated agents (Bevir and Rhodes, 2010). Second, we do not assume that states have fixed objectives like survival or status. Rather, we seek to uncover how the actors that represent states in the international realm see, develop, and alter their objectives. This approach to agency is what makes our interpretive method distinct. To be clear, we are not saying that states or their representatives are autonomous and able to pursue objectives independent of context; quite the opposite. Our claim is that if we want to explain why IOs and small states sought to *both* create a shared constitutive category like SIDS across multiple IOs *and* the diversity of forms that the category takes, then our approach must be able to account for the way individuals interpret intersubjective norms and traditions, and how when confronted with dilemmas their choices shape outcomes. Likewise, if we want to explore how IOs seek to increase the levels and breadth of participation, we need to follow the same approach.

We start from the interpretivist position that there is no way to provide a definitive, Archimedean adjudication between the multiple interpretations of actors about if, when, how, and why somebody mattered on a certain issue in a certain IO. The best we can do is ask a variety of actors – primarily diplomats, international civil servants, and NGO representatives – similar questions about the interaction between IOs and small states, and then report their patterned responses. We made no initial assumptions about what those patterns might be – whether the influence they have would be tightly constrained by institutional rules, follow the logic of utility maximization, and so on – albeit we had hunches that these things were important based on past work and a close reading of the existing literature. We simply sought to understand how the people who make IOs work saw the world and acted in it. Our logic is that understanding what mattered to them can help us explain why they act the way they do, and that if we understand why they act, then we can shed some light on questions like whether influence in IOs is centralized or dispersed.

The emphasis on multiple states and IOs builds on recent thinking about the comparative interpretive method (see Boswell et al, 2019). The key to this approach to comparison is the aforementioned empirical focus on dilemmas (see Boswell et al, 2019: Chapter 3). Dilemmas thus function as an intellectual skeleton key for empirical work:

> when we ask why actors act, we create an opportunity for reflection on alternative meanings and actions, and the pros and cons of each. By reflecting *with* actors, we uncover the choices and questions they confront. By understanding how they *see* these choices, as a reflection of the webs of belief in which they are embedded, we are able to explain why actors do what they do. (Boswell et al, 2019: 4, original emphasis)

Revealing the extent to which dilemmas recur across contexts is a key task of interpretive political science. We do not expect that dilemmas will be universal or that individuals will respond to them in identical ways. But empirical research reveals time and time again that they often share elective affinities or a family resemblance (see Boswell and Corbett, 2017).

Cases: which small states and which IOs?

Our approach to comparison is pragmatic and opportunistic. We started with a hunch, based on our previous research, on both IOs and SIDS, that there was something interesting to say about how their interactions were changing. We then set about exploring this hunch empirically by talking to the actors involved in both arenas. The decision to focus on SIDS and the extent to which their activism could be explained using the same strategies that scholars had identified as important for European small states emerged as we gathered our data. We therefore selected the IOs in part based on how the category was formed and adopted: first at the UN, then the economic institutions, and finally in a nascent form in the WHO and WIPO.

Small size is thus a 'perceived' category (Maass, 2009) that varies from IO to IO. There is nevertheless a core group of countries that all of these definitions encapsulate, as outlined in Table 1.1.

This book thus takes the position that being 'small' in part depends on self-perception and in part on the collective decision of IOs who rank and label states according to their 'size' (sometimes population, sometimes economy), often with different results. Given that who is defined as small is not pre-fixed, we examine why some countries seek and are given the label, and how and why the label matters in some IOs but not others. Our analysis therefore pays specific attention to how self-perceptions shape collective processes (Maass, 2009; Baldacchino and Wivel, 2020). Given the trend towards ever-smaller states (Lake and O'Mahony, 2004), irrespective of any firm definition, the number of small states seems to have steadily grown in recent decades. Comparing between IOs allows us to recognize this trend. In doing so we add to the literature on IOs which has tended to focus on specific organizations (for example, Gilbert and Vine, 2000; Marshall, 2008; Xu and Weller, 2009 on the World Bank; Xu and Weller, 2004; vanGrasstek, 2013, Laker, 2014 on WTO; Uvin, 1994; Weitz, 1997 on the FAO; Burci and Vignes, 2004; Chorev, 2012 on the WHO; and Standing, 2010, Kott and Droux, 2013 on the ILO).

An empirical focus on the social construction of labels and groupings allows us to side-step the perennial 'who and what is small' question. But it proves cumbersome when undertaking the practical task of writing about specific countries that we now call SIDS and IOs. To overcome this, we employ a slight of hand: we use the label SIDS to describe *both* the specific label in the UN system and as a shorthand for a group of countries. This is not a perfect solution: it means that on occasion we talk about how the SIDS (a UN label that includes Singapore) created the label SVEs (a WTO label), or the existence of a 'SIDS agenda' before IOs had created the label. In these cases, the shorthand refers to the group of countries that are members of each of these different groupings and labels in different IOs (see Table 1.1): small islands in the Caribbean, Pacific, Africa, and the Indian Ocean regions. We hope that readers will forgive us for this imperfect but pragmatic solution.

Table 1.1: Small state groupings in IOs

	United Nations (Small Island Developing States)	United Nations (Alliance of Small Island States)	United Nations (Forum of Small States)	The Commonwealth Secretariat	World Bank (Small States Forum)	World Trade Organization (Small and Vulnerable Economies)	World Health Organization (Small Countries Initiative)
Definition	Est. 1992 at the Rio Earth Summit. Defined as developing countries facing specific social, economic and environmental vulnerabilities. 38 are UN members and 14 are non-UN Members or Associate Members of the Regional Commissions.	Est. 1990. An ad hoc negotiating body established by SIDS at the United Nations. 44 States and observers.	Est. 1992 by Singapore. Informal group for countries with populations of less than 10 million.	Est. 1997 (but first designated in 1977 and initially defined in 1985). 31 Commonwealth members with a population size of 1.5 million people or less and larger member states that share similar characteristics with them.	Est. 2000. The Bank defines small states as countries that: (a) have a population of 1.5 million or less; or (b) are members of the Small State Forum (SSF). The SSF currently has 50 members.	Est. 2001 as part of the Doha Declaration. SVEs are defined as WTO members that account for a small fraction of world trade and are particularly vulnerable to economic uncertainties and environmental shocks but do not qualify as LDCs. The SVEs has 26 members.	Est. in 2013 at an informal meeting in Turkey. The group comprises eight countries in the WHO European Region with a population of less than 1 million people.

(continued)

Table 1.1: Small state groupings in IOs (continued)

	United Nations (Small Island Developing States)	United Nations (Alliance of Small Island States)	United Nations (Forum of Small States)	The Commonwealth Secretariat	World Bank (Small States Forum)	World Trade Organization (Small and Vulnerable Economies)	World Health Organization (Small Countries Initiative)
Members	UN Members: Antigua and Barbuda, Bahamas, Bahrain, Barbados, Belize, Cape Verde, Comoros★, Cuba, Dominica, Dominican Republic, Fiji, Grenada, Guinea-Bissau★, Guyana, Haiti★, Jamaica, Kiribati ★, Maldives★, Marshall Islands, Federated States of Micronesia, Mauritius, Nauru, Palau, Papua New Guinea, Samoa★, São Tomé and Príncipe★, Singapore, St. Kitts and Nevis, St. Lucia,	Members: Antigua and Barbuda, Bahamas, Barbados, Belize, Cape Verde, Comoros, Cook Islands, Cuba, Dominica, Dominican Republic, Fiji, Grenada, Guinea-Bissau, Guyana, Haiti, Jamaica, Kiribati, Maldives, Marshall Islands, Mauritius, Nauru, Niue, Palau, Papua New Guinea,	Members: More than 100	Members: Antigua and Barbuda, The Bahamas, Barbados, Belize, Botswana, Brunei Darussalam, Cyprus, Dominica, Fiji, Grenada, Guyana, Jamaica, Kiribati, Lesotho, Mauritius, Namibia, Maldives, Malta, Nauru, Papua New Guinea, Samoa, Seychelles, Singapore, Solomon Islands, St Kitts and	Members: Antigua and Barbuda, The Bahamas, Bahrain, Barbados, Belize, Bhutan, Botswana, Brunei Darussalam, Cabo Verde, Comoros, Cyprus, Djibouti, Dominica, Equatorial Guinea, Estonia, Fiji, Gabon, The Gambia, Grenada, Guinea-Bissau, Guyana, Iceland, Jamaica, Kiribati, Lesotho, Maldives, Malta, Marshall Islands, Mauritius, Federated States	Members: Antigua and Barbuda, Barbados, Belize, Bolivia, Cuba, Dominica, Dominican Republic, El Salvador, Ecuador, Fiji, Grenada, Guatemala, Honduras, Jamaica, Mauritania, Nicaragua, Panama, Papua New Guinea, Saint Kitts and Nevis, Saint Lucia, Saint Vincent and the Grenadines,	Members: Andorra, Cyprus, Iceland, Luxembourg, Malta, Monaco, Montenegro, San Marino

Table 1.1: Small state groupings in IOs (continued)

St. Vincent and the Grenadines, Seychelles, Solomon Islands★, Suriname, Timor-Leste★, Tonga, Trinidad and Tobago, Tuvalu★, and Vanuatu★. ★Also, LDCs **Non-UN** **Members:** American Samoa, Anguilla, Aruba, British Virgin Islands, Commonwealth of Northern Marianas, Cook Islands, French Polynesia, Guam, Montserrat, Netherlands Antilles, New Caledonia, Niue, Puerto Rico, and US Virgin Islands	Samoa, Singapore, Seychelles, Sao Tome and Principe, Solomon Islands, St. Kitts and Nevis, St. Lucia, St. Vincent and the Grenadines, Suriname, Timor-Leste, Tonga, Trinidad and Tobago, Tuvalu, Vanuatu **Observers:** American Samoa, Netherlands Antilles, Guam, US Virgin Islands, Puerto Rico	Nevis, St Lucia, St Vincent and the Grenadines, Swaziland, Tonga, Trinidad and Tobago, Tuvalu, Vanuatu	Of Micronesia, Montenegro, Namibia, Nauru, Palau, Qatar, Samoa, San Marino, São Tomé & Príncipe, Seychelles, Solomon Islands, St. Kitts And Nevis, St. Lucia, St. Vincent And The Grenadines, Suriname, Swaziland, Timor-Leste, Tonga, Trinidad And Tobago, Tuvalu, Vanuatu	Samoa, Seychelles, Sri Lanka, Tonga, Trinidad and Tobago **Observers:** Bahamas

Source: Corbett, J. et al (2019) 'Norm entrepreneurship and diffusion "from below" in international organisations: How the competent performance of vulnerability generates benefits for small states', *Review of International Studies*, 45(4): 647–68. Reprinted with permission from Cambridge University Press, Copyright © British International Studies Association 2019.

Sources and data

We draw on three forms of data to uncover how actors see, experience, and attempt to resolve dilemmas:

1. **Public documents and archival sources**: extensive information on policies, resolutions, positions, and working procedures provided by IOs and those member states studied here. They include, for instance, policy papers, agenda decisions, and records of meetings at all relevant IOs. Data were collected *inter alia* on the history of changing memberships of IOs, their rules, working procedures and practices, level and means of participation, and qualifications and career paths of those in small states involved in making decisions on IO representation and participation, and the positions taken by small states across these IOs on the issues we focus on.

2. **Interviews**: we have undertaken more than 80 in-depth interviews for this project, including with staff in IOs who manage relations with the small states, with the ambassadors and representatives of the small states to the IOs, as well as their diplomats and politicians at home. The book also builds on a data bank of interviews (around 200) on the processes of the WTO, the World Bank and the WIPO, FAO, WHO, and IMF undertaken for previous books on IOs (Xu and Weller, 2004, 2009, 2018) and a similar number of interviews for books on the domestic politics of small states (Corbett, 2015; Corbett and Veenendaal, 2018). We employ quotes selectively throughout to illustrate key themes but they only represent a fraction of the material consulted. The level of specificity we provide to identify quotes – that is, attribution at the SIDS-, region-, or country level – depends on the permissions provided by interviewees.

3. **Observation**: while some aspects of multilateralism are inaccessible, many of the ordinary day-to-day activities can be observed. Doing so added to our understanding of how small states participate in IOs by providing a layer of detail not obtainable via interviews. Observing international elites does not involve spending years in the field as with conventional anthropological ethnography. Rather, we undertook 'yo-yo ethnography' (Wulff, 2002; Rhodes, 2011), moving in and out of multiple field sites for intermittent periods timed to coincide with key events. We did not undertake this type of work in every IO, but we grabbed opportunities when they arose. For instance, we spent a week attached to the Kiribati mission to the UN in New York (from which the opening vignette is drawn), attended sessions at the IMO in London, and a meeting of the LDC/SIDS Trust Fund at the UNHRC in Geneva. Our analysis has been enriched by these experiences.

The interview sample was snowballed – we started with present-day diplomats who then put us in touch with their predecessors. As mentioned, we made no effort to define 'small state' but rather talked to diplomats from states who acted under that label in IOs, specifically in the UN system, WTO, World Bank, IMF, WIPO, and the WHO. At IOs we talked to the senior officials whose interest included small states and we then sought out officials in these IOs who work on small state issues to gain their perspective on the strategies being adopted.[3] When selecting small states our aim was to gain a breadth of perspectives – rich and poor, different regions, different levels of engagement in IOs, and so on – so as to ensure our analysis was holistic.[4] We also spoke to diplomats from larger states who support small states in pursuing their issues.[5] Given the emphasis on SIDS, we primarily rely on that interview data here (more than 60 interviews were conducted with diplomats from SIDS, SVEs, or their IO counterparts).

All case-selection strategies have limitations and ours is no exception. Our choice of IOs is in part a reflection of our previous work (Xu and Weller, 2004, 2009, 2018) but it also allowed us enough variation in institutional rules (one vote per state versus weighted voting) and between those IOs in which the SIDS label and grouping is active and important (the UN), somewhat active (the WB and IMF, and the SVEs in the WTO) and of limited relevance (WHO and WIPO), to make meaningful comparisons. We chose SIDS because they often have *both* small populations and developing economies, which means they are extreme cases for arguments about the impact of both size and economic wealth on participation in IOs. As such, any influence small states such as SIDS have, and any strategies from within IOs that succeed in involving them, are likely to also be effective when cohorts of slightly larger and wealthier states are considered. But this is conjecture, albeit we think plausibly so given the existing scholarship that we build on, as the book does not include analysis of all states or all IOs. Further empirical research is required to test whether the dilemmas we identify and the approach we adopt is relevant for other states and IOs. It may well be that the 'competent performance of vulnerability' is only relevant to developing countries, for example, just as the pursuit of 'throughput legitimacy' by IOs may be most effective when employed to justify the inclusion of SIDS.

Analysis

Our analysis follows the interpretive method of 'abduction' (Schwartz-Shea and Yanow, 2013: 46–9); we move back and forth between theory and data, seeking a holistic answer to the research puzzle. The result is a historically orientated description of the practice of small state participation across IOs over more than two decades that reveals the common dilemmas outlined previously. In abductive research, analysis is intertwined with data collection. Our interview questions focused on the everyday practice of small state diplomacy, both within national delegations and within the IOs themselves – we wanted to know when and how SIDS participate in IOs; in which IOs and on what issues; and what the challenges and opportunities of participation are. We then augmented their account with documentary records (for example, major reports on SIDS by IOs, reports from United Nations Conference on Small Island Developing States (UNSIDS) conferences, regular WTO reports on the SVE work programme, and so on. We use conventional citations for these sources. When interviewees gave us instances of when and how their participation had mattered in IOs, we followed this up by accessing formal agenda, minutes, and voting records. We then went back to interviewees to confirm the accuracy of the written account.

The patterns we uncovered are not seamless. There is conjecture and multiple interpretations. Some small states, including SIDS, are active in IOs and believe their efforts are significant. Others are not, either because they are sceptical of the difference they can make or because they choose to employ scarce resources elsewhere. Some IOs successfully incorporate small states in their discussions; others try but find it hard to induce them. As much as possible we differentiate between them by reporting the diversity of responses while also acknowledging patterns where they exist. While we interviewed more than 80 people specifically for this book, our sample is not representative of anything other than these were the people who agreed to talk to us. We consciously sought a diversity of views. But we do not deny that if a different group of researchers asked more than 80 different people similar questions they might come up with different patterns. We hope one day somebody else will try.

The desired outcome of this type of research is a heuristic not the naturalist goal of generalizability or predictability. In this case, the heuristic is that we can explain the rise of the constitutive category SIDS by way of two distinct strategies – the competent performance of vulnerability and throughput legitimacy – which in turn reflect dilemmas inherent to multilateral diplomacy. Heuristics are an intellectual shortcut – a rule of thumb – that can help us better understand the topic at hand. They are the map that allows us to make sense of the complexity around us and in doing so may inform practical political reasoning.[6] They are not law-like or predictive as their meaning and function is always open to revision and reconsideration: 'Heuristics are not about truth or falseness, but about discovery, finding new ideas' (Abbott, 2004: 161; see Wagenaar, 2011: 241 onwards). But they are also more analytically parsimonious and theoretically orientated than 'mere description' (Gerring, 2012). We hope that others will be able to use our heuristic to understand and explain cases that we have not included here. We also expect that if and when they do so they will refine our categories and interpretations.

Structure of the book

The structure of the book follows this abductive logic. Part I explains why IOs seek to include small states and why small states participate in IOs. Chapter 2 tells the story from the IOs' perspective. We first outline how the widening participation of members in processes and practices has led IOs to pursue throughputs as a means of enhancing their legitimacy. We then discuss the different features of throughput legitimacy as applied to the participation of SIDS in IOs: promoting norms and principles; upholding rules and traditions; and facilitating mutual assistance and cooperation.

In Chapter 3 we distinguish between different motivations for why small states participate in IOs: sovereign recognition; resource extraction; and the maintenance of a permissive LIO. We then outline how the competent performance of vulnerability enables them to achieve these goals, albeit recognizing that participation is always dynamic: different states, and different representatives of states, place different emphasis on each and are constantly revising their approach based on perceived successes and failures.

Part II encompasses three chapters that illustrate how these dilemmas and strategies interact. In Chapter 4 we take the 'most likely' case for SIDS influence: climate change. We show how the competent performance of vulnerability and the quest for throughput legitimacy have enabled SIDS to become champions of progressive action on this issue. We show how the label SIDS has enabled them to do so, not only in the UNGA and UNFCCC processes but also how they politicized an IO like the IMO that had previously been a predominantly technical institution. The success of SIDS in drawing attention to their vulnerabilities to achieve progressive action on climate change demonstrates how their participation in IOs can matter.

In Chapter 5 we focus on the three Bretton Woods institutions: the IMF, WBG, and WTO. Both the IMF and WB have recognized the condition of SIDS and tailored projects and programmes for them. Likewise, gaining recognition of the challenges facing the SVEs at the WTO provided some small states with an opportunity to present their interests and demands as a group, which would not be available to them otherwise. But these successes have been circumscribed by a system that advances the interests of each member rather than common goods. Thus, the voice and influence of small states in the Bretton Woods institutions has not been as significant as at the UN.

Chapter 6 focuses on the WHO and WIPO. SIDS have only rarely been active in these IOs despite persistent efforts, by other states, IO leaders, and the secretariat, to include them. We explain their absence in similar terms to their stalled efforts in the economic institutions – capacity deficits, existing rules and traditions, and the absence of friends and allies. The limited successes that have occurred stem primarily from the normative imperative of IOs to balance their inherent dilemma.

In the concluding chapter, we consider what these interactions amount to for small states, IOs, and the LIO writ large. We argue that while SIDS only represent a fraction of the world's population and economic wealth, and absorb only a very small proportion of IOs' time and resources, their participation is nevertheless significant because of what it tells us about the values and principles of international society. SIDS are often portrayed as the canary in the coal mine of climate change. But the metaphor works for the LIO too. If SIDS see value in participation, and other states are inclusive of them, then we know that the principles of sovereign equality and the right to development matter. These efforts may be primarily symbolic. But a society that completely ignored its smallest members would strike many as illiberal. By studying the participation of small states in IOs we learn something about the nature of liberal internationalism, too.

PART I

Actors

2

Why Do IOs Encourage the Participation of Small States?

IOs are facing serious challenges in continuing their active role in managing collective problems, whether being climate change, migration, cybersecurity, pandemics, or economic and financial stability. Diagnoses range from: 'the growing gap between yesterday's structures and today's problems' (Goldin, 2013: 3); that the large, rich, and powerful states continue to use a combination of options – threat to exit, voice, and the creation of alternative institutions – to dominate the agenda (Morse and Keohane, 2014); the increasingly diverse number of members have caused constant gridlocks and impasses that paralyse decision making; that IOs have become 'the Frankenstein problem' themselves – that is, they develop preferences independent of the governments that created them, leading states to fight back by refusing to cooperate (Newman, 2010; Guzman, 2013); that a lack of popular elections and insulation of organizational leaders and bureaucrats creates a 'democratic deficit' (Koppell, 2008; Hurd, 2008); and the inability of IOs to manage the challenges stems from a lack of leadership, especially leadership of leading powers. All of these statements have some merit and capture aspects of the development of a complex IO world.

Our intervention starts with the straightforward point that the inclusion of the countries we now call SIDS in IOs has occurred against this backdrop. In the next chapter we show how SIDS sought to pursue their agenda in IOs. In this chapter we explain why IOs accommodated their involvement. We argue that the key reason they have created groupings like SIDS is that it contributes to their ongoing attempt to resolve these challenges, all of which threaten to undermine their legitimacy as authoritative global actors. To be effective IOs needed to be trusted by their member states to represent their interests. Without legitimacy, nothing will be achieved;

legitimacy is a necessary condition for success but not a sufficient one. The significance of this research agenda derives from Buchanan and Keohane's (2006: 407) argument that '[t]he perception of legitimacy matters because, in a democratic era, multilateral institutions will only thrive if they are viewed legitimate by democratic publics'.

The legitimacy of IOs is the subject of intense academic debate (Agne et al, 2015; Gronau and Schmidtke, 2016; Lenz and Viola, 2017; Tallberg and Zürn 2019). Specifically, scholars have sought to identify the strategies IOs employ to increase their legitimacy among different communities – for example, member states, other IOs, NGOs, and the public at large – while remaining bound to the centuries-old principle that sovereign states are the fundamental units of the international system. In doing so they have also sought to specify the precise mechanisms by which legitimation or delegitimation occurs.

Typically, when analysing how IOs generate legitimacy for their operations, scholars differentiate between 'inputs' and 'outputs' (Uhlin, 2010; Agné et al, 2015; Tallberg and Zürn, 2019). We extend these arguments by focusing on what Schmidt (2013) calls 'throughput' legitimacy. We show how involving SIDS in everyday processes and practices enables IOs to balance inputs and outputs by way of throughputs. By including SIDS in the processes and practices of decision-making, IOs fulfil their mandate to be inclusive while at the same time they share responsibility for outcomes by increasing ownership and buy-in from all players. The point is that IOs have legitimation strategies (Gronau and Schmidtke, 2016) that they enact to generate support and these strategies have to be seen to serve multiple constituencies. SIDS are only one such constituency but they are nevertheless symbolically important given their size and practically significant because of their numbers.

IOs, membership, and throughput legitimacy

IOs have always had to manage two competing demands: to be inclusive in representing and promoting the interests of their members, they must also be able to move cooperation forward in either rules and standard setting or/and in assisting member states in one form or another. In other words, IOs must be seen as not only legitimate through their inclusiveness and participation but also by being able to achieve something. Historically, a few countries dominated IO organizational structures, agenda setting, and their operations; as our interviews noted, some middle-ranking countries were known to be 'friends of the system' willing to compromise and build alliances to make multilateral cooperation a political reality, a small number of countries were known as spoilers who could rock the boat at critical times, and a fourth group, a large number of small and/or developing countries, remained largely inactive or acquiescent (Keohane, 1969: 295–6; see Long, 2017a, b for further discussion).

Some of the extensive discussions on the legitimacy of IOs are normative; some are practical. The issue comes up primarily because in joining IOs, states cede part of their autonomy in return for some rights and benefits. The IMF constantly reminds its members that when they decided to become members, they agreed to 'cede part of their economic sovereignty to the Fund … and their most general obligations are to pursue economic policies that are consistent with the IMF's purposes, and to collaborate with the Fund and with other members to assure orderly exchange rate arrangements and to promote a stable system of exchange rates' (Mountford, 2008: 5). Those IOs that emphasize the ceding of 'sovereignty' tend to 'intrude' on domestic politics and policies more than those that do not. States then demand IOs to be inclusive in their decision-making. They insist on some degree of 'fairness' in both what IOs do (substance) and the way of things are done (processes) (Gelphi, 2010; Zürn, 2018). Given that the 'commonality of interests' of member states is always in question, meeting the perception of fairness to their diverse members is important but difficult. This is especially the case when structurally not all members have an equal input in decision-making. An IO still can 'accumulate legitimacy through effectiveness: It produces "goods" for relevant actors, but how it does so may be opaque' (Kahler, 2006: 258). All IOs have been struggling to find a balance to be accountable to all their members by being inclusive, sometimes in decision-making and sometimes in outcomes, and to be effective in producing key outputs, whether decisions or service delivery.

In the past 70 years or so, the number of IOs has expanded exponentially. The public and governments constantly either attribute progresses in, or blame for failure on, multilateral cooperation to IOs. In the past 20–25 years, all IOs have experienced significant changes in their membership and in their way of operating. While the threat of exit remains an option of a very few yet important member states, as in the US decision to leave the second-oldest IO, the United Postal Union (UPU, founded 1874), a range of diverse states have increased their participation in IO activities. The 'increasing assertiveness' of some small states in the areas of their concern can obstruct IO operations and may even surprise and frustrate a few large and powerful ones, but the interests need to be balanced at IOs nonetheless. The practice of consensus decision-making, regardless of the formal rules, only exacerbates the paralysis of the operations of some IOs, as seen in the prolonged Doha round of trade negotiations at the WTO, the divided membership in the leadership elections in the FAO, or ILO in 2012, or the way H1N1, Ebola, or COVID-19 were managed at the WHO. Some of the world's smallest states have tried to exert influence with the support of large numbers of other members and/or IO staff to place their concerns on the international agenda, as seen when Botswana, in close cooperation with Sweden, placed discussion of the funding rules on the agenda at the WHO, or the climate change issues at the UN Security Council discussed in the opening chapter.

For many small states, IOs are important forums because they are at their most vulnerable when 'only might makes right' (Lupel and Malksoo, 2019). When they decide to challenge large states through IO mechanisms and get support from international civil servants, IOs may get the blame, not them. IOs may be 'democratic in principle, as exemplified by the judicial equality of states, but in practice it is impossible to erase differences between its members' (vanGrasstek, 2013: 558). Their legitimacy depends to a large extent on the perception and experience of each member state of some degree of fairness (Bradford and Linn, 2007). IOs have always been under pressure from their member states to 'promote a formal display of equality among nations that are in reality profoundly unequal' (Niezen and Sapignoli, 2017: 12). How do IOs manage the balance of the *numbers* (the chairs) that are necessary condition for their legitimacy and the *weight* (the shares) to achieve their commitment at the expense of ignoring the numbers?

Much of the politics and activities in IOs are organized around this theme. All IOs we consider, with the exception of the IMF and WB, work on the principle of sovereign equality and majority rule. Despite the existing structures of IOs, especially those whose decisions are still calculated as a balance between chairs and shares, most IOs in practice try to reach their decisions through consensus. This practice gives their member states a sense that their participation is valued and IOs a sense of legitimacy.

To explain how IOs balance their inherent dilemma between inputs and outputs we adapt the term 'throughput' legitimacy from the work of Vivian Schmidt (2013) and analysis of the EU (for example, Iusmen and Boswell, 2017). Schmidt (2013: 3) uses the term 'throughput' to describe decision-making conducted with, rather than for (output) and by (input), citizens. Likewise, Uhlin's (2010) work on the democratic legitimacy of transnational actors distinguishes between input legitimacy, defined as the relationship between the actor and its constituencies, throughput legitimacy, defined as the procedures for decision-making, and output legitimacy, defined as the consequences of decisions. Obviously, small states, as members of IOs, are not directly equivalent to the citizens in Schmidt's conceptualization or Uhlin's transnational actors. But long-standing assumptions about their structural disadvantages in the international system mean they face similar challenges of unequal knowledge, access, and influence. Indeed, the common view is that, despite their membership, small states have no influence on IOs and in this sense their participation (or lack thereof) cannot be explained away by reference to inputs (Drezner, 2008). In which case, by extending the 'throughput' idea to include the smallest members of the international system we are better able to identify the diversity of ways that IOs seek to enact legitimacy, and the trade-offs involved in focusing institutional reform efforts on one dimension rather than another (Oates, 2017: 200).

We therefore adapt the essence of Schmidt and Uhlin's definitions to the study of member state participation in IOs. Where the latter sees throughput legitimacy as characterized by transparency, accountability, participation, and deliberation, we focus primarily on participation in institutional processes and practices to empirically demonstrate the way IOs, as strategic actors (Gronau and Schmidtke, 2016), seek to generate throughput legitimacy via the inclusion of groupings such as SIDS. Our rationale is that all four characteristics may be important from the standpoint of some transnational actors, like NGOs, but they are not all relevant to member states, large or small. In doing so we assume that 'international organisations are instruments of change' in their nature (Blokker and Wessel, 2005: 1). Or, citing Michel Camdessus (2000), former managing director of the IMF, 'the hallmarks ... of the IMF are its universality and its adaptability. It is a perennially "self-reforming" institution, very mindful of its obligation to its entire membership.' The point is that IOs have adopted various measures to bridge the gap between the formal rules and structures paid down decades earlier and the shifting interests and priorities of their expanding membership.

The term 'throughput' brings our attention to the processes by which decisions are made in institutional contexts. It draws on the idea of 'feedback' articulated in Easton's (1965) seminal systems theory and turns on a version of Beetham's (1991) dual meaning of 'legitimacy': it is something that actors believe in and express. It has normative aspirations – Schmidt (2013: 6) sees a need for administrative systems to shore up 'the quality of the governance processes as established by their efficacy, accountability, transparency, inclusiveness and openness to interest intermediation' – but, we argue, it also has important empirical purchase as it invites us to open up the black box of daily interactions between actors in IOs.

A focus on 'throughput' legitimacy differs from much of the extant literature on IOs. The growing interest in the roles of IO secretariats as bureaucracies among constructivist scholars (for example, Barnett and Finnemore, 2004) asks whether their tendency to pursue their own interests may mean that dysfunctional behaviour thwarts the best intentions of their member states. At the least, this literature illustrates that IOs are made up of more than just competing member states, and great powers in particular; other actors, such as secretariats and NGOs, also shape outcomes. Studies, nonetheless, typically do not focus on small states. We contend that their participation is also an important component to generating 'throughput' legitimacy for the mandate and practices of IOs.

We posit that a focus on 'throughput' requires a different set of perspectives than conventionally used by IR scholars because it draws our attention to the processes and practices of decision-making (for example, Wildavsky, 1978; Kingdon and Thurber, 1984; for analogous studies in IR, see Pouliot, 2010). In these studies, decisions spring from the interplay between the actors who (some temporarily, some for longer periods) have access to strategic levers of influence, whether formal authority, information, communal memory, or expertise. Institutionalized processes create networks of ambitions, enmities, and disappointments. At different times, temporary coalitions seek to dictate what the IOs should do. The point is that practitioners, whether member state representatives or secretariats, take small states seriously, even if most scholars do not.

That is not to say that our analysis of 'throughput' legitimacy neglects the role of member states – quite the opposite. It just does not exclusively focus on 'great powers'. Some of this work is underway. But outside the EU, the literature has barely kept up with these developments. But if IOs are institutions whose processes are shaped by a host of actors, including secretariats and NGOs (for example, Finnemore, 1996; Martin and Simmons, 1998), then we would expect that even the world's smallest states, individually or collectively, could have an influence. And, if their participation is significant to understanding how IOs have sought to manufacture legitimacy outside the usual 'input–output' logic presumed in past studies, then this influence matters.

The evolution of legitimation practices

To demonstrate the way that IOs interact with small states like SIDS to increase their throughput legitimacy we focus on three aspects of their engagement with them. The first is the promotion of norms and principles. As outlined, the fact that SIDS are members of IOs reflects prevailing norms of the LIO, including: the sovereign equality of states and the right to development. These norms create the imperative for IOs to be inclusive of a broader and broader range of voices. The second is the rules and traditions of IOs. These can be contained in their formal charters, handed down decades ago, but they also incorporate informal practices and conventions. Rules, practices, conventions, and traditions can help explain why some IOs have had more success in incorporating SIDS than others. Finally, IOs exist to facilitate cooperation and so it should be no surprise that SIDS have friends and allies in IOs who champion their cause. As the UNSC example we started the book with illustrates, these friends and allies can be larger states (like Sweden), the leaders of IOs, the secretariat, as well as NGOs. The ability of IOs to facilitate cooperation can help explain why SIDS bridge the gap between their agenda, limited capacity, and the standards of competent performance.

Promoting norms and principles

IOs are not new. The oldest – managing copyright and postal services – hark back to the 19th century. The first regional organization for health was created in response to an epidemic in the Americas 40 years before the WHO itself in 1948. Yet most of the key ones today were created at the end of the Second World War with the intent of preventing any repetition. They were founded on the assumption that institutional mechanisms were required to regulate aspects of relations between states (Inis, 1956: 21). The initial steps were in areas where the needs were most apparent: trade and financial systems. The membership was limited, and the commitment of those few had much in common. Gradually decolonization and the emergence of new states changed the imperatives. Development became an integral part of their activities. Here we are concerned with the way in which the processes and practices that sought to integrate national sovereignty with international action were extended to notions of the right to develop, finally enshrined in the UN Declaration of 1986.

These norms have altered a number of practices. It is widely accepted that all members have the right to be represented at IOs, for example. These institutions are typically referred to as 'member-driven organizations' who serve all states. Decisions are made by consensus. The secretariat is supposed to be neutral and there is an increasing emphasis on the representativeness of its staff. Leaders of IOs are elected and serve limited terms. And non-members are permitted to join providing they agree to the terms and conditions of participation. The point is that these core norms operate across the multilateral system. They encapsulate the ideas of how IOs think they should be run, although they are invariably different practices between them that can make myths out of the visionary propositions. We do not expand on them here, but will return to these practices as appropriate. The key point is that these norms and practices have been permissive of small states. Indeed, over the last two decades they appear to have become increasingly conducive to them.

Around the turn of the century, many IOs had to reconsider their condition. The three economic IOs were facing some shared and unique challenges. The relevance of the IMF came into question as borrowing demands had significantly declined in part because of the way the IMF had managed the Asian financial crisis and in part because of the conditionality imposed on borrowing. Competition from the regional banks undermined its centrality and raised questions about its continued presence. The IMF faced dwindling lending as emerging economies started accumulating foreign reserves to avoid potential future 'rescues'. The WB had been the subject of continuing campaigns. '50 years is enough' was one NGO war cry. Its conditions on lending, including the concessional lending from the International Development Association (IDA) along the ten principal lines of the Washington Consensus, had forced even some African countries away. It was no longer the only player too. The WTO was looking for a role after the completion of the Uruguay Round and the occasionally violent demonstrations against its presence. The member states were determined that the new WTO would not be dominated by a small Quadrilateral Security Dialogue (QUAD) as the General Agreement on Tariffs and Trade (GATT) had been; they wanted influence in the new organization and more member states were becoming active participants. The lack of progress in the new Development Doha round raised questions about whether it still had any influence. The three were suffering from widespread public protests, as seen in Geneva, Seattle, Genoa, and Washington. Other IOs were struggling. The WHO and the FAO had stalled under unimpressive leaders. The WIPO seemed to have lost its position as the lead agency on intellectual property when the WTO took responsibility for Trade-Related Aspects of Intellectual Property Rights (TRIPs). The WIPO's long-time leader had never made the transition to seeing IP as an economic issue. He regarded it as an exclusively legal question; unimpressed by the WIPO's inability to enforce its policies, many countries forum shopped and decided the WTO was a better location for settling disputes because its tribunal had teeth.

An example of when these issues – the development agenda and the changing norms in IOs – came together was September 2000 when the membership of the UN endorsed the call to reduce the extreme poverty. Known as the Millennium Development Goals (MDGs), these ambitions consolidated efforts to draw attention to small and developing states, to acknowledge their specific structural characteristics and increase assistance. The multilateral game had new imperatives and the positioning of small states in the IO universe needs to be understood against this backdrop. By understanding first how the IOs responded to the bigger issues, we can then better appreciate the context for the decisions about, and relations with, SIDS.

These changed conditions for IOs provided opportunities for new initiatives, new ground on which they could work. The 'club' nature of IOs was being replaced with a bazaar of big and small, developed and developing players, open to NGOs and different agendas. It was not a forum where all players were equal, far from it. SIDS, constituting the smallest of the small, had a difficult hand to play, but given skill, opportunities were there which had not existed in earlier formulations of the IOs' working worlds. These new circumstances provided a contested environment in which 'small island developing state' could become a label and an established grouping. In a similar way labels and groupings of small states, such as SVEs at the WTO, could emerge in other IOs, even when forums like the G20 and G7 explicitly sought to marginalize them. Small states had to fight but IOs – the membership and the secretariat – were more receptive to their condition because they needed to redefine their own position. The door was ajar. There were those within IOs who saw greater participation and inclusiveness as a way to resolve their inherent dilemma. It could be seen as a win-win situation. SIDS, BRICS, and other groupings found fertile ground in which to plant ideas and be heard.

In sum, the key point is that the norms and principles of IOs were always somewhat conducive to small states. But the practice of them under the old club model meant that their promise was rarely realized. Part of that was due to the lack of participation (Chapter 3). But there were also changes in IOs. As the old club model waned, the 'epistemic virtues' (Buchanan and Keohane, 2006: 406) of IOs were reimagined in ways that might enhance their legitimacy. Part of this shift was a renewed focus on the development agenda, as represented by the MDGs, but it also ushered in a greater emphasis on procedural fairness (Tyler, 2001).

Upholding rules, conventions, and traditions

The norms and practices that govern IOs and the preference for consensus might appear to advantage the smallest; the rules and traditions often favour the largest and richest who created them decades ago. The dilemma this creates for reformers in IOs can help explain why a shift in the principles that favour inclusion does not lead to seamless change across the multilateral system. Rather, ad-hoc and incremental adaptations to the existing rules, conventions, and traditions is the common pattern. In turn, this give and take can explain why there is variation between IOs in the way they have accommodated the growing demands of small states for greater participation in their activities. Three aspects of IOs' operations illustrate this: groupings, decision-making, and leadership elections.

Groupings

IOs have always had exclusive groups to discuss key issues before they were brought to the table or before the final decisions could be worked out among the member states. This practice is nothing new; it is a practical way for countries to conduct their diplomacy in a multilateral environment, as Rodrigo de Rato (2006: 128), the former managing director of the IMF, explained: 'I am a strong advocate of transparency, but ... I think quiet diplomacy, as some have characterized it, has produced good results.'

The problem with groupings is that while large groups have more clout they also have greater difficulty coordinating positions. The inverse is also true: small groups have an easier time reaching consensus but have less clout. Moreover, each faces the problem of exclusivity – that is, those who are not included frequently complain about being excluded. Club decision-making creates serious legitimacy issues for IOs, as explained by Michel Camdessus (2000), another former managing director of the Fund: 'The problem is not that we are not accountable, but that we are not seen to be accountable, and that some member governments from time to time find it convenient not to express their public support for actions they have supported behind closed doors.'

An important starting point in relation to the core message of this chapter is that there is no monopoly on forming groupings: the rich and powerful states have used groupings to achieve their objectives, and so have smaller states. Groupings are double-edge swords for multilateral cooperation: they can facilitate it through consensus building; they can also be stumbling blocks for cooperation. Initially, IOs channelled SIDS participation via existing groupings. However, reflecting the perennial tension, SIDS felt that groups such as G77 (formed in in 1964), the African, Caribbean, and Pacific Group of States (ACP) (formed in 1974), or G33 (formed in 1987), did not sufficiently promote their interests on either climate change or S&DT in trade. Despite some opposition, for the most part IOs have accommodated their desire to create new groupings of their own. We will discuss this further in relation to the UN in subsequent chapters (see also Panke, 2013). Here we provide examples from the economic IOs.

As interests became more specialized and identified, more exclusive groupings began to emerge, using a wide variety of tactics. Some groups worked within the existing system while others took their issues to forums outside IOs. These developments often led IO leaders or other players either to expand the number of groups or institutionalize the processes. Small states have both added more groups and been included into quasi-formal discussion and deliberation processes. One often-cited example is the 'Green Room' meetings started at GATT and continued today in the WTO. The Green Room was the WTO Director General's (DG) conference room, the place where he could hold small meetings of key member states to seek common ground and thrash out possible compromises; it was a sort of inner sanctum, informal but strategic. Scholars have called the meetings there an example of 'the club model of multilateral cooperation' lacking democratic legitimacy (Keohane and Nye, 2001). Those practitioners involved in multilateral cooperation tend to see them as normal means of diplomacy. In the early 1980s, during the preparatory stage for launching a new round of trade negotiations, there were serious differences among contracting parties about the issues to be negotiated and in what order. As some major trading countries, especially those in Asia and in the Middle East, showed little interest, the US and EC convened numerous times to work out their differences because without cooperation negotiations would stall. When the two did agree, other parties with their combined efforts (usually small and/or developing states) 'had no real prospect of altering the outcome' (Winham, 1989). The agreement of key powerful players might be a necessary condition for multilateral cooperation, but not sufficient, as their (dis)agreements often frustrated middle and small members. Progress then depended on the coalitions of smaller states, as the 'cafe-au-lait' led by Switzerland and Columbia in 1986, and, more importantly the IO secretariat to defend multilateralism and promote interests of small and large alike (Xu and Weller, 2004: Chapter 4). This was the process that lead to the launch of the Doha Development Round in 2001 too (Harbinson, 2009). 'Consensus is built in committees and within small groups', explained one former DG of the WTO, but broader support is needed. This is often when the interests and demands of small states are brought into the picture either with their combined efforts, which do not happen often, but by large states speaking on their behalf and more often than not by the IO secretariat.

The IMF has multiple groups working inside or outside its formal procedures: G2, G4, G5, G10, G20, G24, G77 (Van Houtven, 2001). In 1946, when the IMF became operational, there were 12 executive directors (EDs) at the Executive Board (EB) – five appointed and seven elected representing a group of countries each. Officials of G10, however, often took the discussion on expansion of the financial resources of the IMF and arrangements and conditions to borrow outside the Board room and entered an agreement and then presented it to the management at the Board meetings. As major countries ran into arguments about the role of the US dollar and the sustainability of the gold standard (de Vries, 1976; Parboni, 1981), G10 became more active in discussing the role and the options of the IMF to stabilize the economy of its member states. The formation of this small and informal group to discuss in detail matters that would affect all IMF members outside the Executive Board caused great resentment among those who were excluded. Access to core decisions can never be taken for granted, even by middle powers, let alone small states; in particular, the latter had to work through these middle-power executive directors. When access is granted it may still be no more than tokenistic. 'The Australian executive director at the Fund complained that G-10 was "a very exclusive club" … [after] Australia and Portugal unsuccessfully demanded admission' (Mountford, 2008: 9).

After their own groups (G77 and then G24) failed to have any impact, developing countries (including small ones) demanded transparency and inclusiveness. While demand for 'one state, one vote' might help small states get their voice heard, it could not go anywhere as that arrangement would 'overweigh the citizens of the smaller countries' and might undermine the ultimate objectives of multilateral cooperation as the 'influential members' or 'structurally important members' can 'exercise a credible threat to exit and form their own clubs, such as the Group of Seven, the Group of Ten and the Organisation of Economic Co-operation and Development (OECD)' (Kahler, 2008: 136). While 'the largest countries argued that exchange rates and policy coordination were too sensitive to be discussed in a wide forum' (Boughton, 2001: 192), often they could not reach agreements among themselves. Back then the US was unhappy with G10 where Europe was overrepresented. They turned to IMF management for endorsement to ensure a sense of legitimacy as multilateral efforts and for help in providing global information and alternatives. This was when major players agreed to institutionalize the informal groupings and practices to meet the demand. G10 was then enlarged to the Committee of Twenty (C20) that was formalized into the Interim Committee in 1974 when a joint Development Committee of the IMF and the WB was formed to advise the Board of Governors on 'transfer of real resources to developing countries'. Upgrading the advisory bodies to a political level of ministers or their deputies might not have stopped informal groups of large and powerful states from working behind the scene. It did nonetheless bring issues concerning the small to the attention of the international community in general. In the process, IO leaders and the secretariat could play an important role in promoting their interests.

As informal groupings expand in size, countries seek help from the secretariat. "Once they expanded from G7 to G20," explained one senior IMF staffer, "they needed a bit more structure and more information, they started looking for input from us". This is the case with the large as well as the small states. The same staffer said:

'Our job is to facilitate understanding. Some EDs do not get a lot of help from their capital because people in the capital are not really focused; they focus on things briefly and they turn to something else. We explain things to EDs, they then can help facilitate process.'

If large states prefer to work through informal groups because they believe it is easier to bargain behind closed doors than in public, small states work through informal groups because, as individual members of IO, they do not have the weight or the capacity to make a difference in IOs. The challenge is 'how do you get everyone into the action and still get action?' (Keohane and Nye, 2001: 170).

In the 1990s, small states, despite their vulnerabilities, did not draw much attention or resources from the WB because they were relatively rich in terms of GDP per capita in comparison with many developing countries (see Chapter 5). As the WB explained, 'The relatively high standards of living were attributed to substantial external aid targeted at the social sectors, "affluent" subsistence systems, and large inflows of worker remittances in some Pacific economies' (The World Bank, 2005: iii). But by the end of that decade this perception would begin to change. In the early 2000s, the WB management 'established a Small States Secretariat within the Operations Policy and Country Services, with the objective of increasing the visibility and corporate attention to small states' (IEG World Bank, 2016: xi). Operations Policy and Country Services (OPCS) is known as the 'plumbing' department as it coordinates both regional and sector departments in a matrix system.

In 2004, the IMF's Policy Development and Review Department outlined an operational guidance on access under the poverty reduction and growth facility. In the guidance note, some small island developing countries were considered as potential targets for help, such as Kiribati, Vanuatu, St Lucia, St Vincent and Grenadines, and Samoa. In the past two decades, the IMF staff have produced a series of studies and reports examining the situations of the small, especially micro, states and what assistance they might need and how to assist them. One consistent message is the diversity of the group despite common challenges.[1] After the global financial crisis in 2008–09, renewed efforts were made that led to the IMF featured event in Samoa in September 2014 on 'Coping with Natural Disasters: building macro-fiscal resilience in small island states', with one of the deputy managing directors attending the event. While the IMF joined other IOs in working on climate change, sustainable development, and aid for trade, it is more removed from providing direct assistance to small states. Its work by and large remains in producing reports and studies.

Decision-making

Who makes the crucial decisions and where are they made? Any analysis needs to take into account both the official forums, even where they do no more than legitimize agreements made elsewhere, and those informal processes through which issues can be settled in advance through often lengthy negotiations. Consensus may be a desirable means of making decisions, but consensus is often the result of lengthy and hotly contested debates across multiple meetings.

At the IMF and the WB, members of the executive board make decisions on behalf of their constituents. At the WHO, 34 elected member states appoint qualified individuals to serve at the executive board that deliberates and makes most decisions over health issues. The Council of the FAO with its 49 elected member states exercised all the delegated power from the entire membership. Other IOs have a similar organizational structure with an elected smaller body in charge of decision-making. Therefore, decisions are not always made by a few powerful actors behind closed doors. The power and influence of small states are often in proportion to their size and their contribution but their interests and concerns are better promoted and represented at IOs than they would do individually in dealing with the larger states. This is the nature of multilateral cooperation.

Take IMF as an example: in 1945 only 29 countries signed on the initial Articles of Agreement and by 2020 its membership has grown to 198. In the 1960s, 48 states joined IMF and they were nearly all newly independent states. Small states in the Caribbean region joined in the 1970s and 1980s while those in the Pacific did so only in the past two decades. When representation (chairs) and voice (shares) were adjusted over the decades the main controversies were not over these small states, rather on the representation of the large ones, either regarding their population or size of their economy. The IMF and WB are governed by Executive Boards. The vote of each member is weighted, and is related to its contribution. Small states therefore have minuscule formal voting power. Some EDs represent single countries; others speak for groups of members. Small states had their choice which group they would like to join so that their interests could be better represented by the middle powers who provide the ED and who represent the group. Tonga and Fiji, for instance, joined the group whose largest shareholders were Singapore and Malaysia; most other Pacific island countries joined the group where Australia, New Zealand, and South Korea rotated in ED and Alternate positions. Back in the 1980s, Fiji belonged to the group where Indonesia and Thailand were the two largest shareholders and was able to serve as Alternate ED (1978–80, 1986–88). It would have been very unlikely to have had that opportunity if it were in the Pacific group where Australia, New Zealand, and South Korea rotated as ED and Alternate. Timor-Leste is in the same group as some Latin American countries, a reminder of its colonial past. This choice is important for small states with limited capacity, as they can decide with whom they shared 'common economic and political interests' (Boughton, 2001: 1042).

After independence, an increasing number of small states joined IOs to bring their special challenges to their attention. For instance, many small island states, especially in the Pacific region, did not join the IMF until the 1990s or later: Marshall Islands (1992), Micronesia (1993), Palau (1997), Timor-Leste (2002), Tuvalu (2010), and Nauru (2016). By 2015, more than a fifth of IMF members are countries with populations of under 1.5 million; three out of four small states are islands or widely dispersed multi-island states. They may be a diverse group of member states at the IMF, representing all income categories, but they all face size-related constraints that translate to a common set of development challenges, such as higher fixed and variable costs of providing public goods, with little scope to exploit economies of scale, and more importantly, natural disasters and other external shocks. 'The heightened interest in their concerns began when several of the IMF's Executive Board members created an informal working group on economic issues in small states', acknowledged the former deputy managing director of IMF. 'Internally collaboration has increased since a small islands group was formed to facilitate the sharing of insights and lessons learned by staff working on small states' (Zhu, 2013).

The WTO is often used as an example of consistent gridlocks. Given that decisions made at the WTO bind state actions and trade is accepted as an engine for economic development, countries large and small pay to ensure their presence and participation. The evolution of their presence in Geneva reflects the change.

The WTO's predecessor, the GATT, had only a few national missions dedicated to its activities: just four in 1982 and ten in 1992, with a total staff across those offices of 19 and 71 respectively. Under the WTO the numbers expanded fourfold, to 29 in 2002 and 39 in 2012 (with a total of 138 and 297 staff respectively). In addition, the number of country missions that incorporated the WTO representatives within a broader UN office grew from 71 in 1982 to 97 in 2012 (and from 215 to 560 staff in total, vanGrasstek 2013: 88). Negotiations in Geneva have become more crowded: more missions, more agents, more interests, and more demands.

Increasing membership has complicated the task of reaching agreements at IOs where formal or informal consensus is the norm. A broad consensus is necessary to make even modest progress as seen in the governance reforms at the IMF and the WB or at the WTO ministerial meetings since 1999. 'Overlaid on the increased number of participants is the reality that participating countries vary widely in population, economic output, and interests' (Porter et al, 2001: 12). Numbers matter where interests are sufficiently common that agreed positions can be settled. In this instance countries felt they had more to gain from bilateral incentives than from common action.

Leadership elections

The leaders of IOs have often been champions of small states. Their advocacy is both a mixture of benevolence and self-interest. Many are committed to the idea of sovereign equality, the increased participation of all members, improved performance for developing countries, and the overarching goal of increasing the legitimacy of global governance. They also need votes in leadership elections and small states represent a considerable constituency. They are therefore a group worth courting and investing resources in.

In the UN specialized agencies, member states vote. There is no weighting for size of population or economy; the US, China, the Marshall Islands, and St Lucia each have one vote. Given that there are far more small states than large ones, elections provide the occasion where small states should matter. Obviously, this is not the case in those institutions where there is no election. The US government chooses the president of the WB. Technically, the US executive director places a nomination before the Executive Board and it is endorsed without a vote. In the IMF the Europeans settle on a candidate, in the past from one the larger powers, usually from France or Germany, even though the most recent is from Bulgaria (via the WB).

In the WTO there is a complex process of developing a consensus candidate. A triumvirate of the heads of the three key committees runs a process of consultations, asking each country to select its preferred candidate from the list of those who were formally nominated by their country (the only way a person can be considered). Gradually the list is winnowed down, until one 'emerges' as the preferred nominee. In asking member states their opinion, the triumvirate asks for a list of names but not for reasons for the choices and not for negative choices; that is, vetoes. Each consultation is very brief. In the last occasion the triumvirate spoke to all the members who had a delegation in Geneva. For those who did not, all of whom were small states, it arranged a phone call to the capital to seek the choice of the country. In the contested process in 2013 there were three rounds, taking the field from nine, to five, to two. In deciding which candidates would survive the triumvirate took into account not just the numbers, but also the geographic spread of support and the size of the economies. Small states are consulted, but size militates against the weight of their vote. A majority constructed of the 55 per cent of the membership, but all of whom are small, for instance, would not guarantee any selection. Groups do not vote; member states do and the voting can be hard to coordinate when no numbers are ever presented.

When the position is vacant, that is when the incumbent DG is not seeking a second (or in earlier days a third or fourth) term, the process is strongly contested. Some member states commit extensive time and resources when they seek the support of other members. Small states are an obvious target. Commitments to build electricity grids or cricket grounds are rumoured to be offered in exchange for votes. Candidates are flown around capital cities to talk to ministers. In such contests small states do not have the resources to fund a campaign that has to touch over 150 member states who can vote. Candidates could not fly around the globe and commitments cannot be made. Even candidates from middle-income member states have complained they had nothing to offer. An ambassador noted that in one ballot the order in which the candidates were eliminated reflected the size of the GDP of each candidate's country. Small states need not apply. While African members such as Senegal, Togo, Mali, and Kenya have headed some of the less high-profile IOs, as have a number of smallish European countries, there is not a single example of a small state in the Caribbean, the Pacific, or Central America that has successfully run a candidate in the IOs we cover.

Decisions about elections are made in the capitals. Delegations may provide information, and even recommendations about which candidate should be supported. This recommendation may be approved, but the prerogative remains with foreign ministers and sometimes heads of state. At the IOs, ballots are often run on a system of repeated votes. The bottom candidate is eliminated and further votes are held until there are just the two remaining. These can happen quite quickly. If the capital has the capacity, they may try to calculate the alternative scenarios that will emerge. So, if our preferred Candidate C is eliminated, we will vote for Candidate B, until there is just a choice between two. Occasionally candidates go backwards, as delegations realize that, although not yet eliminated they will not win and their support shifts elsewhere in the hope of being identified with a winner. Discretion in second and third choices may be delegated to the person in the room; more often it will require a quick phone call home. These second and third rounds are "the only time you need to have them on speed dial", said a Geneva-based diplomat.

The larger the numbers voting, the more likely is it to be dominated by blocs, not individuals. In the WHO, said an observer, the dynamic changed when it went from the Executive Board with 34 votes to the Health Assembly with over 150. In the former candidates had to compete for votes, in one ballot the EB was tied 17–17 for a series of ballots until one member state switched its vote. In the Health Assembly the ballot was dominated by regional politics. The African Union had long claimed it had been ignored and that now it was its 'turn'. It had a good candidate who duly won easily. In the WIPO the Coordination Committee in 2008 elected Gurry by one vote out of 81; the split was said to be on developed versus developing state lines.

There can be no surprise if in some cases small states put a price on their vote. "If a candidate brings pot of money, lots of promises, then small states have become skilful at playing different cards. It may not be ethical to make promises to favour candidates but that's politics." An FAO DG once stopped off in Nauru for a lunch with a group of Pacific island agriculture ministers while en route for New Zealand. An FAO official wondered at first why he bothered as it required a long detour. Then he realized that sitting at the table were seven votes for the DG's next re-election. It did not take expensive commitments to tie in the votes. Small states can be satisfied they were being remembered with small targeted funds that are within a DG's discretion.

Bloc votes do not always hold. Even when the African Union has a nominated candidate there can be no guarantee that another African country will not still nominate one of their own and split the vote. But the tensions are still there. A WHO official recalls the occasion when the delegate from Liberia claimed that the DG election was a Western conspiracy. "No sooner said, you could see the room divide and you could see the frenzy, the thirst for blood ... The statement forced everyone to take a position." It was an example of how small states could have an impact. The delegate never claimed it was his government's position, but the statement once made could not be retracted.

Facilitating mutual assistance and cooperation

So far, we have outlined how the norms and principals of IOs have been able to encourage increased participation of the small states we have come to call SIDS, and how their inclusion has been channelled via existing rules, conventions, and traditions, and varies because of them. In this final section we outline how promoting a SIDS agenda suits a number of other actors in IOs, including some larger states, the secretariat, and NGOs. The caveat, again, is that we are not saying that SIDS do not have opponents in IOs when, as we will illustrate in subsequent chapters, they do. Rather we want to highlight that they also have important friends and allies. And the ability of all states to work through friends and allies to build peaceful coalitions on key issues is the *raison d'être* of IOs.

Larger states

Robert Keohane's (1971: 163) observation that 'America's crusading spirit presented small allies with bargaining influence' at IOs, identifies the broader truth that small states will often work with larger countries to achieve their objectives. Supporting the demands of small states is still occasionally used by the US to resolve its differences with the European states, but a few large and small European countries have become quite active supporters and even the champions of SIDS. Part of this is a pragmatic calculation by larger states: in institutions where consensus is the convention, co-opting the support of SIDS provides crucial weight in numbers. Indeed, they can be among the cheapest votes to attract. But other motives are important too, including a sense of responsibility, particularly on the part of former colonial powers, and shared interests, especially on climate change. We provided a climate change example in the opening vignette to the book, and will revisit that discussion in Chapter 4. Here we illustrate how larger states can sometimes seek to promote the interests of the smallest out of a sense of responsibility.

The development agenda has few outright opponents. But not everyone is in favour of S&DT for SIDS (see Chapter 5). Some larger states and individual leaders have been crucial to their cause. We provide one illustrative example: Gordon Brown and his commitment to development. Of course, his core interest was on heavily indebted poor countries (HIPC), but his continuing championing of the development in general contributed to a context in which the SIDS agenda could be advanced. Many working at the IMF and the WB attributed the development agenda at both institutions to Gordon Brown. After several years of operation behind closed doors, major powers decided to formalize informal decision-making by establishing the International Monetary and Financial Committee (IMFC) in 1997. 'Although the IMFC has no formal decision-making powers, in practice, it has become a key instrument for providing strategic direction to the work and policies of the Fund' (Mountford, 2008: 9). It also gives political weight to the Board. The chairman of IMFC plays a key role in setting up the agenda for the Fund with close collaboration with the Fund management. From its beginning in 1999 to 20 October 2007, all 15 IMFC meetings were chaired by one person – Gordon Brown. The Committee met twice a year and Brown took an active leadership and resorted to 'the greater use of more relaxed and informal meetings at both breakfast and lunch' to prepare for the meetings.

There was close collaboration between the Fund and Brown's office. IMF management proposed the draft provisional agenda to the Executive Board, normally after informal staff-level discussion with the Chairman's office. After the Board's review, and before sending the agenda to the IMFC, the Chairman's agreement was obtained. 'Gordon Brown always sought to have a low-income country item on the agenda' (Shakow, 2009). This emphasis overlapped with those at the joint IMF–Bank Development Committee, where four ministers of international development played a key role. In 1998–2002, four development ministers, all women, were active at roughly the same time: Clare Short of the UK, Hilde Frafjord Johnson of Norway, Eveline Herfhens of the Netherlands, and Heidemarie Wieczrok-Zeul of Germany. At the IMF/WB joint development committee meetings they joined forces to push forward development agendas. These active ministers made a difference in shaping the agenda on development, inclusiveness, and equality. That was also the time when developing countries in general, large and small alike, had shifted their historical position of being 'as aloof as reasonably possible in accepting [IO] obligations' to more active and assertive participants in making concessions with the expectation that others would fulfil their promises too. Consequently, they had gained a much greater stake in IOs and "a greater right to assert their interests", explained Julio Lacarte Muró, Uruguay career diplomat who served the GATT/WTO, the United Nations Conference on Trade and Development (UNCTAD), the International Bank for Reconstruction and Development (IBRD), the United Nations Educational, Scientific and Cultural Organization (UNESCO), the UN Committee for Development Planning, and other multilateral institutions. IOs responded to the combination of these developments, such as the WB working closely with the WTO on trade and development at the Doha ministerial meeting and became a partner of the newly launched MDGs in 2000.

This example highlights how leaders from larger states can be important allies of the smallest. But the caveat is that relying on the support of these types of individuals is a high-risk strategy for SIDS. Democracy ensures that these leaders are only ever temporary and there is no guarantee their successor will be of a similar mind. They also win elections primarily on the basis of their domestic performance not their role in assisting former colonies overseas. Indeed, their international efforts may count against them at home and so when push comes to shove, they will likely prioritize their constituents. Moreover, much of the implementation of their vision is left to their diplomatic service, who have their own culture and outlook in relation to SIDS. Specifically, for diplomats from large states working on SIDS issues and taking postings in SIDS capitals is usually at the very bottom end of the hierarchy when it comes to career goals and aspirations.

In sum, friends and allies can be fickle, especially when they are personalized, but they are nevertheless an important part of this story, and our explanation of variation in the interactions between IOs and small states on different issues in particular.

The secretariat

The secretariats of IOs are always faced with a dilemma. They have expertise, experience, and a collective memory with which to assist member states.

Yet, they are meant to be the servants of the member states, responding to their initiatives. That IOs are member-driven is a ubiquitous mantra. Meanwhile, secretariats have the opportunity, and occasionally requests from member states, to devise tactics that allow their expertise to be utilized without it appearing they are pulling the strings. 'Esse, non videri' was the description of their role by a WTO director ('to be, but not to be seen', was his translation, cited in Xu and Weller, 2004). Deep knowledge and rich experience can empower the secretariats, but they know they can only exercise their influence as the guardian of the multilateral system and supporters of the member states.

In recent years, scholars have paid more attention to the secretariats of IOs and started appreciating the work and influence of these 'faceless' professional staff. In respect to small states in IOs, they need to fulfil a number of special roles: they should defend and protect the multilateral system; they need to be inclusive by engaging with all states, large and small; they need to maintain impartiality to all even while small states need more help; and they need to ensure both the effectiveness and efficiency of the system. These demands on the secretariat may not always be compatible. The secretariat requires judgement and skill to maintain the image of impartiality that allows them to fulfil their role. At the same time, they have a direct interest in the efficient functioning of their institution and its processes and practices. Both are key to their legitimacy. And this dilemma is compounded by the development agenda because small states such as SIDS are likely to be long-term clients. So, secretariats have increasingly dedicated time and resources to assist small states such as SIDS. They are careful not to appear to advocate for them but they also know that if they do not facilitate a minimum level of participation it will be to the detriment of IOs as a whole. As a result, the secretariat of IOs is an important factor in why small states are able to be more active than they once were.

The capacity of the secretariat varies from institution to institution. International civil servants (ICSs) at technical organizations enjoy more 'freedom of manoeuvre' vis-à-vis their counterparts in political organizations, such as the UN (Jonah and Hill, 2018). 'This relatively broader authority has, for instance, allowed the WHO secretariat to change and adapt its operational activities incrementally without the involvement of its policy-making organs' (Burci, 2005: 439). This is the shared practice in all technical IOs. They adapt because other things change. The WHO secretariat was able to identify and respond to 'the dark side of the pervasiveness of market and corporate values' that created the so-called '10/90' divide – 'only 10% of investment is destined to the research and development of medicines for diseases affecting 90% of humankind' (Burci, 2005). That anomaly made those working at the WHO feel obligated to seek new ways of managing those 'neglected diseases'. This was not a response to the demand of small states; rather it was a response to what many in a technical organization saw as a threat to the health of the millions that their profession is supposed to help.

The secretariat are often a key ally of SIDS in IOs. On occasion they also use them to pursue their agenda. A director asks a delegate to move a motion at a members' forum that asks for more funds for a given programme. If it passes without opposition then the director is able to argue that the membership has asked for greater emphasis and that the organization should duly provide more funds. Some DGs dislike the way that the secretariat lobbies small states and think they could keep their distance. The process is called 'serial ventriloquism', putting ideas and words in the mouth of delegates from small states. There is often a shrug and the comment that 'that's politics'. Not all members of the secretariat agree there is anything wrong. They say that the IO does not have an agenda, it's a member states' agenda. Trying to advance that agenda is what they should do. 'It's leadership, right?' If a DG has defended a vision, 'we explain it to member states and ask how we can respond within these promises'. Proposing ways that small states can advocate their interests is part of the process. Whether it is leadership or ventriloquism is a matter of perspective.

When a small state does wish to advance a cause by moving a resolution, then secretariats can assist with tactical advice, both in terms of writing the motion and how to gain the support of the 'like-minded'. If some lobbying is not pursued then it is unlikely any proposal would progress. It can be easy to slow things down. One example was the proposal in the WTO for a policy of global value chains (GVCs). It had been mandated by ministers. When the secretariat wanted to start writing a background document, the US first wanted to approve an outline. That took a year. As long as there were instructions, there was little the secretariat could do. Whether other countries could have the same effect is open to question; it is unlikely a small state would even try. The ICS response also depended on organizational culture: in the FAO where the secretariat had a practice of proposing and driving subjects through, it was easier to move an initiative along.

At times ICSs were able to advance ideas that came from elsewhere too. IOs must ensure these initiatives to be seen as legitimate in the eyes of international community. For example, a development agenda was first proposed at the WIPO by Brazil and caused a lot of angst among members as well as ICSs; the WIPO had to work out a strategy to bring the interest of small to the negotiation table – it did so by stressing the need to help the vision impaired and mainly targeted those in small states. ICSs tend to be more sympathetic to the challenges facing small states; for a long time, for instance, many Americans who joined IOs came from Peace Corp – "once you are Peace Corp, you are Peace Corp for life", commented one of the long-serving officials at the FAO. Their views of small states may not be shared by those representing the US in IOs.

Sometimes ICSs could pursue an innovation that assists small states for their own reasons – the IMF probably is the last organization that one would expect to do anything for the smallest as it is first and foremost an organization of 'the rich'. As discussed, the IMF faced increasing competition from their peer institutions in the aftermath of the Asian financial crisis. The leadership had to adapt to remain relevant as a global institution and as a facilitator of international monetary cooperation. A former undersecretary of the US Treasury emphasized that 'The IMF governance structure should ensure that every member has a voice' and must do everything it can to 'ensure universal representation' while protecting the weighted influence of a few, from which the IMF drew most of its financial resources (Adams, 2006: 134). The IMF secretariat started a series of initiatives as they sought to adapt to ensure their legitimacy in two senses: normative – by pursuing 'common interests', and professionally by their impartial exercise of authority. In both cases, it involved the issue of representation – who decides and how are decisions made on what 'common interests' are.

There is an implicit model for relations between national capitals, delegations to IOs, and the IOs' secretariats. There is an expected routine. Issues are discussed in national capitals, instructions are delivered to the delegations, with agreed levels of negotiating discretion. The secretariat provides information but not advice. These routines may work effectively in wealthier countries where national capitals have the resources and expertise to service the multiple IOs and their ever-continuing negotiations. It works too where the delegations have the depth and expertise, whether in trade, intellectual property, or health, to make recommendations to the capitals. The attachés in these areas are often seconded from the line departments, have connections in national capitals, and a deep technical understanding of the issues. It makes sense to delegate a degree of negotiating discretion within prescribed limits to them. In this formulation there is little need for assistance and therefore little role for the secretariat. As a generalization, the ambassadors from big countries are on a short leash.

There are of course distinctions between IOs. Those that are high profile, such as the WTO or the UNHRC, are likely to generate closer relations between delegations and capitals. Others are much less close. A WHO official in Geneva argued that they did not work through the local delegations but through their regional and country offices. If the Geneva delegation asked them for something, they would first check back with the country office and only then provide a response. "We have a county briefing ... but we are told of demands from country offices, not local diplomats ... we do not operate through them. They are Foreign Affairs. We deal with Health."

And another: "I want to talk to experts in capitals." Their lines bypassed the central agencies and foreign affairs and through the local offices dealt directly with the health department in the country.

The secretariat could potentially be more involved. The staff there are aware of the imbalances and the limitations within capitals. They are also aware of the divisions within national administrations, between foreign affairs and line agencies and between finance department and line departments. These tensions are most obvious at the Heath Assemblies or other annual meetings where delegates who come from the capitals take precedence over the national delegations based in the city. The latter may feel aggrieved when patiently negotiated compromises are discarded for technical, not diplomatic reasons.

Most secretariats try to assist small member states because they are concerned that, if they do not, then the small states will be more likely either to be co-opted by the larger states or by NGOs. There is an innate suspicion of NGOs who are active on the periphery of most negotiations. The NGOs, members of the secretariat suggest, often take the high moral ground; they will draft statements, sometimes become members of delegation, arguing that 'they represent the people'. IOs are more sceptical. They are never sure whom the NGOs represent, or who funds them; they see them often as voice without responsibility. When they represent the medical or industry agencies, they find their protestations shady. So IOs believe that they need to be available to help the small states overcome their lack of capacity, always conscious at the same time that it is in the interest of the IO to do so effectively because if they fail then the small states will look elsewhere for assistance. The officials state that their door is always open and that are there to assist but note that they don't often come; there is a suspicion about the secretariat's motives that creates a level of frustration, the feeling that "we could help but are not asked".

A simple example is that when the WHO in the early 2000s decided to put all formal documents and communications online, small island states, especially those in the Pacific complained that they did not have the stable and reliable access to online resources, the WHO immediately decided to continue mailing the documents to them, regardless of the extra costs. After finding out that "only some 30 member states here have health attachés represented in Geneva and those that claim to represent the interests of small states may or may not have the interests of small states at heart because we do have a heavy presence of large pharma and large food industries here," explained one senior official at the WHO, "we are obligated to think on behalf of the interests of small states." At the WHO, there is a division dealing with member states and managing all activities in Geneva, the World Health Assembly meeting, Executive Board meetings, and committee meeting. "The other part of the job of this division is to help member states understand the issues, get their way around, or understand how to get things done here", explained a former director:

'While many states have a lot of support from their capitals, I'm like the entry point for small states to make connections with the technical department; then also to support them in preparing for and during any of the meetings. We hold mission briefings maybe four or five times a year. The boilerplate ones on the Assembly and the Executive Board saying these are the big issues. Then on logistical stuff but also giving them an opportunity to ask questions or flag if they are going to bring up issues themselves. So basically I am supporting them, guiding them through what they need to do, preparing them for the various meetings. Two areas concern me: one is Pacific Islands and another is the Caribbean. They are not here in Geneva; there are very few that have missions here. So that for us is always an issue. We try and use our regional offices a lot. That is the other part of my work – working with the regional offices. There are about 27 or so member states that don't have a mission here. Most of them are either Pacific Islands or Caribbean. I will let them know if there is something really important happening here. I will do special pre-sessions and briefings when their officials come for the WHA meetings. I think it is a struggle sometimes for some of them, but individuals also make a difference.' (Interview with former WHO director)

NGOs

While IOs have sought to help SIDS overcome capacity deficits, their participation has also been affected by the rapid increase in the number of NGOs, which grew from 6,000 to 26,000 in the 1990s alone, and their involvement in IOs. NGOs can help solve the capacity deficits SIDS experience by funding technical expertise and assistance, and by underwriting some of the logistical costs of their presence. Their assistance rarely comes without strings attached as SIDS are expected to advocate for their agenda. The same is true for corporations. For example, many SIDS have large shipping registries who represent them at the IMO where they become a proxy for the industry's voice in that organization. The result is that external actors like NGOs represent both a blessing and a curse for IOs: they can facilitate 'throughput' legitimacy by increasing the capacity of SIDS to represent themselves, but they can also provide an avenue for marginal voices to be magnified within IOs, thus complicating decision-making.

Public protests of NGOs and civil societies against the WTO in Seattle in 1999 and in Geneva a few months later shocked ICSs who had sincerely believed that they had been working for the common goods and global interests. After being in the position of DG for just little over three months, Michael Moore had to face the challenge at Seattle. 'This increasing civil society activity – though sometimes orchestrated to mischievous ends – is not fake', admitted Moore – 'it reflects the growing public hunger in the West for involvement in these issues' (Moore, 2003: 205). Since then, the numbers of NGOs behind actions and proposals of the small states were rising too – some were 'legitimate' supporters of the causes of the small states while others were fighting for their own interests. The difficulty was how to distinguish them and how to work with those that do have interests of small states in mind. This was a genuine and generic challenge for all IOs.

Some speak with their special interests while others fight for what they consider as common goods. Some have made a business of fighting for what they consider as being small, developing, or vulnerable. Four relatively small least developed countries in the world – Benin, Burkina Faso, Chad, and Mali – successfully challenged cotton subsidies in the US, in part because of the assistance they received from some powerful NGOs, such as Oxfam's Geneva-based advocacy team aligned with Céline Charveriat and Romain Benicchio and others at the International Centre for Trade and Sustainable Development. Their efforts were combined with organized support by governments in developed countries and together they provided the right strategies to take on the large states. Small states managed to ensure that cotton was included into the Doha trade negotiations (Eagleton-Pierce, 2013). In the same vein, the Marshall Islands' initiatives to place climate change on the agenda of the IMO were very much work supported by NGOs (discussed further in Chapter 4).

In the 1990s, the NGO encirclement, visible in the streets around the headquarters of the IMF, the WB, the GATT/WTO, the WIPO, and elsewhere, presented a very difficult challenge to IOs as these 'missionary' NGOs also 'encircled the parliaments of aid-giving governments'. Cutting through the encirclement would mean breaking the grip of donors, while giving in to the demands of these northern NGOs meant IOs were 'losing touch with developing countries', leaving IOs setting agendas to suit northern activists rather than their client member states. Sebastian Mallaby (2004: 6, 294) bluntly put it: 'an army of NGOs, especially those from developed countries, pounds upon the World Bank's doors, demanding the Bank projects bend to particular concerns ... These constant NGO offensives tie up the World Bank, frequently disabling its efforts to fight poverty; despite their diminutive stature, the Lilliputians are winning.' A similar development occurred in the WHO too. One senior official put it: "There are 34 members of the Executive Board. We used to have a full attendance of the EB room that fits 300 or 350 including galleries. Now our usual list of participants has 800–900." There are people from capitals of member states but there are much more representing NGOs. The upshot is that those from developed countries continue to dominate.

How to balance the relationship with the shareholders, NGOs, and stakeholders has been such an important and difficult challenge for all IOs. In front of the WTO building, NGOs demonstrated with posters, such as 'Michael Moore Starves the Poor'. Mike Moore (2003: 190), the then DG of the WTO responded: 'I just wish I had the power I was always accused of having.' Nonetheless, he and IOs had to take NGOs and stakeholders seriously while protecting the integrity of IOs serving all their members – that is, 'NGOs should have a voice, not a vote in the process' (Moore, 2003: 193). To do so, all IOs started the practice of allowing accredited NGOs to participate, often alongside member states' meetings.

The number of NGOs that were accredited to attend WTO ministerial meetings every two years dropped from its peak of 1,065 in Hong Kong to a more stable number of a little over 200. An overwhelming number of them came from a small number of countries: Belgium, Canada, India, Switzerland, and the US. A few countries always had NGOs present: France, Germany, Norway, and the UK. While NGOs from developed countries continue to have a dominant presence in most IOs, IOs have been consciously maintaining a balance of the demand from NGOs for participation and the interests of their member states. This is also because member states are reluctant to deal with NGOs themselves, especially those from their own countries. "Pro-NGO member states who were fed up with some NGOs told us that this is the organization of member states, member states only." They 'delegated' NGO contacts to the secretariat. One senior official at the WHO explained:

> 'Unlike with the tobacco companies that we could stop dealing with, we cannot cut entirely our dealing with pharmaceutical industries or physician and patient associations. After a long process of consultation, we decided to publish a list of those NGOs, whether those for public interest (PNGOs) or business (BNGOs) that engage with us, their membership, missions, finance, etc. so that they cannot hide.'

While IOs need to be 'democratic' by including voices of NGOs, in part to keep their parliamentarians happy, it is equally important for IOs to focus on the demands of their member states and work with their member states. 'It is necessary to make institutions relevant and more legitimate', explained Moore (2003: 232–3). 'Otherwise we risk further control of the agenda

Table 2.1: Participant accreditation and IOs

WTO Ministerial	Accredited	Represented	Number of participants
Singapore 1996	159	108	235
Geneva 1998	153	128	362
Seattle 1999	776	686	1500
Doha 2001	651	370	370
Cancun 2003	961	795	1578
Hong Kong 2005	1065	812	1596
Geneva 2009	435	395	490

IMF World Bank	MC 8 (2011) Geneva	MC 9 (2013) Bali	MC10 (2015) Nairobi	MC 11 (2017) Buenos Aires
Accredited NGOs	234	346	232	251
Country	59	66	48	52
Host	34	19	45	42
Belgium	14	13	7	13
Canada	28	29	11	16
India	17	28	23	19
Switzerland		26	18	20
United States	14	38	17	24

Source: Compiled by the authors from websites of WTO, IMF and national missions.

passing to some NGOs which – despite their claim to speak for the people – are largely unaccountable, except for themselves and their agenda, or as they would put it, their principles.' Each IO now designates individuals to assist member states, especially the smallest, in getting their interested topics on the agenda. "My office works closely with health attachés of member states", one director at the WHO explained.

'A country was interested in non-communicable diseases or another one on disability. They tend to be small without much capacity to do so but wanted to put a resolution to the General Assemble or the executive board. They came to us. I would find them the right technical people here and facilitate the process. If they need other assistance, I would get together a team from technical department, from the budget and other department, and then organise it. Sometimes I feel I am almost like a mother hen with them.'

While many NGOs have supported the causes of small states, as it is seen in the case of Seas at Risk supporting the Marshall Islands at the IMO, the role of NGOs in 'promoting' and 'protecting' the interest of the small states can be extremely controversial too because of the unbalanced power and capacity between them and NGOs. Small states are vulnerable to manipulation of powerful NGOs because of their 'limited financial resources' and 'institutional capacity constraints' and also because 'small states often lack clarity with regard to precise strategic and policy objectives' (Laurent, 2011: 220).

Conclusion

An environment that permits small states is one thing but the idea that it might be conducive to their influence is quite another (Long, 2022). This chapter asked why IOs have accommodated the countries we now call SIDS. It sought to explain how the mission of IOs shapes their approach, how IOs manage the capacity deficits experienced by the small states in terms of information and participation, and how they ensure their involvement, balancing the interests of the small states against the broad need to ensure that the objectives of the organization are, to an extent, achieved. The key point is that increasing the participation of small states like SIDS has been part of the agenda of all IOs since the late 1990s due to growing concern about their legitimacy. Larger states, as well as IO leaders and staff, have thus all sought to engage them in the everyday processes and practices.

The reason they have done so, we have argued, is that they know that if they solve their legitimacy dilemma in favour of inputs – increased participation – they increase complexity and risk gridlock, thus undermining their ability to deliver outcomes. If they solve it in favour of outputs, they risk being unrepresentative and unresponsive. SIDS thus present IOs with an opportunity to balance inputs and outputs by way of 'throughputs' – they encourage the active presence of members in the processes and practices of IOs so as to both be seen as more inclusive while simultaneously sharing responsibility for outcomes. To be sure, the existing rules and traditions of IOs have often proven a barrier to the inclusion of SIDS. But the normative imperative has ensured that IOs have searched for ways around these problems, even if many of their attempts have proven more symbolic than substantive. By doing so they have created an opportunity for SIDS to advance their agenda.

3

Why Do Small States Engage with IOs?

The long-standing assumption in the IR literature is that small states have very little influence in IOs. Or, if they do appear to have influence, their impact is a chimera that masks the power of larger 'system influencing' states who are the ones really determining outcomes. If this is correct, why do small states participate in IOs at all? The creation of a large number of small states in the second half of the 20th century has seen the membership of IOs expand rapidly. The Pacific state of Samoa, for example, which has a resident population of little more than 200,000 people, is a member of 33 IOs (not including numerous regional organizations, sporting, religious, and other social organizations), while Vanuatu, which has a similar population size, is a member of 36: crude but impressive measures of this expansion (Corbett and Connell, 2015: 442). The aim of this chapter is to explain why some SIDS have sought to participate when their limited capacity would appear to favour free-riding or opting out of multilateralism altogether.

The short answer is that small states see their participation in IOs as serving their interests. But to understand this we have to differentiate between different types of small states and the ideas they have about their interests. We distinguish between three common narratives about how SIDS see their participation. At the most basic level, small states participate to secure sovereign recognition of their status as states. That is, participation is a form of conformity that incidentally secures survival (Sharman, 2015, 2017). For some SIDS this is the sum total of their engagement with IOs and their membership of different organizations is tightly bound to those that will maximize this objective at the lowest cost (that is, the UN). This has led to the perception that they get a 'free ride' (Olson and Zeckhauser, 1966). A second reason is they participate because they believe it will contribute to their development. These states engage selectively on certain issues and in certain IOs where they believe they are likely to either extract the most resources or gain S&DT for their economies. The majority of SIDS are in this group. The final reason is that SIDS have the greatest stake in the function and continuity of the LIO. A select few SIDS thus engage heavily in IOs as part of a broader strategy of ensuring the international system remains permissive of their presence (see also Getachew, 2019). By differentiating between SIDS and their interests we are able to explain why participating in IOs matters and makes a difference *to them*.

The second half of the chapter explains how the latter two groups of states work to achieve their goals in IOs. We use the phrase 'competent performance of vulnerability' to describe how, since the late 1980s, SIDS have accentuated their vulnerabilities in service of their goals and objectives. Performing vulnerability is potentially at odds with the first aim of promoting conformity to secure legitimacy. Two features of IOs are important for explaining this apparent contradiction: (1) in a permissive liberal order state death is rare. By implication, once membership is gained IOs are unlikely to withdraw it; and (2) *competent* performance is a form of conformity that promotes legitimacy. In which case, to secure advantages from IOs SIDS have to enact the core requirements of membership. This is no easy feat given their well-documented capacity constraints. The point we seek to emphasize is that on some issues, and in some IOs, they have proven very adept at getting what they want. These successes, while rare, are seen by many SIDS diplomats as a vindication of their decision to participate in IOs despite disproportionate costs.

Sovereign recognition

The basic puzzle that small states present realist IR scholars in particular is why they exist at all (Fox, 1959). A permissive LIO is often invoked as an explanation (for example, Sharman, 2017 and Maass, 2017): despite being regularly conquered and incorporated within colonial empires prior to the Second World War, state death by violent elimination is rare even when the smallest have extremely limited (or non-existent) military capabilities. In which case, one of the major functions of IOs is to allow all states, including the smallest, to shape the norms of international relationships through alliances with 'great powers' (Keohane, 1969: 297). Recent examples of this argument, like Bailes and Thorhallsson (2013), contend that the basic security imperative for small states is to secure survival by means of 'shelter', usually from powerful allies (see also Veenendaal, 2017). In this account they have some discretion over *whom* they seek shelter from; but they must gain it from somewhere. This argument echoes the early literature on small states in IOs

(Vital, 1967, 1971; Benedict, 1967; Reid, 1974), which posited that given external constraints small states could rarely act autonomously. Indeed, one of the reasons why decolonization of the smallest was delayed was fear that small countries would become nothing more than pawns of larger states, which can help explain why foreign relations were the last area of policy to be handed over to local control (Ince, 1976). By implication, membership of IOs was a way that these new states asserted their independent status from larger states, including their former colonizer. In which case, while SIDS membership in IOs demonstrates the increasing permissiveness of the international system, it also highlights the willingness of the very smallest to assert their independence.

The simultaneous desire for shelter and independence can help explain why many joined the UN soon after becoming sovereign states, as one Caribbean diplomat explained:

'You need an umbrella. You're going out on your own but there is a degree of comfort to be had by you looking to associate yourself in the wider world. Because you know you can't make it entirely on your own without some form of support. So ... [you] join the UN, which we did weeks after we became independent, then join the Organization of American States, which was the regional body and in fact you could not join the Inter-American Development Bank if you were not first a member of the Organization of American States at that stage ... [it was] the early phase of decolonization. Therefore, you gravitated within those groupings towards the Group of 77. In other words, what you would consider to be like-minded. I would doubt that there was any analysis of whether or not those were natural groupings for us. Basically, we were all becoming independent together. Whether it was Barbados or Ghana, we thought we had an affinity ...' (Interview with Caribbean diplomat)

This trajectory was not uniform. Western Samoa (now Samoa) did not join the UN until 14 years after independence. Tuvalu and Kiribati waited more than 20 years and Nauru waited 31 years. Sharman (2015: 208) explains that the latter initially chose to ignore international affairs on the basis that, being the same size as a small town, it wasn't worth the effort (the country was also fabulously rich and so had little to gain economically from participation). But timing aside, increased participation has become the norm.

Any time lag between independence and membership can partially be explained by the end of the colonial period and the fact that some small states were jettisoned by empires who no longer wanted or needed them (Aldrich and Connell, 1998; Larmour, 2005). In which case, proxy representation by the former colonizer was acceptable as an interim measure. Where small states had to fight harder to gain independence – Vanuatu, for example, or more recently Timor Leste – they tended to be much quicker to seek UN membership. The other factor is that capacity constraints meant that it took time for small states to create the diplomatic apparatus required to participate at all. Regardless of the timing of their membership, the key point, as exemplified by Nauru, is that eventually they all end up joining an increasing number of IOs due a combination of international pressure exerted by IOs seeking legitimacy for their operations (discussed in Chapter 2) or out of a desire to realize potential benefits (Nauru, for example, is no longer a wealthy state).

Learning to play the game of multilateral diplomacy takes time and initial entry was often daunting for small states, as a former head of government from Kiribati relates:

'It is very intimidating, coming from a small [country]. At the big meetings, like the Commonwealth Heads of Government Meeting … I observed the big leaders talking and performing and I must admit I regarded it as a learning thing for me. People like Lee [Kuan Yew] from Singapore, when they talk they are articulate and confident … It also depends on your personality as well, because there are people who find it easy … I found it uncomfortable in that sort of environment, as it were. I mean coming from the village background and the island situation, it was quite a new world so it is not easy.' (Cited in Corbett and Connell, 2015: 445)

But, as we will show, confidence and an understanding of the best ways for small states to navigate the multilateral world grew.

'So, I think it took more than a decade into the mid-80s, going into the 90s, when there were enough small states emerging within the international community to realise we have our own issues.' (Interview with Caribbean diplomat)

The combination of presence and confidence is therefore significant, as we will outline extensively throughout Part II of the book. Sovereign recognition is said to create numerous benefits for small states. The most obvious is access to foreign aid and financial capital that they would not have were they non-members (discussed in the next section). But small states have also found inventive ways to sell their sovereignty, including: trading votes on issues in which they have little interest (for example, Seychelles sold its representation on the international whaling commission to Greenpeace – Sharman,

2017: 571); the lease of land and territory with, for example, Marshall Islands leasing a portion of Kwajalein Atoll to the US, while Nauru leases a portion of its island to Australia as a asylum seeker detention facility (Mountz, 2011). Elsewhere, small states sell sovereign recognition (many Pacific states have been rewarded for recognizing either Taiwan or China, for example; see Van Fossen, 2007); passports and economic citizenship; shipping registries; Internet domain names (Tuvalu was advantageously granted .TV); while philately and numismatics have been a lucrative business for small states, albeit revenue from this source is declining. Other forms of revenue can take their place, however, with small states increasingly home to online gaming operations, for example. Marshall Islands recently launched its own cryptocurrency. Many small states have functioned as tax havens, albeit the financial services industry has been more lucrative for non-sovereign jurisdictions that have remained overseas territories of former colonizers, and some of these ventures in sovereign states have come under growing pressure since 9/11 and the 2008 global financial crisis in particular because they have proven unprofitable (Vlcek, 2008).

The financial services example reveals one of the great paradoxes of sovereignty for small states: sovereignty can bring economic benefits but non-sovereignty has tended to be much more lucrative (Baldacchino, 2010; Rezvani, 2014). Across the world, but most apparent in the Pacific and Caribbean, small non-sovereign jurisdictions (SNIJs) perform consistently better in economic terms than their sovereign neighbours. Advantages for SNIJs include: welfare transfers, concessional market access, and freedom of movement. Being a SNIJ is not without disadvantages: there is a trade-off between these benefits and autonomy with SNIJs often forced to adopt policies that suit metropolitan powers but enjoy little local support. A recent example is same-sex marriage legislation that has been very unpopular in the Caribbean (Schields, 2018). But on balance, most SNIJs are comfortable with this pact: few of those still on the decolonization list are agitating for independence and those that have held referenda invariably prefer to remain a SNIJ.

The SNIJ example illustrates that inherent dilemmas of SIDS: self-determination is desirable but statehood creates disproportionate costs for the very smallest, of which international representation hitherto undertaken by colonial authorities is only one area in which they are disadvantaged by diseconomies of scale (Campling and Rosalie, 2006). Sovereignty sales could be construed as an argument for why small states are not real states (that is, Jackson, 1993). But as Sharman (2017: 572) notes, the smallest have in general delegated less authority than EU members and most have not granted permanent authority over their territory, diplomatic alliances or citizenship to other states or supranational bodies. In either case, the important point for our purposes is that sovereign recognition has both symbolic and practical value for the smallest and membership of IOs is the easiest way to secure it. Small states do not have to bear the costs of an embassy in New York to achieve this; having their head of state or government attend UNGA once a year and give a speech has sufficed. But they do have to perform this minimum level of participation.

Economic development and technical assistance

The value of sovereign recognition, both as a means and an end, explains why small states are members of the UN. It does not explain why they are increasingly members of other IOs or indeed why they have established diplomatic missions in New York and Geneva in particular. We argue that small states establish a presence via their missions and join multiple IOs because they see advantages beyond sovereign recognition. Indeed, there is considerable variation in the IOs that small states are members of, which reflects the extent to which they are seeking to realize diverse interests and agendas (see, for example, Braveboy-Wagner, 2007; Corbett and Connell, 2015). Expansion and variation in membership implies a number of things, including that: (1) small states are strategic about their diplomatic relationships; (2) they have some control over their participation in IOs; (3) that they see themselves as being able to realize their interests above and beyond survival on certain issues and in certain IOs; and (4) that in some cases they are willing to incur what are, to the very smallest at least, disproportionately high costs of establishing and maintaining diplomatic missions to do so (see Ince, 1976; Corbett and Connell, 2015).

Small states are acutely aware of the trade-off of their increased participation in the multilateral world. Consequently, many diplomats from SIDS in particular articulate that the primary purpose of their missions is to raise revenue. Indeed, they rank missions according to their ability to do so:

'The UN is the least productive – it's the most prestigious diplomatic posting you can have but it's the least productive in terms of bringing money home. The most productive is Brussels because of the EU.' (Interview with Caribbean diplomat)

Aside from the fact that it is often their 'mission to the world', the main instrumental value of a presence in New York is for those countries seeking to avoid or delay graduation from LDC to middle- or high-income status:

'As a Small Island Development State, my real challenge now is that because my country has been graduated as a low and middle income countries in 2008, because we exceed the GDP criteria and the Human Development Index criteria, but not the economic vulnerability criteria. For me, that should be a mandatory criteria as part of the two out of the three for graduation.' (Interview with diplomat from Cape Verde)

Outside the UN, recent and often very heated domestic debate about the accession of Tonga, Samoa, and Vanuatu to the WTO illustrates the extent to which SIDS consider the costs and benefits of their participation in terms of their ability to generate substantive developmental gains (Gay, 2005; Grynberg and Joy, 2006; Wallis, 2010). Speaking at a dialogue organized by the Samoan Chamber of Commerce in late 2012, the DG of the WTO, Pascal Lamy, outlined the benefits of membership in the international trading regime for Pacific SIDS. While acknowledging that the accession process was not easy, and that membership was not a panacea to development challenges, he argued that it provides:

> a tapestry of opportunities to use trade as a development tool. In a world where we are becoming increasingly interlinked through more efficient and effective technologies and logistics and where actions in one part of the world will have an impact in other parts – to remain an outlier is an illusion. (*Samoa Observer*, 1 December 2012)

Lamy's presence, and the tenor of his pitch to Pacific SIDS, reflected the length of their accession processes. On 24 August 2012 Vanuatu became the 157th member of the WTO over 16 years after it first began the accession process in July 1995. The push for membership only commenced in earnest from 1997 with the implementation of the Comprehensive Reform Programme (a structural adjustment package) undertaken in agreement with the Asian Development Bank (for discussion, see Gay, 2005; Grynberg and Mickey Joy, 2006). In 2001 accession was suspended. Officially, this was due to 'technical reasons' but several other factors, including local political dynamics, the capacity of the negotiating team, growing awareness about the costs of accession, and concerns about the ability of Vanuatu to fully participate in the WTO as a member state (Gay, 2005; Grynberg and Mickey Joy, 2006), were also at play. The latter two reasons were expressed forcefully by key business interests, NGOs, and church leaders right up until August 2012, fuelled in part by increased awareness of how other Pacific member countries – Fiji, Papua New Guinea, Solomon Islands, Tonga. and Samoa (which acceded in May 2012) – fared in the WTO. In 2008 Vanuatu reopened negotiations and while the 16-year time period is somewhat unique (Samoa took 13 years) their accession story reveals the contestation within small states about the benefits of participation in IOs.

Despite WTO members theoretically having an equal voice, accession negotiations do not operate on this basis. The first hurdle that prospective member countries must clear is an examination of their trade regime by existing members who determine whether the applicant is compliant with WTO regulations. This process, Grynberg and Mickey Joy (2006: 693) argue, is systematically abused by member states who place numerous demands on new applicants. In the aborted 2001 process, Vanuatu's regional neighbours, Australia and New Zealand, sought specific concessions, including opposition to agricultural export subsides. Daniel Gay (2005) argues that because these countries are major aid donors, Vanuatu felt pressured to acquiesce to their demands. Indeed, Grynberg and Mickey Joy (2006: 701) go as far as arguing that WTO members were totally uninterested in Vanuatu's development status during these negotiations. Rather than benefitting Vanuatu, they maintain that concessions hurt the poorest farmers who 'bear the full brunt of price fluctuations in a distorted and volatile edible oil market'.

The key point is that the interests of larger states aside, participation in IOs presents a capacity challenge to SIDS who often have only a limited pool of experienced staff capable of dealing with the demands of accession and membership. As a result, small states have to enmesh themselves further and further in global processes to generate the resources and they need to gain development, but at the same time they are being stretched in terms of their human resource capacity. There were five staff on Vanuatu's 2001 negotiating team and none of them had experience on prior negotiations or with the WTO (Gay, 2005). Consequently, SIDS struggle to negotiate with bigger players as most lack a deep pool of skilled personnel required to sustain long-term engagement (Panke, 2013; Corbett and Connell, 2015). The WTO is not unaware of these challenges and reflecting the imperative to generate throughput legitimacy have instigated some initiatives to counter this trend, which we will discuss further in Chapter 5. But even so, the costs of negotiating – travel and accommodation expenses – are disproportionately high for SIDS like Vanuatu who do not have permanent missions in Geneva, often leading to disengagement with the multilateral process (Bowman, 2005), a sentiment recognized by then head of the Vanuatu Association of NGOs, Dickson Tevi (cited in Gay, 2005):

One of my concerns is our ability to participate effectively in WTO meetings. For instance our parliament has fifty-two members, but you only ever hear three talking throughout the year. How confidently can we participate? If we can't participate effectively we might as well not be included.

The WTO is not unique. In several instances, pressure has been placed on small states to join IOs where there are no obvious economic advantages. Reflecting on why he rejected an application from a national senior bureaucrat to attend a meeting of the International Atomic Energy Agency (IAEA), one minister from a small Pacific state maintained:

> We have a practice of signing up to anything, and then not being able to pay the dues so we have huge arrears to all of these organisations. It is idiots who just want to travel and get the allowance you know. It is an issue that the Ministry of Foreign Affairs has looked into. We have to rationalise our membership. I think we can gain a lot from our membership of international organisations but we have got to know what we want. (Corbett and Connell, 2015: 44)

As the final line makes clear, aside from diversity of interests there is also variation in terms of how well developed the domestic understanding of what those interest are.

In sum, while IOs have encouraged the participation of small states, the dramatic expansion of their presence in IOs cannot be explained by supply side factors alone; small states will choose to join IOs if they believe it will improve development outcomes. But as the previous section on sovereign recognition highlights, compared with EU members they are much more likely to retain sovereign control so they can sell it. On this basis Sharman (2017: 571) concludes that small states practice hierarchy 'à la carte'. In which case, SIDS participate because they have specific interests that they seek to realize in IOs, and the variation in membership across the group illustrates they have some discretion over how they do so. Moreover, as we will show in subsequent chapters, SIDS change the level and nature of their participation in response to assessments of whether their participation is achieving their chosen objectives. In which case, the acuteness of their participation dilemma is the main difference between them and larger states.

Maintaining a permissive liberal order

> 'Some small states come here but they just listen and write notes and say nothing. Whereas you've got to participate. You've got to know what you want. And you've got to say it. You've got to be articulate in the way you put your case on the table. If you don't open your mouth, nobody will listen. If you make sense, people will come onboard with what you're trying to do.' (Interview with Mauritian diplomat)

In the previous chapter we highlighted how a permissive LIO had both enabled the proliferation of small states but also encouraged them to participate in IOs. In this section we argue that SIDS have also sought to uphold and maintain the LIO in order to ensure it remains permissive of their presence. Indeed, while IOs provide the smallest states with the opportunity to align themselves with their powerful allies (for example, Veenendaal, 2017) who provide them with 'shelter' (Bailes and Thorhallsson, 2013), we would also expect them to be among the most enthusiastic participants of IOs because, *ceteris paribus*, they have the most to gain from the persistence of a LIO that upholds the principle of sovereign equality. By implication, we can gauge how liberal the international order is by investigating how permissive it is of sovereignty claims made by the very small communities.

The rise of the SIDS label and the recognition of the differentiated impact of climate change illustrates the capacity of even the very smallest countries to have an influence on IOs when they are present, coordinated, and active. In some respects, however, climate change is unique as it invokes a shared existential threat. The lesson from this example, however, is that under certain conditions small states will move from joining IOs to secure sovereignty and extract resources to actively participating as a means of buttressing a multilateral system that is permissive of their presence (Súilleabháin, 2014). We see this influence as expansive and creative (see also Getachew, 2019). But it has also been identified as defensive: 'little more than a corollary of their security predicament' (Bueger and Wivel, 2018: 5). In this view a rules-based order limits the 'action space' of larger states, thus levelling the playing field (Neumann and Gstöhl, 2006). We will return to this discussion in the conclusion of the book. Here, we focus on a select few small states who are often highly active and visible in IOs, including those that are not directly involved in climate change issues, and are therefore capable of acting as a 'honest broker', 'lobbyist', and 'norm entrepreneur' (Smed and Wivel, 2017: 82).

Active SIDS tend to share several characteristics. They are not the very smallest – that is, those with populations of less than 100,000 – and therefore have a minimum level of bureaucratic capacity required to be active in IOs. They tend to have a foreign service of at least 50 or more staff, for example. This may seem ridiculously low compared with the US or China but what it allows for is a core analytical capacity at home and missions of 3–4 staff in strategic locations – New York, Geneva, London, Washington, and increasingly Beijing. Any less than 50 and renders this coverage impossible. They also tend to be middle- or upper middle-income countries, rather than LDCs, have stable governments, and are predominantly English-speaking countries with a Commonwealth heritage. This partially reflects our bias – we are from the Anglophone world and Anglophone institutions and so these are the countries more likely to speak to us – but also the linguistic bias in most IOs. Indeed, small non-English speaking states feel they are doubly disadvantaged in IOs because of the preference for English.

We do not want to be overly prescriptive about this classification – it is a heuristic rather than a set of necessary and sufficient conditions – but it does provide a sense of the type of SIDS that is likely to be an active participant across multiple IOs and beyond single issues of immediate interest. When we ask diplomats of larger states or members of the secretariat who the active small states are, and in particular which small states participate in the operations of IOs via leadership elections and so on, invariably the same group of countries emerges: Jamaica, Mauritius, Seychelles, Barbados, Maldives, and, in coup-free periods over the last three decades, Fiji. For many of these active small states Singapore, who created the Forum of Small States at the UN in 1992 for countries with a population of less than 10 million (105 of 193 members) with the explicit aim of buttressing 'a predictable, stable rule-based system' (cited in Chowdhury, 2012: 6), is a model for the type of impact they can have in IOs.

Superficially, what is interesting about these states is that in contrast to accounts that emphasize dependence on a larger neighbour or former colonial power, they tend to eschew the protection of a larger ally and instead see their interests, be they survival or economic development, in terms of maintaining a permissive liberal order. Consider these three quotes from active small states:

'Barbados basically feels that as a small state we have no choice but to assert ourselves at the multilateral level. We have to take refuge within a multilateral system; we can't project the kind of power that larger states can, and we don't have the economic influence that other states have. So we try to project ourselves within the multilateral fora as a place that the rule of law, promotion of international law, certain norms and standards that should be adhered to internationally. Because that is really the only refuge for small states, where you promote international architecture that lends itself to good governance and an understanding of the vulnerabilities, really, of small states. So this is where we have to push, and also we have to make sure that within the context of the global international agenda, that small states like Barbados are not left behind … our first prime minister essentially said, we will be "friends of all and satellites of none". I still think that that's the guiding principle of our foreign policy.' (Interview with Barbadian diplomat)

'Why are we proactive? Because we have nothing else in Mauritius. Mauritius is a resource-less country. We have nothing in the ground or above the ground. There are no mineral resources, gold and so on. Even our sea is not fish-rich and so on ... We are a country which is dependent on trade completely. We are a net exporter ... so that's why [we are proactive] on all the trade fronts ... national, regional and big bilateral and also multilateral. We have no choice.' (Interview with Mauritian diplomat)

'The culture of the foreign service when I joined is one of always seeking to position Jamaica in the international community, such that regardless of size our voice counts. So we have actively pursued areas that are of particular concern to the nation as well as to the region. Wherever we are, if we can lend the authority which we have plus the reputation that we have towards having a leading role, we do that. That is something that is taken very seriously. If an issue comes up where in Mission's view this is an opportunity for Jamaica or for the region to be able to influence a matter, we would then recommend it to Kingston and request permission to do, and more often than not it is encouraged.' (Interview with Jamaican diplomat)

Taken together these quotes highlight why these small states see active participation as imperative to their sovereign and economic survival, but also why this leads them from participating on certain issues in certain IOs, and acting as veto players on matters of immediate interest, to seeking leadership positions and attempting to project themselves as partners in, rather than dependents of, IOs. Indeed, the language of partnership is often key to how these states perceive themselves relative to small states who primarily attend multilateral meetings to extract benefits. The upshot is that these small states nearly always find themselves as candidates for leadership positions in IOs (Braveboy-Wagner, 2007: 144 calls them 'high joiners' who believe that 'visibility can be maximised' in IOs). Taking on leadership roles in IOs is not a simple task for any state but the costs are magnified for the smallest given capacity constraints. They overcome these constraints by adopting the same types of 'smart' strategies that scholars who work on small states in the EU in particular have identified. A key difference to European small states and others like Singapore, however, is that SIDS have sought to do so by emphasizing, rather than offsetting, their vulnerabilities.

The competent performance of vulnerability

SIDS seeking to increase their economic development or maintain a permissive LIO deploy similar tactics and 'smart' strategies to larger and richer small states whose activities and achievements are increasingly well documented. But they are also different in one key respect: where European small states seek to 'offset' inherent disadvantages by accentuating the positive features of smallness – 'innovative', 'active', and 'smart' – and exert influence that is disproportionate to their size, which in turn increases their 'status' (de Carvalho and Neumann, 2015), SIDS have sought to draw attention to their vulnerability to gain S&DT. This appeal to vulnerability has been especially successful in relation to climate change, which has an internationally recognized discourse in which SIDS are prominent (Moore, 2010; Kelman, 2020). But SIDS have pushed the idea of vulnerability beyond Intergovernmental Panel on Climate Change (IPCC) discussions and in doing so have championed a particular constitutive norm – differentiated development – 'from below' (Towns, 2010, 2012). That is, SIDS have sought economic and security benefits by moving down, rather than up, a hierarchy in which large is stronger than small. This emphasis on the benefits of moving down a hierarchy can help us explain why there has been a marked increase in the participation of SIDS in IOs over the last three decades and their subsequent ability to create distinct labels and groupings in IOs that recognize their unique condition. The important point on which our contribution to these debates turns is that SIDS pushed for these categories themselves as a vehicle that would facilitate their participation and allow them to realize developmental gains. This competent performance of vulnerability has three distinct features – rhetorical action, collaboration, and active participation – and so we conclude the chapter by detailing what they are.

Rhetorical action

SIDS have used rhetorical action (Schimmelfennig, 2001; Browning, 2006) of the type identified by scholars working on the agency of African states in the international system (Jourde, 2007; Lee, 2013; Laker, 2014) to draw attention to their unique economic and environmental circumstances and the need for S&DT. In doing so they have invoked two existing norms – the right to development and the sovereign equality of states – in order to advance a new understanding of 'differentiated development'. The constitutive norm of differentiated development, once accepted, would eventually result in SIDS increasing their rank on development indices (or at least that is the aim). Nevertheless, maintaining the benefits (that is, trade concessions at the WTO) that could enable this to occur would be contingent on continued acceptance of their vulnerability and thus a lowly rank in the related hierarchy, defined by size, in which large is stronger than small.

SIDS claim to enduring vulnerability is based on their: (1) ongoing struggle with diseconomies of scale resulting from the fact that they have a narrow export base (usually a combination of tourism and financial services) that is uniquely vulnerable to global economic fluctuations; (2) that they are caught in a 'middle income trap' that sees them receive few of the concessions and development assistance of other developing countries, while having little prospect of becoming industrialized nations; and (3) are often crippled by high levels of indebtedness as they need to regularly rebuild after extreme weather events; a cycle that will increase with climate change. To be sure, the group is diverse: many of these states are small islands, some PSIDS receiving considerable development assistance, and some experience few natural disasters (Vleck, 2008; Bishop, 2012). But the general appeal is commonly made on behalf of the group nonetheless.

The constitutive norm (Finnemore and Sikkink, 1998) of 'differentiated development' is thus avowedly an appeal that there is no one-size-fits all growth model: what works for China or India will not work for SIDS. In which case, if SIDS are to pursue their right to development IOs need to differentiate between types of developing states, defined by their unique structural conditions, in order to maintain the principle of sovereign equality. This argument is buttressed by the observation that the current definition of development used by IOs includes everyone from the BRICS to Tuvalu, thus disadvantaging their smallest members.

The evidence that this norm entrepreneurship has been persuasive is the creation of groupings like SIDS and SVEs in IOs – these groups would not exist unless IOs recognized the unique vulnerability of these states and by extension the principle of differentiated development (see Table 1.1). As Wiener (2014) argues, constitutive norms both reflect and create new categories of actors and actions, identities and interests in specific contexts. In turn, SIDS have used recognition of their vulnerability to gain benefits. We dedicate Part II of the book to a discussion of these benefits and challenges. Here we highlight several of them to illustrate the point that by creating the label 'SIDS' these states have improved their position in IOs.

In process terms, the labels and the groupings they represent have changed the operation of IOs by allowing SIDS as a group and as individual member states to:

1. Create working groups, convene conferences and taskforces, and initiate reports and declarations, and secure work programmes, that draw attention to their unique needs (that is, the Barbados Programme of Action or the SAMOA Pathway).
2. Gain entry to key decision-making arenas (that is, the WTO Green Room).
3. Win positions on boards and key committees (that is, the Clean Development Mechanism; the Adaptation Fund; and the Green Climate Fund).

4. Gain subsidies for their participation in IO activities (that is, the LDC/SIDS Trust Fund at the HRC or the Commonwealth Secretariat Small States Office in New York and Geneva).

This has further pluralized the decision-making of IOs. In policy terms, the label has resulted in SIDS:

1. Providing leadership in decades of climate negotiations. They have not acted alone and they have had considerable technical support from NGOs, but they have unequivocally been key participants in the processes, usually via AOSIS. They are thus able to contribute to, for example, SDGs on Oceans and Climate; the 2017 UN Ocean Conference and appointment of former Permanent Representative to the UN for Fiji, Peter Thomson, as UN Special Envoy for the Ocean; and the 2018 UN Security Council debate on climate change (2014 was even the International Year of the Small Island Developing State).
2. Working under a label strengthens their ability to become a potential veto player across IOs. At the WTO, for example, the SVEs could insist they had a dedicated work programme as part of the Doha Round in the knowledge that their interest could not be just ignored in a process that required consensus. The WTO Committee on Trade and Development now meets regularly to discuss and review their work programme.
3. Presenting their case in a way that meshed with trends in the WB and IMF to re-evaluate the way they think about the types of lending they provide and projects they finance. Rather than off-the-shelf solutions, staff are increasingly aware of the need to tailor projects to the scalar dynamics of development in SIDS.
4. Responding to approaches from IOs that had previously shown little interest; that is, the WIPO/WHO.

Several caveats are important. These lists are not exhaustive and SIDS have not had it all their own way (for example, Jackson, 2012). Indeed, we will go to great lengths in subsequent chapters to show how these achievements are shaped by IOs and larger states too. These successes would pale in significance if SIDS were able to win 'loss and damage' compensation for the disproportionate impact of climate change, which in many respects is the holy grail of the vulnerability claim. Moreover, some SIDS diplomats do not like being associated with vulnerability and its negative connotations (poor and weak), which has in turn inspired recent moves to identify as Large Ocean States. But for now, the important point is that the rhetorical performance of vulnerability over several decades has produced successes, at least on some issues in some IOs.

Collaboration

The second core attribute of their strategy is collaboration or coalition building to take advantage of the principle of sovereign equality and the preference for consensus within IOs (Deitelhoff and Wallbott, 2012). Groupings are beneficial for all states but they are especially important for SIDS:

'We are small but together we are heard ... if there are 30 something countries that are small asking for a minimal mention in a declaration and we still don't get it and they're willing to block the outcome document, then you have the strength of being part of the group.' (Interview with SIDS diplomat)

Belonging to groups provides small states with information, access, and a voice. It enables burden sharing: diplomats from small states, especially those from the same region like the Caribbean or the Pacific, build up strong working relationships based on trust and reciprocal interests within groups that allows them to compensate for their capacity deficits. The SVE members of the WTO, for instance, meet and coordinate who will act as focal points on which issues and attend which meetings, reporting findings back to the group. This is especially important for small posts as often meetings run in parallel. It helps that small states often have similar interests and thus have less to lose from sharing information with like-minded countries.

Individually SIDS are members of numerous groupings in IOs (Carter, 2020b). They may be a member of the ACP (African Caribbean and Pacific), the G77, or the Non-Aligned Movement, for example. They also participate in regional groupings – CARICOM, Pacific Islands Forum Secretariat (PIFS), and the Organization of American States (OAS). The importance of collaboration for small states is why they pushed to create a grouping called SIDS in the UN and SVEs in the WTO. Participation in each of these groupings is a pragmatic response to the circumstances in which small states find themselves. It is also a key means of developing and prosecuting their agenda. The membership is different from IO to IO but as Table 1.1 in Chapter 1 illustrates, there are core states in the Caribbean, Pacific, and Indian Ocean that are present in each definition.

Groups need leaders and for the most part small states have been led by the active small states discussed – Barbados, Fiji, Jamaica, Seychelles, Mauritius, and Maldives. Invariably, whenever small states play a significant role in an IO's deliberations it is because a diplomat from one of these countries is prepared to dedicate time and effort to making it work. Ambassadors admit it takes time to learn the job, as one reflected:

'It takes a good 18 months to get to know the system within the organizations, and so then after the first 18 months then you get your money's worth for the next five years. So yes, then you become pretty au fait with the procedures and the history of the issues, and you can then meaningfully participate in the discussion.' (Interview with a SIDS diplomat)

Those who are especially skilled carve out a reputation for themselves that transcends the state they represent, as one diplomat reflected on a Caribbean PR:

'She was incredibly active. She went everywhere … she made a point to attend as many events as she could, she always made herself known … she just had a way about her, people loved her. This gave her access and contacts which she in turn leveraged for the benefit of the mission.' (Interview with a Caribbean diplomat)

This type of description of active SIDS diplomats was consistent across our research. As we will discuss further in Chapter 5, the SVE grouping emerged due to the effort of Barbados, one of the member states that was prepared to dedicate resources to the communal good. While the Doha modalities were being negotiated, Barbados, on behalf of small states, asked that there be recognition of the particular problems of small economies, that an annual session of the General Council would be dedicated to their issues, and that the coordinator of SVEs would be when appropriate be invited to the Green Room negotiations. That was the price of their support. As one official wryly commented, "Who was going to say no to Barbados in those circumstances?" Whether they did, or in reality could, threaten a veto was probably just theatre. The DG was always onside.

Two positive features of SIDS diplomacy enhances their ability to leverage groups to their advantage. The first is the relative autonomy of their diplomats from their capitals. Here, the small size of the diplomatic service, and indeed the small size of the national bureaucracy in general, means that diplomats are often given much greater latitude and autonomy than counterparts from larger countries. One diplomat recalled being told early on in their career by their ambassador:

'Analyse your situation, use your very best judgement and just do it. If you're wrong but you have done your homework and you can justify to me why you took that position. I back you a 100 per cent. Just go do it. So, I never forgot that.' (Interview with a SIDS diplomat)

The result is that many diplomats from small states think they have more latitude than diplomats from larger states.

A second feature of SIDS diplomacy that facilitates their collaborative efforts is the longer tenure afforded to their diplomats. Autonomy is risky but SIDS offset this by having longer rotations through key posts – usually no less than four years and often considerably longer. Indeed, some of the longest-serving representatives at IOs, many of whom have been involved in each organization for a decade or more, are from SIDS. Tenure provides these diplomats with considerable institutional memory. In turn, this long-term historical knowledge offsets the endogenous weaknesses of favouring generalist staff, legitimizes their authority in meetings and negotiations, and results in diplomats from small states being sought out for leadership roles. All states could adopt longer rotations but in larger services the demand for postings and the need to broaden the skill set of specialist officers makes this unworkable. Diplomats from small states are always generalists and human resource capacity constraints mean there are often few candidates to fill each post. Thus, while long tenure is a function of necessity it has distinct advantages for small states, providing the diplomat in question is good at their job.

The inability of SIDS to represent themselves on every issue across every IO, combined with the pressure on IOs to include them, means that alternative means of representation have to be created for them. We consider these at length throughout the book. The SIDS and SVEs label is one such mechanism that provides them with a greater opportunity for coordination. The WTO also allows the Organization of Eastern Caribbean States (OECS) and PIFS states to be represented jointly – when one speaks other WTO members know they speak for the group. The point is that these methods of collaboration have been institutionalized as a way for the very smallest to increase their participation.

Collaboration has long been touted as a panacea to the problems of smallness. As we will discuss further in Chapter 5, the West Indies Federation (1958–62) is perhaps the most ambitious attempt to increase economies of scale by pooling resources. It collapsed after the larger states (Jamaica and Trinidad and Tobago) decided they did not want to be burdened by the smallest (Mawby, 2012). CARICOM is the more modest successor to this configuration and the CARICOM states coordinate positions in IOs (Payne, 2008). The Pacific has never attempted a federation and arguably the PIFS is even more fragmented than CARICOM due to the presence of Australia and New Zealand (Fry, 2019). In recent years the PSIDS at the UN have started to work on their own because, as one of Manoa's (2015: 92) interviewees argues, in the previous Pacific Group, which included Australia and New Zealand:

'PSIDS issues were never at the centre, the agenda was dictated by those that held the purse strings. If the issues were at all addressed, they were addressed sub-standardly. Within the region, the same actors and institutions are still at play, so why not form a different entity in New York at the UN to address the real challenges of the PSIDS.'

And, as outlined in the introductory vignette and discussed further in Chapter 4, the success of the PSIDS on climate issues has occurred despite little change in their resources and because they have distanced themselves from Australia in particular (Carter, 2020a). The OECS has the deepest level of integration and coordination (Byron, 1999; Lewis, 2002): aside from Geneva, they have joint diplomatic representation in Brussels and Morocco, as well as a liaison service for seasonal workers in Canada. In this case, collaboration is aided by a shared Anglophone heritage, albeit broadening to include the French-, Spanish-, and Dutch-speaking Caribbean is on the agenda (Lewis et al, 2017). Regional variations and nuances aside, the more general rule is that regional groupings of small states have been less prominent in IOs like the UN and WTO than the global SIDS and their joint claim to vulnerability.

Active participation

The advantages of collaboration are difficult for SIDS to realize unless they are active participants (Panke, 2012b, 2013) in the processes and everyday practices of IOs, including proposing initiatives or motions; holding leadership positions, taking up positions on boards, and other decision-making bodies; coordinating positions; drafting text; holding press conferences and issuing press releases; briefing ministerial groups, delegations, and taskforces; and attending workshops, meetings, and conferences. It is via involvement in these activities that SIDS are not only able to realize the advantages of their condition but also demonstrate their competence. The problem is that active participation on even a few issues and within even a small number of IOs is disproportionately costly.

The reason participation in the processes and practices of IOs is a necessary condition in our explanation is that the presence of SIDS in IO decision-making cannot be assumed due to well-known capacity deficits (Panke, 2013; Corbett and Connell, 2015). Large states can have missions and delegations for most if not all IOs, whereas SIDS membership is often defined by their absence. A focus on the smallest and most peripheral members reveals, therefore, that influence is contingent on *presence*. SIDS embassies typically have 3–4 staff, of whom two might be diplomats (see Braveboy-Wagner, 2007: 145–8). In New York or Geneva there may be

50 meetings being held across multiple IOs in a single day in addition to routine consular matters. The logistics do not work. For those IOs such as the WHO and WIPO whose activities may not be a top priority unless there is a crisis, it can be hard to attract the desired attention. The daily work of the small state official is often rushing from one meeting to another, from one subject to another, catching up on details from colleagues from other states.

In addition to collaboration, SIDS have two primary strategies for offsetting these disadvantages. The first is prioritization. This is the core coping strategy for all SIDS. Active small states have a larger appetite for engagement but they still prioritize. They take leadership opportunities where they think they can have an impact. Fiji turned down the opportunity to be Chair of the ACP because it wanted to prioritize climate change and COP, for example. Prioritization can also be about how to spend time *within* negotiations rather than about which issues to get involved in. One diplomat reflected that a reason why active small states are often considered aggressive negotiators is that they are time poor:

'We don't have the time, cut to the chase please ... we are not going to sit and argue with you over the placement of a comma ... We have other meetings to go to, other things to deal with.' (Interview with Caribbean diplomat)

The second strategy is flexibility. Because they are few in number, diplomats from small states are invariably generalists. They move from issue to issue, IO to IO, often multiple times during their work day. This flexibility enables them to identify strategic linkages and affinities between agendas. The small size of bureaucratic apparatuses in capitals also means that gaining cross-institutional approval for positions is quicker than larger states. Size thus enables small states to adopt flexible positions and be nimble enough to realize advantages when they arise. Technology has been a real asset for SIDS in this work. As the UNSC vignette in the introduction illustrates, messaging services like WhatsApp and Viber are used regularly to coordinate between SIDS as well as between post and capital. These services are free and, according to most SIDS diplomats, secure enough for their purposes.

The final way that small states are able to participate is via assistance from IOs. We discussed why IOs do this at length in the previous chapter. For now, the important point is that IOs have taken a number of steps to help SIDS deal with the disproportionate costs of participation. Several larger Commonwealth countries have funded office suites in New York and Geneva, for example. Both cities are expensive to live in and so these facilities allow SIDS to rent a small office or one or two rooms. In Geneva

Table 3.1: The number and location of SIDS overseas missions

	Groups	New York	Washington	Geneva	Brussels	Vienna	London	Paris
Antigua and Barbuda[1]	SIDS/SVES	Yes	Yes	No	Yes	No	Yes	No
Bahamas[2]	SIDS/SVES	Yes	Yes	No	Yes	No	Yes	Yes
Bahrain	SIDS	Yes	Yes	Yes	Yes	No	Yes	Yes
Barbados	SIDS/SVES	Yes	Yes	No	Yes	Yes	Yes	Yes
Belize	SIDS/SVES	Yes	Yes	No	Yes	No	Yes	Yes
Bolivia	SVES	Yes	Yes	Yes	Yes	Yes	Yes	Yes
Cape Verde	SIDS	No	Yes	Yes	Yes	Yes	No	Yes
Comoros	SIDS	No	No	No	Yes	No	Yes	Yes
Cuba	SIDS/SVES	No	Yes	No[3]	Yes	Yes	Yes	Yes
Dominica[4]	SIDS/SVES	Yes	Yes	No	Yes	No	Yes	Yes
Dominican Republic	SIDS/SVES	Yes	Yes	No[5]	Yes	Yes	Yes	Yes
Ecuador	SVES	Yes	Yes	Yes	Yes	Yes	Yes	Yes
El Salvador	SVES	Yes	Yes	Yes	Yes	Yes	Yes	Yes
Fiji	SIDS/SVES	No	Yes	No	Yes	No	Yes	No
Grenada	SIDS/SVES	Yes	Yes	Yes	Yes	Yes	Yes	No
Guatemala	SVES	Yes	Yes	No[6]	Yes	Yes	Yes	Yes

Table 3.1: The number and location of SIDS overseas missions (continued)

	Groups	New York	Washington	Geneva	Brussels	Vienna	London	Paris
Guinea–Bissau	SIDS	No	No	No	Yes	No	No	Yes
Guyana	SIDS	Yes	Yes	No	Yes	No	Yes	No
Haiti[7]	SIDS	Yes	Yes	Yes	Yes	Yes	Yes	Yes
Honduras	SVES	Yes	Yes	Yes	Yes	Yes	Yes	Yes
Jamaica	SIDS/SVES	Yes	Yes	Yes	Yes	Yes	Yes	No
Kiribati	SIDS	No	No	No	No	No	No	No
Maldives	SIDS	No	No	Yes	Yes	Yes	Yes	Yes
Marshall Islands[8]	SIDS	No	Yes	No	No	No	No	No
Mauritania	SVES	No	Yes	Yes	Yes	No	Yes	Yes
Mauritius	SIDS	No	Yes	Yes	Yes	Yes	Yes	Yes
Federated States of Micronesia	SIDS	No	Yes	No	No	No	No	No
Nauru	SIDS	No	No	No	No	No	No	No
Nicaragua	SVES	Yes	Yes	Yes	Yes	Yes	Yes	Yes
Palau	SIDS	No	Yes	No	Yes	No	No	No
Panama	SVES	Yes	Yes	Yes	Yes	Yes	Yes	Yes
Papua New Guinea	SIDS/SVES	No	Yes	No	Yes	No	Yes	No

(continued)

Table 3.1: The number and location of SIDS overseas missions (continued)

	Groups	New York	Washington	Geneva	Brussels	Vienna	London	Paris
St. Kitts and Nevis[9]	SIDS/SVES	No	Yes	Yes	Yes	No	Yes	Yes
St. Lucia[10]	SIDS/SVES	Yes	Yes	No	Yes	No	Yes	No
St. Vincent and the Grenadines[11]	SIDS/SVES	Yes	Yes	Yes	Yes	Yes	Yes	No
Samoa	SIDS/SVES	No	No	No	Yes	Yes	No	No
São Tomé and Príncipe	SIDS	No	No	No	Yes	No	No	Yes
Seychelles	SIDS/SVES	Yes	No	No	Yes	Yes	No	Yes
Singapore	SIDS	Yes	Yes	Yes	Yes	No	Yes	Yes
Solomon Islands[12]	SIDS	Yes	No	Yes	Yes	No	Yes	No
Sri Lanka	SVES	Yes	Yes	Yes	Yes	Yes	Yes	Yes
Suriname	SIDS	No	Yes	No	Yes	No	No	Yes
Timor-Leste	SIDS	No	Yes	Yes	No	No	Yes	No
Tonga[13]	SIDS/SVES	Yes	No	No	No	No	Yes	No
Trinidad and Tobago	SIDS/SVES	Yes	Yes	Yes	Yes	No	Yes	Yes
Tuvalu[14]	SIDS	No	No	No	Yes	No	No	No
Vanuatu	SIDS	No	No	No	Yes	No	No	Yes

[1] Brussels: Embassies of the Eastern Caribbean States (OECS) to Belgium and Missions to the European Union (EU).

[2] Consulate in Zurich.

[3] Both embassy and consulate are located in Bern.

4 Brussels: Embassies of the OECS to Belgium and Missions to the EU.

5 Embassy is located in Bern. Two consulates are located in Bern and Zurich.

6 Embassy and consulate is located in Bern. Another consulate is located in Zurich.

7 Brussels: Embassies of the OECS to Belgium and Missions to the EU.

8 Consulate in Zurich.

9 Brussels: Embassies of the OECS to Belgium and Missions to the EU.

10 Brussels: Embassies of the OECS to Belgium and Missions to the EU.

11 Brussels: Embassies of the OECS to Belgium and Missions to the EU.

12 Permanent missions of the United Nations in New York and Geneva function as embassies.

13 Consulate is located in Zurich.

14 Consulate is located in Basel.

Source: Compiled by authors from national websites.

the Commonwealth secretariat also funds a trade adviser who can assist the national officials in the technicalities of trade negotiations. The Swiss government, effectively the landlord for all delegations in Geneva, sometimes helps to pay the rent, funds a number of ad hoc visits, and can even second experts to work with the small states. When these countries also have delegates to the EU in Brussels they will sometimes fly in for particular meetings, using the office space provided. That can give them a presence; there are still a number of small countries who are members of the UN and the WTO but who cannot afford to maintain even a minimal office in Geneva or other posts. As a WHO official reflected: "We have to remind ourselves that we have only consulted members who have a presence here."

The secretariat can also assist SIDS by providing technical advice. Again, we will discuss the where and why of this in greater depth throughout Part II of the book. For now, the important point is that while asymmetries between states are an important context to our story, there are also asymmetries between the secretariat and their members. Indeed, small state delegations to IOs and the secretariat of IOs are polar opposites. The former are usually limited in numbers, stretched in capacity, temporary in position, technically circumscribed, rushed in activities, but politically authoritative. The latter have depth in knowledge, continuity in tenure, and technical expertise, and are concentrated in subject matter, but politically dependent. IO officials can be caged tigers, knowing what they think needs doing, versed in the long history of the subject but reliant on member states to come to a similar appreciation of what might be done. It is, in many respects, the traditional mismatch found in domestic policymaking where the experience of the continuing civil servants acts as an uneasy balance with the temporary political masters. But there are additional complications: the lack of a single political authority and the difficulty of gaining authoritative decisions from a medley of 180 plus member states with different views and opinions is coupled with a suspicion among small state representatives that the secretariat really only serves the rich and powerful members. The images are contradictory but can be held by different members about the same officials in the secretariat.

Thus far we have told a fairly positive story of how SIDS are able to overcome these capacity deficits on some issues and in some IOs. We will nuance this story as we go. It is also important to note here, however, that despite the successes there is an ongoing debate within SIDS about whether active participation is worth it. We went back to talk to Mauritius some years after the previous quote about how their interests were served by taking a leadership position in trade negotiations in particular. The team and the strategy had changed; they were disillusioned with the value they received from taking on such a prominent role. Specifically, they felt because of their leadership role in the Doha round they were required to seek consensus rather than push their own position. The decision to step back had consequences for the larger group of small states. Because historically few small states have been represented in Geneva the burden has fallen on the countries we identified earlier to act as representatives for the group. If one steps back then a larger burden is placed on the others. Some SIDS diplomats were angry at Barbados for allowing Guatemala to take over the leadership of the SVEs at the WTO, for example, as their interests are seen to be too different. The result is that there can be resentment by these more active small states of the more passive members of the group who essentially free-ride on their labour. Low-level Caribbean grumbling about the Pacific SIDS, who, Fiji aside, have historically not maintained a presence in Geneva, is a case in point.

This problem is not as acute in New York where nearly all small states are represented. Here, a small Pacific state like Nauru has taken on multiple leadership roles, including of AOSIS and the PSIDS. Having a presence in New York – their 'mission to the world' (Mohamed, 2002; Braveboy-Wagner, 2007: 152; Súilleabháin, 2014) – is also important for conducting bilateral business and trading votes across the entire multilateral system (Brazys and Panke, 2017). SIDS are adept at trading their votes. Indeed, they even use their relatively small size to their advantage, as this diplomat describes leader's week where each country is granted six seats in the UNGA:

> 'Another example of a cheap favour is during leader's week, especially the first few days, the hottest commodity in town is [seats in the UNGA] … I don't need six people all the time. So one of the biggest black markets – it's not selling, it's literally giving out favours. [They come to me]: "My PM is here, how many passes can you give me?" I don't need all of them. "I can give you three. But afterwards I need you to give them to this delegation because they needed to make sure to get it back to me." Very cheap favour, but very popular.'

Conclusion

To account for the diversity of small state participation in IOs we have differentiated between: (1) small states who seek membership in IOs to gain sovereign recognition often with a view to selling it; (2) small states who maintain a presence in certain IOs to extract resources and influence on specific issues that are central to their development; and (3) those select few that actively participate in the operations of multiple IOs so as to contribute to the maintenance of a permissive LIO. This latter group most closely resemble European small states and the strategies and tactics they employ.

We therefore extend those accounts by showing that SIDS, who are much smaller in both population and wealth, can also overcome the limitations of size to influence multilateral diplomacy. But to do so they have drawn attention to their vulnerability in the belief that it will generate S&DT based on their unique condition.

PART II

Interactions

4

Differentiated Vulnerabilities, Climate Change, and the UN Agencies

Climate change is the policy issue most commonly associated with the influence of small states and SIDS in particular. It is therefore a 'most likely' case (Eckstein, 1975) for their influence. Climate change magnifies the common dilemma for small states – that they have to fulfil the minimum requirements of modern statehood with limited resources or capacity. It also represents a significant challenge to the legitimacy of IOs because the smallest members will bear the disproportionate impact while the largest and richest are responsible for the vast majority of emissions. The impact of climate change on SIDS thus infringes on two key norms of the LIO – the sovereign equality of states and the right to development.

The consequence is that the creation of the SIDS category and the prominence provided to SIDS in climate change negotiations and policy suits both small states and IOs: it allows the countries we call SIDS to 'perform vulnerability' while also enabling IOs to generate 'throughput' legitimacy. But to understand this we have to recognize that the category SIDS is not a neutral or technical label. It is a political tool designed to realize specific ends. The creation of the label SIDS, the associated groupings at different IOs, and the fact that actors talk about a 'SIDS agenda', is the most compelling evidence we have for the way these states have altered the practices of IOs.

This chapter tells this story from both sides. We start with small states and show how they have pressured IOs to recognize their unique vulnerabilities. We then tell the story of IOs and how they have responded to these concerns. Small states, acting as a group, have been central to each of the major climate summits since Rio. They are key negotiators at COP. They were integral to the formation of the High Ambition Coalition (HAC) in the lead up to the Paris COP and thus played a central role in the subsequent agreements. This story is well documented so we pay particular attention to the IMO and the way SIDS have recently positioned themselves to achieve greenhouse gas (GHG) reductions. The IMO discussion is revealing because it illustrates how the SIDS agenda has spread throughout the network of UN agencies, and in doing so has politicized IOs typically considered to have a technical focus.

Climate vulnerability and the rise of the SIDS

The countries that we now call SIDS were engaged in international affairs long before they assumed a distinct label. As we saw in Chapter 3, on achieving independence in the decades after the Second World War they joined the UN. Many of them are members of the ACP, for example, which has been in existence since 1975. They have also been members of the G77, regional groupings, and the Commonwealth (1985, 1997). SIDS make up two thirds of the Commonwealth's membership; the Commonwealth therefore has a vested interest in these states and their issues. Section XIV of the 2013 Charter of the Commonwealth commits to addressing the needs of SIDS. The Commonwealth has also provided an office for SIDS seeking to represent themselves in New York since the 1980s. The Commonwealth held the first Ministerial Group on Small States (MGSS) in 1993. The MGSS met six times between 1993 and 2006. It has been replaced by an Open-ended Ministerial Group on Small States. The Commonwealth also began holding a Global Biennial Conference on Small States in 2010. The Commonwealth has altered its definition of small states during this period (Sutton, 2011). As per Table 1.1, the 1997 definition includes states with populations over 1 million who share similar characteristics and regional links with small states (that is, Papua New Guinea and Jamaica). The important caveat therefore is that in this chapter we are not claiming to tell the story of each small state, or indeed the multitude of ways the countries we now refer to as SIDS engage in diplomatic affairs. Rather, we seek to tell the story of how the countries we now call SIDS have created and utilized the label – a constitutive norm – to pursue progressive action on climate change.

Rhetorical action

'[For] the Maldives, a mean sea level rise of 2 metres would suffice to virtually submerge the entire country of 1,190 small islands ... That would be the death of a nation.' (Gayoom, 1987)

It is impossible to determine a precise date when the label small state came into common usage in IOs as it has emerged iteratively in everyday diplomacy. 'Microstate' is a term that has been used at the UN since at least the 1960s and the United Nations Conference on Trade and Development (UNCTAD) set in motion studies on 'developing island countries' in the 1970s (Sutton, 2011: 143). This reflects that there has been a long conversation among economists about the development challenges of small countries since at least the end of the Second World War. But by and large, recognition of the special development needs of small islands dissipated during the 1980s and 1990s (see Chapter 5). One veteran SIDS diplomat reflected, "Up until the climate change negotiations, the small island countries in particular had been, if anything, systematically forgotten about."

By contrast, group consciousness in IOs was heightened by international recognition of climate change. As the previous quote illustrates, the Maldives, a low-lying atoll nation in the Indian Ocean, claims to be the first country to talk about the impact of climate change on small states at the UN in 1987. In 1989 the first Small States Conference on Sea Level Rise was held in Male, Maldives. The conference was jointly funded by the Commonwealth and Australia. The vulnerability of islands and low-lying islands in particular to sea level rise was later recognized by the 44th session of the UN General Assembly (resolution 44/206) in 1989, which expressed concern that:

> sea-level rise resulting from global climate change could lead, inter alia, to abnormally high tides, which could intensify flooding and the erosion of coastal areas and damage infrastructure on islands and in low-lying coastal areas.

and recommended:

> that the vulnerability of affected countries and their marine ecosystems to sea-level rise be considered during discussions of a draft framework convention on climate as well as within the framework of the United Nations conference on environment and development to be held in 1992 and during the preparatory process for the conference.

As we will outline further, this understanding of the impacts of climate change gave rise to the label SIDS. Rhetorical action based on emphasizing the unique vulnerability of small islands to the most detrimental effects of climate change has been repeated by these countries ever since – to the extent that they have come to symbolize the planet's moral voice for progressive action on this issue.

The rhetorical action of SIDS in relation to climate change negotiations is well established in the literature so we will not revisit it here (but see Ashe et al, 1999; Chasek, 2005; Beztold, 2010; Benwell, 2011; Betzold et al, 2012; Deitelhoff and Wallbott, 2012; Panke, 2012a; de Águeda Corneloup and Mol, 2014; Jaschik, 2014; Carter 2015, 2020a; Manoa, 2015; Ourbak and Magnan, 2018; Petzold and Magnan, 2019). Instead, we will show how the creation of the SIDS category has enabled these countries to pursue their agenda outside the General Assembly and UNFCCC processes to more marginal and technical arenas of global governance like the IMO. In doing so they have become more than a symbol of victimhood; they have become leaders on this issue in their own right. Indeed, the late Tony de Brum, veteran politician and activist from the Marshall Islands who was instrumental in the achievements of the HAC at the Paris Climate Conference and subsequent agreement in December 2015, declared during the UNFCCC COP18 held in Doha in December 2012, 'It is time the world focused not only on our vulnerability, but on our leadership' (SPREP, 2012).

Tony de Brum is a key actor in the SIDS story because he led the effort to take the SIDS agenda from the UNFCCC to the IMO. In 2012 de Brum was elected as 'Minister in Assistance to the President' and Minister for Foreign Affairs in 2014 (for the third time), and sought to enhance the Republic of the Marshall Islands' (RMI) technical progress in the UNFCCC negotiations; raise the state's international profile through IOs (such as the security council) and other public and academic events, as well as to 'make noise in the international media'; and finally, to make climate change the central message of every diplomatic opportunity (de Brum, 2014). Indeed, as one diplomat from another PSIDS said,

> 'We are kind of almost like an octopus: we put out our tentacles and planted SIDS issues in pretty much anything where we have a chance to do so. Be that in the high-level political forum, the twenty-third-year agenda, you name it we tried to put it there.'

Here we use the IMO as an example of the broader trend. The IMO is especially interesting as, unlike UNFCCC, it has a reputation as a highly technical organization. This should disadvantage small states, who tend to lack human resource capacity in negotiations (Panke, 2013; Corbett and Connell, 2015). But, because many small states maintain large shipping registries, they actually have considerable expertise on these issues and greater structural clout in this IO than they do in virtually any other international forum. For our purposes, the point is that in this case the formal rules and traditions favour SIDS.

Created in 1948, IMO is one of the 15 special agencies of the UN, delegated with responsibilities to create regulatory frameworks on 'practices relating to technical matters of all kinds affecting shipping engaged international trade; to encourage and facilitate the general adoption of the highest practicable standards in matters concerning the maritime safety, efficiency of navigation and prevention and control of maritime pollution from ships' (Biermann and Siebenhüner, 2009). The Assembly of all members meets once every two years. The Council of 40 elected members is the executive body in charge of policy deliberation and decision-making when the Assembly is not in session. The Marine Environment Protection Committee (MEPC) is a standing committee of the Assembly with the responsibility to adopt and amend legislation governing marine pollution from ships. As in most IOs, decision-making at the IMO follows the principle of one-state-one-vote, yet in practice consensus is the norm.

Given the nature of shipping operation (for example, in open seas, beyond national boundaries) and the system of ships being registered in states with open registration, international regulation is especially important. The RMI has an open registry which means any ship can carry its flag regardless of its country of origin. The RMI is currently the third-largest shipping registry in the world. Income from the registry accounted for approximately 10 per cent of RMI government revenue in 2018.[1]

By convention, states, both developed and developing, large and small, either grant shipping registries a formal position as delegates to represent them at the IMO or bring corporate officials from shipping registries as advisors. The formal delegates put forward proposals, participate in debates, and vote on final decisions on behalf of their states. As result, 'the shipping industry has substantial opportunity to influence the shape of global maritime climate change policy' (Influence Map, 2017: 11). One environmental organization commented:

> The bigger your registry, the bigger clout you have at IMO – when new legislation is being negotiated, everyone is looking in the room to see what bigger registries are thinking and doing. You can design amazing environment legislation, but if the registries don't want to play then it's worthless. (Cited in Hayer, 2016)

Until recently the RMI was represented at the IMO by its registry, International Registries Inc. (IRI), which had started operations in 1948 and become a privately owned and operated corporation in 1991.

As in many environmental issue areas, there has been a widespread delegation of authority to NGOs (Green, 2018); at the IMO, over 80 NGOs have received consultative status. These NGOs include representatives of the ship-owners and operators, industry trade associations, cargo owners and charters, and environmental organizations (Karim, 2015). Although

Table 4.1: IMO assessed contribution

Ranking	Country	Amount GBP	% of total assessment
1	Panama	4,896,058	16.26
2	Liberia	2,943,744	9.77
3	Marshall Islands	2,803,537	9.31
4	Singapore	1,829,757	6.07
5	Malta	1,482,973	4.92
6	Bahamas	1,322,304	4.39
7	United Kingdom	1,237,591	4.11
8	China	1,236,270	4.10
9	Greece	942,964	3.13
10	United States	831,412	2.76
Total		19,526,609	64.82

Source: Corbett, J. et al (2020) 'Climate governance, policy entrepreneurs and small states: explaining policy change at the International Maritime Organisation', *Environmental Politics*, 29(5): 825–44. Reprinted with permission from Taylor and Francis.

they may not have the right to vote, they can submit documents and often find partners in the 'flag of convenience' (FOC) states, such as the RMI:

> Their main influence comes via IMO Member States who also share similar interests. The presence of FOC countries in the leading position of IMO created a further avenue for shipping companies to exert influence on the IMO law-making process, as they virtually have a client–service–provider relationship with those countries. (Karim, 2015)

With heavy participation of shipping industry players, in formal and informal positions, the IMO had achieved little since it was granted the responsibility to regulate GHG emissions from shipping by the countries that signed on the Kyoto Accord in 1997. Meanwhile, in 2007–12, shipping GHG emissions rose to 2.8 per cent of total global emissions, and they could grow by up to 250 per cent by 2050 (Smith et al, 2015). As a result, some NGOs turned their attention to the IMO as part of their broader fight to reduce GHG emissions. PSIDS had not previously acted as a grouping at the IMO. Indeed, unlike other IOs, and with the important exception of the EU, the IMO has not had a culture of strong groupings (multiple interviews). But the point is that the rules of the IMO meant that this IO provided considerable scope for PSIDS once they became more active and organized.

The IMO was identified as one such diplomatic opportunity where they could exert influence disproportionate to their size and push forward their interests for two main reasons: (1) even though politically controversial issues, such as regulating GHG emissions from maritime transport had been excluded from the discussion at the IMO due to the interests of the shipping registry industry and other trade associations, the IMO was nonetheless delegated by the Kyoto Agreement to regulate its emission; and (2) the RMI has been a 'large' stakeholder at the IMO (Influence Map, 2017).

> our cards from the beginning have been a small country, loud voice. We don't really have that kind of leverage on anyone. Even our shipping registry, although large and of substantial importance to our economy, its voice is in the IMO context, and that is still a sort of mystery to small island countries: what the IMO does, how it conducts its business. There's a lot of insistence on anonymity, protection of identity, and all of those things that make working within the IMO not an easy or pleasant task for small island countries. (Tony de Brum interviewed in Yeo, 2015)

In May 2015, during the 68th session of the MEPC de Brum arrived in London and gave an impassioned speech which incorporates the appeal to unique vulnerability that has become a hallmark of SIDS:

> Our islands lay just an average of two meters above sea level. Day after day, climate change and the resulting sea-level rise and tropical storms take grip on our homes, on our security and on our livelihoods. My colleagues here from our fellow atoll nation of Tuvalu can tell you what it looks like. And Minister Bule, here all the way from Vanuatu, can tell you how it feels to have 70 percent of your capital city wiped away by a cyclone whose winds were whipped up by the quickly warming Pacific Oceans. Any country here that lives an island existence or that has big populations living along low-lying coastlines can, and will increasingly be the victim of such events. (IMO, 2015)

As Benwell (2011: 208) claims, the unifying theme of this advocacy is that climate change is a global public good problem and SIDS are the 'canary in the coalmine' in a tragedy of the commons scenario. de Brum's speech at the IMO was dismissed by some as a stunt – ministers do not usually attend highly technical IMO sessions. But attention-grabbing stunts have been part and parcel of SIDS activism, justified by the existential nature of their predicament and captured in the catchy phrase '1.5 to stay alive'. In this sense, de Brum was following in the footsteps of Maldives President Mohammed Nasheed who instead of sending a delegation to COP15 held an underwater cabinet meeting to highlight the threat of sea level rise. The images made compelling news items but underneath the attention-grab SIDS diplomats argue that more than other nations their diplomacy must rise or fall on the power of their ideas:

> 'We have no money. We're small economies. Yes, we are sinking and we can mount fairly effective PR campaigns but we generally have to be coming with good ideas ... we can go to France and say, hey former colonial master, do this, and they'll be like, yeah, probably not ... But if we come with a good idea then it matters a little less who the messenger is.' (Interview with SIDS diplomat)

In recent years the 'good ideas' that SIDS have been successful in promulgating include the 'Oceans Agenda' and the importance of the 'Blue Economy' (Chan, 2018).

Examples like the IMO and Oceans have largely been driven by the PSIDS. This is a step change. Maldives and Caribbean states were at the forefront of establishing AOSIS, the grouping that coordinates SIDS issues at the UN (Ashe et al, 1999). Indeed, while Vanuatu was a key player in the establishment of AOSIS their representative was Suriname-born Robert F. Van Lierop. As outlined in Chapter 3, in the late 1980s many PSIDS were not represented at the UN while the former US Trust Territory States had not yet gained independence. In recent years this has changed, as one PSIDS diplomat reflected:

> 'When I came here about 21 years ago I would have to say the mindset or the way that people were behaving was somehow differently. [In the Pacific] if someone says something and you keep quiet it means you don't like it. That's exactly the opposite of what you're doing here. If you don't like something here you yell, you scream, you kick around, you make yourself known. For Pacific people to realize that fact, that took a while.' (Interview with PSIDS diplomat)

The growing assertiveness of PSIDS and their increasing independence from regional neighbours (and aid donors) Australia and New Zealand on climate issues has been well documented (Manoa, 2015; Carter, 2020a). The key point for our purposes is that the additional numbers and rhetorical power of the PSIDS has further amplified AOSIS voice on climate issues.

Collaboration

Rhetorical action is a necessary feature of SIDS influence but it is not sufficient because on their own no country, let alone a very small nation, can change the agenda of IOs where consensus is the norm. The membership of SIDS was decided in the lead-up to the 1994 Barbados conference by a single UN official who recalls:

> 'I said let's make it 10 million and that was that … [it's] the population of Cuba … We wanted Cuba's political strength … the energy that the Cubans would bring to bear … [and] the fact that they were not easily intimidated … They could [also] be a useful nuisance … If Western powers wanted to change something that small islands were putting forward then you had Cuba as a scapegoat … "Look at these crazy Cubans. What can we do with them?"'

The definition has been key to their activism but so too was AOSIS who championed its creation. The 1989 meeting in Maldives and the impending UNFCCC negotiations inspired the formation of AOSIS in 1990, which at the time comprised 24 island states under the leadership of Maldives, Vanuatu, and Trinidad and Tobago. Since then, membership has grown to 39 members plus five observers, all of whom coordinate positions at the UN (Betzold et al, 2012). Member states of AOSIS work together primarily through New York diplomatic missions, with major policy decisions taken at ambassadorial-level plenary sessions (Chasek, 2005). AOSIS has no formal charter or secretariat but receives considerable pro bono technical assistance (Betzold, 2010).

The success of AOSIS in the deliberations on climate change in the early 1990s is well documented (Ashe et al, 1999). In the negotiating committee set up by the UNGA to develop a climate change convention, the chair of AOSIS, Van Lierop, set three goals (Ashe et al, 1999):

1. to devise a common negotiating position at the intergovernmental negotiating committee (INC) for a framework convention on climate change;
2. to focus world attention on the plight of small island countries in the face of the threat of global warming; and
3. to consider strategies to cope with its damaging effects and to ensure that AOSIS's interests were properly addressed by an effective convention.

To achieve these goals, AOSIS had 12 key objectives; in the majority of cases (10 of 12) they were successful in getting their preferred wording in the draft text of the convention. For example, their first objective was that the preamble should expressly recognize the problems and unique vulnerability of small island countries. This position is reflected in the text agreed and adopted at the Fifth Session of the Intergovernmental Negotiating Committee for a Framework Convention on Climate Change on 9 May 1992.

Part of the reason for the success of AOSIS was the considerable goodwill among the international community towards small and vulnerable countries. Van Lierop and John Ashe, the representative for Antigua and Barbuda, argue that the weight of the group and its numbers as a negotiating bloc were also important (Ashe et al, 1999: 219). We might add that AOSIS enjoyed a first-mover advantage vis-à-vis other groups (Betzold, 2010) and that the process of UNFCCC deliberations – six intensive, two-week long negotiating sessions over 14 months leading up to the 1992 Rio Conference – favoured the skilled diplomats who led AOSIS during this period, rather than unwieldy bureaucratic teams.

AOSIS success in the UNFCCC process illustrated the potential of the group. This was confirmed at the United Nations Conference on Environment and Development in Rio de Janeiro 1992 where they again succeeded in inserting their position in the formal text (UNCED, 1992). Agenda 21 makes numerous references to the unique challenges of small islands, designating them a 'special case' (17.123) by virtue of their fragility and vulnerability to environmental hazards. It further noted that SIDS would require cooperation from the international community to meet these challenges (17.126). In addition to a work programme, $130 million funding commitment, and a decision to hold the first ever UN conference on small states, Agenda 21 also urged that other IOs recognize the unique circumstances of SIDS.

AOSIS remains a key voice on climate change issues, as we saw in the vignette from the UNSC at the start of this book. Indeed, it has become increasingly professionalized since 2011–12. Historically, AOSIS hasn't had a secretariat but has instead relied on the mission of the chair. As a result, taking on the chair of AOSIS is a big commitment for individual SIDS as it means adding staff to their missions. Donors have helped by funding fellowships. NGOs have also provided considerable pro bono technical support, as we will discuss later. Interns are common. AOSIS has always been primarily NY-based and UNFCCC focused. But it remains significant to all of the IOs we consider because it serves as a model for SIDS about how collaboration can help them achieve their aims in multilateral institutions. This impact can be seen in the example of how the RMI worked at the IMO.

The RMI does not have the capacity or clout to influence the agenda on its own at the IMO. So, they enlisted support. At the MEPC 68th session, de Brum presented a position paper on behalf of the RMI: 'Setting a reduction target and agreeing associated measures for international shipping' (MEPC, 2015).

> 'for the Marshall Islands, I mean IMO was not going far enough. When they submitted that submission three – four years ago I guess, the – brought back the issue, right, in adopting – I mean stringent measures to reduce CO_2 emission and it's thanks to the Marshall Islands by the way, definitely. It's Tony de Brum who brought back this issue here.' (Interview with a SIDS representative)

The position taken by the RMI was rejected by the MEPC (Baresic et al, 2015; Marke, 2015) for three reasons: (1) it was a last-minute submission even though it was supported by Tuvalu, Vanuatu, and the Solomon Islands; (2) the outcome of the Paris Conference was yet to be settled; and (3) in order to determine the contributions of ships to the emissions, the data collection system that had been under debate for several meetings remained to be finalized (UMAS, 2016). Moreover, as one observer noted (author interview), the RMI had not yet developed the political machine to support their initiatives. Despite the rejection, the call for decarbonization brought the issue of reducing shipping GHG emissions back on the negotiation table at the IMO.

To realize their ambition, and build regional capacity, the RMI had to generate political support for their position. They worked through the PSIDS, a regional grouping of 12 island nations which is a reincarnation of the old Pacific Group that included Australia and New Zealand (Manoa, 2015), as one diplomat explained:

> '[As] each Pacific country becomes stronger, they know their issues and they wanted their issues to be more reflected in international for a. So we've started to realize that our key agendas were not reflected by the Pacific Island Forum Secretariat. Key agendas such as climate change, sustainable development issues are not being really reflected as we wanted. They have always been watered down by our bigger brothers such as New Zealand and Australia because of their differing views. We say climate change is a priority. We say climate change is an existential threat.' (Interview with a PSIDS diplomat)

The PSIDS meet regularly in New York where they coordinate positions and burden share. The group is tightly knit – many diplomats live in the same suburb and they have regular social events. They consider this cohesion and camaraderie as key to their success. The main point from our perspective is that while SIDS benefit from mutual cooperation with larger states, as discussed later, the PSIDS have had more success on this issue by striking out on their own.

Since 2012, the RMI had worked towards consolidating climate diplomacy in the Pacific region. In 2013 the leaders of the Pacific Island Forum Secretariat, at a meeting in the RMI, signed the Majuro Declaration which committed them to 'climate leadership':[2]

> To lead is to act. In supporting this Declaration, a government, economic entity, company, civil society organization or individual commits to demonstrate climate leadership through action that contributes to the urgent reduction and phase down of greenhouse gas pollution. (Pacific Islands Forum Secretariat, 2013)

Sustainable sea transportation was specifically mentioned in the declaration. That same year, Fiji, which was suspended in 2009 from the PIFS due to its political situation, founded the Pacific Islands Development Forum (PIDF). Sustainable transportation was one of the PIDF's ten priorities. In 2014, the SIDS Accelerated Modalities of Action (SAMOA) Pathway, the outcome of the third UN SIDS conference held in Samoa, included a provision on Sustainable Transportation (SIDS Action Platform, 2014). In 2015, the Suva Declaration on Climate Change – an outcome of the third Pacific Islands Development Forum leaders' summit – included the participating countries' positions ahead of COP21 in Paris, and their wish to see sea transport included in the agreement:

> We the Leaders of the Pacific Islands Development Forum following consultation with and the agreement of all stakeholders at the Pacific Island Development Forum Third Summit therefore call for: … an integrated approach to transitioning Pacific countries to low carbon transport futures, in particular sea transport given its central role in providing connectivity for Pacific Small Island Developing States, including a regional strategy to advocate for and monitor implementation of sector targets through relevant UN agencies commensurate with the 1.5°C threshold. (PIDF, 2015)

Later that year, at COP21, de Brum led the HAC, a grouping of over 100 countries demanding a binding agreement (King, 2016). But GHG emissions for the shipping and aviation sectors were not included in the outcomes of the conference.

Before the MEPC68 in May 2015, the RMI delegation could not rally the support of Western European countries, because the IMO negotiators did not believe that the organization would ever decarbonize (author interview).

But in September 2015, at the next intersessional meeting, the RMI, with the help of academics from University College London (UCL), hosted a meal with European countries (Norway, France, Belgium, and Germany) and other PSIDS (interview with PSIDS diplomat). This led to regular collaboration between some of these countries and the PSIDS in their IMO activity. At MEP69 in April 2016, the Solomon Islands submitted a position paper on behalf of PSIDS, supported by the RMI, together with Belgium, France, Germany, and Morocco. An observer noted that the fact that the Solomon Islands, rather than the RMI, led the submission, added credibility to the call made earlier by de Brum for regulating shipping (author interview).

The submission MEPC 69/7/2 promoted the adoption of a work plan to define the shipping sector's 'fair share' in GHG emission reductions. MEPC69 occurred after Paris; this led to a notable change in mood towards the GHG issue in the room (interview with PSIDS adviser). At MEPC70, an even larger coalition, in addition to the original Solomon Islands, the RMI, Germany, Belgium, France and Morocco,[3] now including Tonga, Antigua and Barbuda, Cote d'Ivoire, Monaco, and Denmark, submitted MEPC 70/7/6. The coalition presented a similar line to the MEPC69 submission, but further clarified that the proposed GHG emissions reductions would be complementary to the three-step approach of the data collection method.[4] During that session, the IMO agreed on a roadmap to adopt a strategy on GHG emissions reduction from shipping by 2018 (and MEPC72): "The small islands they got together; they became a block and then Tony de Brum lobbied for them all. So, it really was the Marshall Islands [paper] and statements that kicked it all off" (Interview with a representative from a large European state).

As the preparations for MEPC72 drew nearer, coordination between PSIDS and some European partners grew deeper. A Shipping High Ambition Coalition (SHAC), a successor to the HAC, was initiated in April 2017 at a side event to the Third Pacific Regional Energy & Transport Ministers' Meeting in Tonga and includes countries from the Pacific and the EU. It has since developed into a 'really well-communicated, coordinated group' (interview with a representative of a small state). The EU helped finance PSIDS representation at the IMO and initiated a 'buddy programme': France is helping Fiji, Belgium is helping the Solomon Islands, Tonga with the Netherlands, and the RMI with Germany. Tuvalu and the UK, and Kiribati and Sweden might set up similar programmes in the future. In February 2018, France and Fiji organized a technical seminar in Suva, with the Micronesian Center for Sustainable Transport (MCST), The University of the South Pacific (USP), and UCL.

Meanwhile, the IMO Intersessional Working Group on Reduction of GHG Emissions (ISWG-GHG) met three times. The first meeting took place in June 2017, and the second was held right before MEPC71, during which they worked on the draft of the strategy. On both occasions, the SHAC, and more especially the PSIDS, were active in the discussions. During the ISWG-GHG, the RMI and the Solomon Islands co-submitted ISWG-GHG 1/2/2 to press the committee to have high ambitions on the issue of GHG emissions reductions (IMO, 2017). At the same session, the two countries also co-submitted 1/2/12, which offered a potential method for quantifying emissions with Belgium, Denmark, France, Germany, the Netherlands, Tonga, Tuvalu, and the International Cargo Handling Coordination Association (ICHCA).

During the second ISWG-GHG, the PSIDS were equally active with two other submissions: Kiribati, the RMI, Solomon Islands, and Tuvalu submitted a draft text for a high ambition GHG reduction strategy, which focused on three objectives: the imminent peaking of GHG emissions at 2008 levels, the rapid decline in GHG emissions starting as soon as possible, but no later than 2025, and full decarbonization (to zero GHG emissions) by 2035 (ISWG-GHG, 2017). The PSIDS mentioned previously also co-sponsored another document with less ambitious objectives, along with Belgium, Denmark, Finland, France, Germany, Luxembourg, the Netherlands, Sweden, the UK, and International Association of Ports and Harbours (IAPH) and ICHCA.[5]

In April 2018, the MEPC met for its 72nd session. Stakes were high, as an agreement was to be adopted on GHG emissions reductions for the shipping sector. Before the session, the PIDF issued a position paper which advocated the need for the upcoming agreement to be consistent with the 1.5° goal and the Paris Agreement. PSIDS and EU states were pushing a 70–100 per cent emissions reduction agenda. In the end, the SHAC managed to get a reduction of more than 50 per cent (with a 2008 baseline). While it was not the 70–100 per cent from their submission, obtaining a decarbonization commitment from the shipping industry was a success, and the outcome was more ambitious than the coalition was expecting (author interview). Aside from the GHG issue, the RMI, Palau, and Vanuatu have submitted (together with Iceland) MEPC 72/15, which invited the IMO to act on plastic marine litter in the context of Sustainable Development Goal 14, and the MEPC has agreed to put it as an output on its agenda (IMO, 2018).

These successes are remarkable for small states, and would have been considered impossible only a few years earlier. SIDS have not had it all their own way since the early 1990s. Indeed, after further success at Kyoto in 1997 (Goulding, 2015), there were fears the SIDS agenda had stalled at the UN (Chasek, 2005; Fry, 2005). Retaining group cohesion has been a problem, especially as the size of AOSIS has expanded (Chasek, 2005; Fry, 2005; Betzold, 2010). These issues were apparent as early as the Barbados conference and were prominent in Mauritius (Chasek, 2005). As a result, SIDS sub-groups, including the PSIDS, the CARICOM Community, and the Coalition of Coral Atoll Nations, have spun off to represent distinct interests (Goulding, 2015; Fry, 2016). Reflecting this diversity, in the same year as the Rio conference, Singapore established an informal grouping of small states in New York known as the Forum of Small States (FOSS).

There are also differences in negotiating styles: the Caribbean and Indian Ocean SIDS are seen as more aggressive while the Pacific is perceived as taking a much quieter approach. The former in particular feel that the Pacific is often compromised by its dependence on foreign aid. More recently, Pacific states feel that the Caribbean has been too aggressive in pursuit of 'loss and damage' on climate change when a more moderate stance might lead to warming being halted at 1.5 degrees and low-lying atoll states being saved from the existential threat of sea level rise. Regardless of whether these generalizations are correct, they point to the fact that despite some common interests, SIDS are a diverse group who often see their participation in IOs in very different terms.

These differences are apparent at the IMO. All PSIDS are uniquely reliant on shipping due to their remote location. As a result, any change that might lead to an increase in the cost of shipping will have a disproportionate impact on consumers in PSIDS. PSIDS are regularly lobbied by members of the shipping industry in this respect and some representatives believe that the people who set policy in capitals are not sufficiently attuned to this dynamic, having been influenced by NGOs. For this reason, some PSIDS like Cook Islands have not joined the SHAC. The technical nature of the IMO renders agreements binding, not mere generic statements, and this characteristic contributes to thwart consensus inside the PSIDS and the SHAC.

But in all cases, whether it is AOSIS in the UN or the PSIDS at the IMO, diplomats draw their strength from numbers. Numbers give SIDS weight in negotiations. Numbers also attract the attention of larger states who, for various reasons discussed in the previous chapters and to follow, may want to align themselves with SIDS on particular issues. This strength in numbers has consistently proven to be the one continuing asset of SIDS in multilateral diplomacy. The caveat is that numbers have proven much easier to mobilize in relation to a common threat like climate change than they have on other issues, like health or intellectual property, as we will see in Chapter 6.

Active participation

The success of SIDS in pursuing progressive action on climate change has been aided by their presence in New York: their 'mission to the world'. As we have seen and will discuss at length in subsequent sections and chapters, SIDS suffer from capacity constraints that limit their participation in multilateral diplomacy (Panke, 2013; Corbett and Connell, 2015). Most have only a handful of missions and small foreign services. But despite their size, virtually all are represented in New York where most of the activity in relation to climate change takes place. Their presence is important as the attendance of leaders at key meetings provides opportunities for rhetorical action. It also makes it much easier to organize collaboration and access technical assistance from NGOs like Islands First (Carter, 2020b: 80). Indeed, at the time of writing many are co-located in a single floor of the Commonwealth Small States Office on Third Avenue. This close proximity has been essential to developing a sense of community that has facilitated working relationships. By contrast, the much smaller SIDS presence in Geneva has stymied their efforts in those IOs.

Presence and active participation were also a key feature of the success of the PSIDS at the IMO. As we saw, the RMI has always been an active participant in IMO activities since it became a member in 1998. But historically it has been represented by its registry, IRI, and thus often co-sponsors resolutions with industry lobbies inside the MEPC.[6] This in part reflects its colonial legacy – as a former US Trust Territory the RMI did not have either the historical connections or trade interests with the UK to justify an embassy in London. The RMI' registry was not always aligned with its climate activism. For example, the RMI has been called out by Greenpeace for its role on registering oil rigs active in the arctic (Greenpeace, 2015). In making the move to represent itself de Brum took advantage of the RMI' position at the IMO to bring global attention to climate change.

Tony de Brum's attendance at MEPC68 was significant on two counts: (1) challenging the long-held protocol that IMO was a technical organization where industry and technical professionals dominate decision-making; and (2) calling for the international shipping industry, from whom the RMI draws a large proportion of its revenue, to decarbonize to save small and vulnerable island states from sea level rise. An informed observer noted three points of significance in this achievement: it (1) challenged the protocol; (2) showed the changing position of the RMI, however reluctantly; and (3) highlighted that the political battle could be fought at a technical institution, like the IMO.

Foreign ministers rarely attend IMO meetings. de Brum was the first minister to address the MEPC (Mathiesen, 2015) and he actively participated at the MEPC 68th session. This was a historic moment for the organization. When he arrived at MEPC68, de Brum was confronted with a protocol issue: 'We had some difficulty convincing the people who were sitting in our seats, literally, that we were the representatives of the Marshall Islands' (Gibbs, 2017). As highlighted the RMI had been represented by IRI at the IMO and was seemingly unaware of de Brum's participation (multiple interviews), and might even have discouraged the government from sending a minister to the subsequent 2016 talks, by suggesting it was far too technical for a ministerial attendance (Gibbs, 2017). According to one delegate, de Brum's attendance at the 68th MEPC session, and the paper submitted by the RMI, transformed the IMO:

> 'it's difficult for all of us … the US delegation is mostly the US Coastguard … the UK delegation is mostly the Maritime Coastguard Agency with colleagues from other departments … the last meeting and the intercessional there was a whole different group of negotiators – the UNFCCC negotiators came to town.' (Interview with a representative from a large European state)

One consequence of de Brum's attendance was that the composition of delegations shifted from technical experts to climate change negotiators. The disruption was intentional, as one other diplomat put it:

> 'Christiana Figueres we organised to come to the last negotiation, and she went and addressed the High Ambition Coalition. Things like that were particularly powerful because again it showed that this was no longer a closed-door, quiet, cigar-smoking lounge on the banks of London that people didn't listen to, and that was important.' (Interview with a representative of a small state)

For our purposes the important point is that presence and active participation matters. SIDS as individual states are often perceived as ineffective in IOs because they do not have the resources or capacity to impact their operations. But when they do commit resources, maintain an active presence, and engage in coalition building and work under the group label, they can have a significant impact. They do not have to have large missions to do so. Rather, like richer European small states, they have to have the ability to act strategically in pursuit of well-defined interests.

Throughput legitimacy and the participation of small members

Thus far we have told a story that highlights how SIDS have pursued a specific strategy in the UN that has emphasized their vulnerability to the adverse impacts of climate change and in doing so convinced larger nations, including those hostile to their agenda, to take them seriously. While SIDS activism is important, we also need to recognize that while they have certainly faced opposition in pursuing their agenda, it also suits IOs to be seen to be taking them seriously. The remainder of the chapter is therefore dedicated to illustrating how the creation of the SIDS category generates 'throughput' legitimacy for IOs.

Promoting norms and principles

The impacts of climate change on SIDS impinges their ability to pursue their right to development. In extreme cases rising sea levels threatens the existence of low-lying atoll states (Armstrong and Corbett, 2021). But even those who are not facing an existential threat are nevertheless likely to be severely impacted, either because of the increased of hurricanes or the inundation of climate related hazards (for example, sargassum seaweed in the Caribbean). Or because the increased regularity of events like pandemics will have a disproportionate impact on tourism sectors. When IOs permitted the creation of the SIDS grouping it represented an attempt to demonstrate that they take the principle of sovereign equality seriously. China (population 1.6 billion) and Tuvalu (population 10,000) will never be equal. But as we saw in Chapter 2, IOs have to maintain the pretence that they are responsive to both. The problem is that doing so is hard because a country like Tuvalu is less able to represent itself. IOs thus increasingly spend considerable time, effort, and resources assisting SIDS to participate. The creation of the SIDS category must be seen in that light.

The creation of an identifiable UN grouping called SIDS, separate but emerging from AOSIS, was not a given. As one Caribbean diplomat recalls:

'We were told then you're never going to get another category within the United Nations. "We're done with categories; there are too many of them already" [they said] ... "it won't happen, it won't happen". We fought for years and years and it did happen.

You just wear them down. In other words, if they say it's not going to be a category. Okay but this what we're doing, we want a plan of action – incrementally, it just sticks. You call yourselves something, you group yourselves ... Then it can't be reversed ...

Because obviously one on one you don't stand a chance. But it is the weight of numbers ... because the issues are so clear cut, the level of coordination and like- mindedness becomes easier. I mean there isn't a whole range of differences or nuances [between small states] where it comes to climate change. Things like that can galvanize a constituency and then they hang together.' (Interview with Caribbean diplomat)

But it did fill a need for both SIDS and IOs. Within the UN system the SIDS label was created for the Global Conference on the Sustainable Development of Small Island Developing States in Barbados, 1994. This conference followed the success of Rio and helped consolidate the emerging group and its agenda by translating the principles embodied in Agenda 21 into specific policies contained in the Declaration of Barbados and the Programme of Action for Sustainable Development of Small Island Developing States. It has been followed by subsequent conferences – in Mauritius and Samoa – and work programmes that consistently reaffirm that assisting SIDS is an expression of the norms and principles of the UN – the sovereign equality of states and the right to development. For example, the preamble of the outcome document from the 2014 UN SIDS conference in Samoa states:

4. We reaffirm that we continue to be guided by the purposes and principles of the Charter of the United Nations, with full respect for international law and its principles.
5. We reaffirm that small island developing States remain a special case for sustainable development in view of their unique and particular vulnerabilities and that they remain constrained in meeting their goals in all three dimensions of sustainable development. We recognize the ownership and leadership of small island developing States in overcoming some of these challenges, but stress that in the absence of international cooperation, success will remain difficult. (A/RES/69/15)

The one area where they have made less headway, however, is 'loss and damage' compensation for those states who are impacted by climate change but have made a negligible contribution to global emissions. AOSIS broached the issue of loss and damage when the UNFCCC was drafted in 1991. But it took 16 years for the term 'loss and damage' to be used in a negotiated UNFCCC decision at the Bali Action Plan of 2007. Loss and damage remains a point of discussion in UNFCCC processes. The 2013 Warsaw International Mechanism on Loss and Damage is significant because key state parties, such as the US, had historically been opposed (Vanhala and Hestbaek, 2016). The Paris Agreement goes the furthest in the SIDS direction, with Article 8 recognizing 'the importance of averting, minimizing and addressing loss and damage'. But an accompanying decision says this language 'does not involve or provide a basis for any liability or compensation' (for discussion, see Calliari, 2016; Ourbak and Magnan, 2018). For many this is a failure and highlights the fundamental limits of both SIDS activism and the norms and principles of IOs. We would caution that this story is not over. And both the activism of SIDS and the IOs response must be considered as part of a broader movement to change the behaviour and policies of states (Benwell, 2011). In which case, it may be that while they do not gain loss and damage the constitutive norm of differentiated development (discussed further in Chapter 5) will remain important to how IOs account for their condition into the future.

Upholding rules, conventions, and traditions

Part of the SIDS success has been the ability to define common positions, speak with one voice, build coalitions with other states, and in doing so ensure their positions are included in the final texts (de Águeda and Mol, 2014: 281). Chief climate change negotiator for the Pacific Island state of Tuvalu, Ian Fry (2016: 106), reflects that:

> In these [CoP] processes, the SIDS tried to use a variety of groupings, processes and tactics to elevate their interests. During 2015, the Republic of the Marshall Islands began convening meetings of ministers in the margins of the preparatory negotiations. The ministers were handpicked 'like-minded' countries who were keen on setting a level of 'high ambition' within the agreement. It included countries from Latin America, the Pacific, Europe (including the EC) and Africa ... This group began as an informal exchange of views on how to drive a high-ambition agenda. Indeed, during the Paris Conference of Parties, it became known as the 'High Ambition Group'. It began to hold press conferences under this banner. Just prior to CoP-21, the US was invited to attend a meeting of the group and joined forces with them. This tended to add theatrical air and political muscle to the group. At one of the plenary sessions of the CoP, the group walked in together under rousing applause and cheers from various well-primed observers. It appeared more like a Presidential rally than a CoP.

In doing so SIDS have used key formal procedures to their advantage, including their votes in leadership elections (discussed later) and the preference for consensus in many IOs. As Deitelhoff and Wallbott (2012) argue, the ability to translate discursive power into measurable effects on outcomes partly depends on the institutional setting of the negotiations and the nature of the issue coalitions. SIDS have held specific seats on the various UN bodies dedicated to tackling climate change, a role on the Executive Board of the Clean Development Mechanism, and the boards of the Adaptation

Fund and the Green Climate Fund (Betzold et al, 2012). Perhaps the most important institutional process achievement by small states was securing a special seat on the COP Bureau, alongside the five UN regional groupings (Benwell, 2011: 204). The exceptional vulnerability of this grouping has been affirmed at the two subsequent SIDS conferences: Mauritius in 2005 and Samoa in 2014. It has also been acknowledged at all of the major UN conferences and summits on economic, social, and environmental issues since 1994. At COP15 in 2009 Tuvalu was able to have the meeting suspended in favour of deeper emissions cuts despite opposition from larger countries such as China and India. As we have seen, SIDS via AOSIS, played a crucial role in the negotiating period during COP21 and the subsequent Paris Agreement (Ourbak and Magnan, 2018). Consistent with more than two decades of activism, they succeeded in highlighting their special circumstances as vulnerable countries and in doing so pushed for ambitious long-term temperature targets. And, as mentioned, they also ensured that loss and damage will be part of the ongoing global discussions about the impact of climate change (Fry, 2016), even if they may never be realized.

As discussed in the previous chapter, one of the reasons why SIDS have been adept at using these rules to their advantage is that they often have long-serving diplomats. We have interviewed many small state diplomats who have been in post more than a decade, for example. This is in itself a reflection of the capacity problems they face – longer rotations are more cost effective. The unintended consequence is that SIDS ambassadors often have significantly more institutional memory than their large country counterparts, and they use this understanding or the rules and procedures to their advantage. For our purposes the important point is that knowledge of the rules and procedures, established decades before SIDS became states let alone active members of IOs, are now being used to overcome inherent disadvantages.

Again, the IMO example is illustrative of the broader trend. As outlined, the IMO is especially interesting as, unlike the UNFCCC, it has a reputation as a highly technical organization. This should disadvantage small states, who tend to lack human resource capacity in negotiations (Panke, 2013; Corbett and Connell, 2015). But, because many small states maintain large shipping registries, they actually have considerable expertise on these issues and greater clout in this IO than they do in virtually any other international forum. The organization of the PSIDS at the IMO is consistent with a wider tendency of Pacific states to raise their profile inside IOs since 2009, such as at the UN in New York, where they secured a stand-alone sustainable goal on oceans (Manoa, 2015). SIDS active participation was the key to the establishment of Sustainable Development Goals (SDGs) 13 (Climate Action) and 14 (Life Below Water), with the latter resulting in the inaugural

United Nations Oceans Conference held in Malta in 2017. The key figure pushing this agenda, now the UN Secretary-General's Special Envoy for the Ocean, was Peter Thomson, formerly Fiji's Permanent Representative to the United Nations and President of the General Assembly in 2016–17. For our purposes, the point is that in this case the formal rules and traditions favour SIDS, which supports the claim that their strategies reflect institutional context but also challenges the assumption that this context will always disadvantage them in favour of larger and richer states.

Facilitating mutual assistance and cooperation

SIDS have numerous supporters among larger UN states, especially on climate issues, as we saw in the UNSC vignette at the opening of the book. Indeed, in recent years an informal grouping of 'Friends of SIDS' has operated in New York and meets regularly. SIDS diplomats are certainly conscious that there is considerable appetite among larger states to be development partners of SIDS, both because they are committed to progressive climate action but also the number of votes that the group represents. A 'Friends of SIDS' function is therefore an opportunity to pitch for support to a large constituency. This approach is part of the culture of the UN, as one diplomat explained: "if someone has their pet project and if you don't care one way or another of course you're happy to help them". The advantage SIDS have is that they only have a narrow range of issues that they care about and so their ability to generate significant goodwill and favours at next to no cost provides them with leverage.

SIDS also receive considerable support from IOs and NGOs to represent themselves in UNFCCC processes. As leader of COP23, Fiji was assisted by Bonn, Germany, which bore costs that ran into hundreds of millions of euros. The idea that SIDS need help to represent themselves is common in climate processes, albeit we will discuss how the norm of sovereign equality has led to similar assistance being provided in other IOs in the subsequent chapters. For now, we highlight that in addition to the UNFCCC, SIDS have also been recognized by the creation in 2001 of the United Nations Office of the High Representative for the Least Developed Countries, Landlocked Developing Countries and the Small Island Developing States (UN-OHRLLS) established under resolution 56/227. At the time of writing the High Representative is Fekitamoeloa Katoa 'Utoikamanu, a Tongan national, and her role includes consultation with and advocacy for SIDS across the UN system.

The United Nations Department of Economic and Social Affairs Division (UNDESA) for Sustainable Development Goals has a dedicated SIDS Unit, which was created following the adoption of the Barbados Programme of

Action during the first SIDS conference in 1994 to monitor, analyse, and assist SIDS in its implementation. The unit continued in this role after the Mauritius conference and it has recently been further enhanced to undertake the work created by the SAMOA Pathway. The unit describes itself as a 'focal point' for SIDS in the UN system that provides technical advice and capacity-building assistance. It has around five staff, many of whom have been SIDS nationals.

SIDS are also assisted by NGOs and interns. At COP23 Seychelles had a 50-strong delegation, for example, but less than a dozen were from Seychelles. As one of their diplomats explains, what happens is that: "people who had worked for us said, 'can you give us a Seychelles badge so we can get where other NGOs can't'". Indeed, as researchers we have benefitted from this liberal approach to allowing outsiders to join delegations. In return, SIDS lean on these outsiders, either at the time or at a later date, for assistance.

Other examples include the 2012 establishment by the UNHRC of a Voluntary Technical Assistance Trust Fund to Support the Participation of Least Developed Countries and Small Island Developing States in the work of the Human Rights Council (Resolution 19/26). By placing SIDS and LDCs in the same category, the LDCs/SIDS Trust Fund – administered by the Office of the United Nations High Commissioner for Human Rights (OHCHR) and funded by 21 countries (Houel, 2017) – provides essential funding, capacity building, and training to support participation in the processes of the UNHRC. Further support for this initiative was provided by resolution 34/40, passed in 2017, which was co-sponsored by 120 states, making it the second most sponsored resolution since the establishment of the HRC in 2006 (Houel, 2017). If nothing else, this illustrates how well accepted the label and the unique vulnerability of smallness have become.

These patterns are also apparent at the IMO. In March 2015, a small team of academics from UCL, USP, and representatives from the NGO 'Seas at Risk' had received funding from the European Finance Foundation to discuss shipping GHG emissions with the leaders of the RMI, including the opposition (author interview). They were met with enthusiasm by de Brum and other Marshellese politicians and diplomats as well as the advisory group Independent Diplomat who provided technical support throughout the process. Together they developed a strategy to push forward climate issues at the IMO by building coalitions among small and vulnerable island states, and gaining broader support, especially from large and rich European countries. The PIDF was also important to this effort because they helped coordinate between the positions of the PSIDS's members by providing briefing documents, guidance, and a position paper before the UN COP sessions, as well as briefings for the IMO MEPC sessions, starting from

MEPC69 (for example, PIDF, 2016). The point in all cases is that SIDS have allies within IOs but also among NGOs seeking influence.

Conclusion

The SIDS label remains somewhat ambiguous in terms of which countries it covers and the exceptionalism it generates is not guaranteed. This is no accident: there is nothing natural or neutral about the SIDS category as it has been created to give voice to the political concerns of a specific group of states. If SIDS had not actively participated in the processes of IOs the label would in all likelihood not exist in the UN, let alone elsewhere. In turn, the SIDS category has provided successive generations of diplomats a platform on the world stage. And, by drawing attention to their vulnerable condition, particularly in climate change discussions, they have shaped global deliberations and set precedents that others have followed.

Climate change is a 'most likely' case for the way we have conceived of the interaction between SIDS and UN agencies. It is an example of a policy issue where SIDS vulnerabilities are clear and acute, thus performing them is relatively straightforward and has generated considerable support from a whole host of progressive actors. It also aligns with existing norms – the sovereign equality of states and the right to development. There has been pragmatic opposition to the establishment of a dedicated group on the grounds that the proliferation of groupings is creating gridlock and delay. And, as we saw in the UNSC vignette that we opened the book with, there is contention about which forum is the most appropriate for this issue. These caveats aside, the story of the SIDS is largely one of sustained success. Aside from creating the label, the SIDS have created working groups, convene conferences and taskforces, and initiate reports and declarations, and secure work programmes that draw attention to their unique needs (that is, the SAMOA Pathway); won positions on boards and key committees (that is, Clean Development Mechanism; Adaptation Fund; and the Green Climate Fund); and gained subsidies for their participation in IO activities (that is, the LDC/SIDS Trust Fund at the HRC or the Commonwealth Secretariat Small States Office in New York and Geneva). In doing so their participation has changed the processes and practices of IOs.

5

Differentiated Development in the IMF, the WBG, and the WTO

The emergence of a distinct SIDS grouping and identity in relation to climate change is a 'most likely' case for their influence on IOs. It is an issue on which they hold the moral high ground as the first and worst effected: the canaries in the coal mine. A much higher threshold for their influence is whether similar strategies would be successful in other IOs and especially those that deal with economic affairs. In these IOs SIDS are not the poorest – most are middle- or upper middle-income countries –and account for a very low proportion of global trade. And yet, they have unique economic circumstances and vulnerabilities that are likely to be exacerbated by climate change.

This chapter documents the interaction between small states and the key economic IOs. The story is not as straightforward as the climate change story; the initiative does not always come from the SIDS; there is as often leadership from other countries; it is determined in part by the mores of the IOs themselves, by their traditional practices, and by their institutional rules, leading to a range of intermediaries speaking on behalf of the SIDS. Despite this complexity, the claim that the countries we now call SIDS have uniquely vulnerable economies due to their heavy reliance on a small number of economic sectors has become orthodoxy in IOs. The WB and IMF both recognize the SIDS agenda. The WTO has created the SVEs. These are important successes for SIDS that emerges from the complex interaction between large and small member states, donors, IOs' leaders, and their secretariats. But there is less evidence that this recognition has been translated into tangible benefits for SIDS or IOs. Our economic story is thus less optimistic about SIDS influence than our account of climate change.

The chapter follows a similar structure to the last. We start by explaining the SIDS circumstance. We show how concerns about their economic viability explain their delayed decolonization and that despite some variations the perception of enduring vulnerability has persisted into the post-independence period. We show how this has become synonymous with an argument about 'differentiated development' – that economic development models designed for large states will not work for small ones. Echoing the success of their advocacy on climate change they have prosecuted similar arguments in the economic IOs, often with the support of key friends and allies. Their more limited success can be in part explained by a combination of the rules and procedures of IOs, and the limited diplomatic presence of SIDS in the key locations where economic IOs operate – Washington and Geneva – but also by the lack of cohesion among small states themselves in terms of objectives, strategy, and capacity.

Rhetorical action

An implicit assumption in most discussions about sovereignty and economic development is that the goal of both is viability. Notions of viability are vague and rarely specified (Connell, 2013) but usually revolve around two ideas (Brisk 1969: 5): (1) self-sufficiency or the potential to generate levels of economic growth that negate the need for external assistance; and (2) the capacity to enact or project statehood in a way that other states will recognize. Based on this common view, during the decolonization period some UN members were sceptical that small island communities could ever become self-sufficient and would therefore easily succumb to the influence of larger powers (Doumenge, 1983). Indeed, the belief that these islands would never turn a profit was one of the reasons why colonial regimes were often desperate to be rid of them, with Mawby (2012: 39, 170; see Cox-Alomar, 2003: 78; Bishop, 2013: 18) reporting that during the 1950s and 1960s British leaders and officials were resigned to the 'most dismal prospect' of being burdened for the foreseeable future with responsibility for the Leewards and the Windwards in the Eastern Caribbean, for example. The UN even created an interim category to deal with their unique condition – associated statehood – but by the early 1980s most of these islands had achieved independence despite little developmental progress, which if nothing else demonstrates how ambiguous contemporary notions of economic viability are.

This orthodox understanding of the relationship between state size and economic wealth is echoed by Alesina and Spolaore (2005) in *The Size of Nations* in which they argue that large states are advantaged by having bigger domestic markets, enabling them to produce cheaper goods and rely less heavily on trade. In turn, economies of scale increase efficiency and productivity, while large size also drives innovation and sectoral diversity. This combination of factors makes large economies more resilient in the face of global financial shocks. The counter argument is advanced in Katzenstein's (1985) classic *Small States in World Markets* in which he argued that while reliance on trade exposed small states to international shocks, the 'democratic corporatism' displayed by these nations was more interventionist and flexible, which enabled governments to respond quicker, and meant they adapted better to new conditions. In doing so they overcame the disadvantages of their size.

Scholars of small states have long debated the merits of these arguments. On the one hand, the economies of small states often perform much better than many expect. This is true of the cases Katzenstein studied – small states in Western Europe (Thorhallsson, 2010) – but it also holds for SIDS too (Easterly and Kraay, 2000; Armstrong and Read, 2003; Baldacchino and Bertram, 2009; Cooper and Shaw, 2009; Baldacchino, 2011, 2014). On the other hand, scholars have argued that vulnerability is not the same as poverty. Most SIDS have above average levels of GDP per capita, yet remain acutely susceptible to external shocks in ways that larger states, regardless of their wealth, are not (Bishop, 2012: 949; see Brigulio, 1995; Briguglio et al, 2009). Moreover, there appears to be a ceiling on their development, with many caught in acute versions of the middle income and debt 'traps' (Paus, 2012; King and Tennant, 2014; Doner and Schneider, 2016) in which graduation from upper middle-income status leads to the loss of concessional finance, which makes them less capable of being able to recover from the next shock, be it economic or environmental. This argument is buttressed by the fact that SNIJs perform consistently better in economic terms than their sovereign neighbours due to a range of advantages, including welfare transfers, concessional market access, and increased confidence for foreign investors in knowing that Washington, London, Paris, or the Hague effectively acts as a guarantor of security and stability (see Baldacchino, 2010; Razvani, 2014).

These economic arguments were being prosecuted long before most of the states we now call SIDS became independent. In the 1950s and 1960s pro-independence activists had to convince metropolitan colonial powers that their islands would be viable should they be granted statehood. 'Industrialisation-by-invitation' was championed by Nobel Prize-winning economist Sir Arthur Lewis (1950) as the route to development for small Caribbean islands (for discussion, see Farrell, 1980). The policy had initial success in the late 1950s and early 1960s. But it proved short-lived. Since the 1960s, Caribbean economists, foreshadowing Alesina and Sploaore (2005), have tended to hold the opposite view: consistently identifying state size as a structural constraint on their development (see famously Demas, 1965) and on that basis arguing that small states cannot possibly achieve self-sufficiency via conventional economic strategies (for review, see Bishop, 2013: Chapter 3).

These arguments were met with some sympathy by IOs in the 1970s as part of the debates about a New International Economic Order (NIEO). The UNCTAD differentiated between LDCs and 'developing island countries' (DICs), for example (Grote, 2010: 168). It chose a wide definition of DICs, which included countries like Indonesia and Philippines, but predominantly focused on structural constraints related to smallness: small population, remoteness from main shipping routes and world markets, exposure to natural disasters, and a narrow and highly specialized export base dominated by foreign companies (Grote, 2010: 170). This list of vulnerabilities is virtually identical to those associated with SIDS today. The reasons why small states now use the nomenclature SIDS, rather than DICs, partly reflects the demise of NIEO, ongoing debate about which countries the DICs category (later Island Developing Countries or IDCs) should cover (a discussion that continues in relation to SIDS), as well as growing hostility during the 1980s and 1990s towards the idea that this sub-group of states deserved special or differential treatment on economic grounds (Grote, 2010; Lindsay, 2019).

Through the 1980s a series of UNCTAD reports and recommendations, as well as UNGA resolutions, addressed the economic problems of small islands (for example, Doumenge, 1983). They tended to be driven by IOs rather than the countries themselves because for the most part the latter were not active participants in multilateral affairs. S&DT was provided for small islands under the package negotiated as part of the Lomé Convention. Here the ACP secured a trading structure whereby they received non-reciprocal preferential access to EU market for their export commodities (Bishop et al, 2013). But the argument that these countries should receive advantageous terms became increasingly unpopular on the grounds that most were not LDCs (Lindsay, 2019). And when the WTO was established, they lost their preferential access, resulting in the rapid demise of the agricultural sector – bananas and sugar – in most SIDS (Connell, 2013). The problem they faced is that trade does not lend itself to the same moral rhetoric as environmental issues. Moreover, some economists claimed that globalization and tourism in particular was increasing the economic opportunities of SIDS and so they are better off moving up value chains than remaining wedded to subsidized agriculture (for example, Easterly and Kraay, 2000).

A number of development models have sought to capture this post-agricultural condition. The following, extracted from Corbett and Veenendaal (2018: 28), summarize them as:

- MIRAB (**mi**gration, **r**emittances, **a**id, and **b**ureaucracy): first formulated by Bertram and Watters (1985) it describes the four pillars of Pacific island economies (see Bertram, 2006; Poirine, 1998). Rather than a strategy for economic growth, Bertram and Watters underscored that MIRAB is a way for small states to survive in the global economic system, basically by living off external funding and resources.

- TOURAB (**tou**rism, **r**emittances, **a**id, and **b**ureaucracy): first developed by Guthunz and Von Krosigk (1996), and later Apostolopoulos and Gayle (2002) in response to strongly growing tourism industries in a number of Caribbean and Mediterranean small states. According to these authors, while tourism offers an important source of income for small states, it is also a highly flexible and unstable economic sector, and therefore cannot compensate for the vulnerability of small states.

- SITE (**s**mall **i**sland **t**ourist **e**conomy): first outlined by Jerome McElroy and his co-authors (McElroy and Morris, 2002; McElroy, 2006; Oberst and McElroy, 2007). The emphasis here is on the fact that small states may actually reap disproportional economic benefits from tourism, because in contrast to larger states, even minor growth in the tourism sector can have major economic effects.

- PROFIT (**p**eople, **r**esource management, **o**verseas engagement, **fi**nances, and **t**ransportation): first launched by Godfrey Baldacchino (Baldacchino, 2006; Baldacchino and Bertram, 2009; McElroy and Parry, 2010) the argument is that instead of focusing on external sources of revenue or a single product like tourism, small states ought to pursue a more multifaceted economic development strategy that exploits niches in the world economy. One example is offshore finance, although this sector has contracted since the turn of the millennium (Hampton and Christensen, 2002).

While small states around the world can be classified as employing MIRAB, TOURAB, SITE, or PROFIT strategies for economic development, the important point in relation to this book is that many leaders and economists in small states have continued to argue that the economic opportunities that were supposed to be a consequence of greater globalization have rarely been realized. Instead, vulnerabilities remain and are indeed magnified by the twin processes of trade liberalization and climate change. Indeed, even a seemingly conventional strategy like tourism has downsides because when an entire country is dependent on a single sector it can suffer rapid downturns (Bishop, 2013; Connell, 2013), as we saw during the 2008 global financial crisis and the 2020 COVID-19 crisis. The industry is also uniquely vulnerable to climate change, which may reduce air travel and increase the frequency and intensity of hurricanes, cyclones, and tropical storms. Since 2011, the Caribbean has also experienced an annual inundation of noxious sargassum seaweed on east coast beaches, with climate change a possible catalyst.

These types of problems are likely to increase and may ultimately make the current tourism model unviable. Tourism also creates social problems, restricts access to land, and much of the revenue does not remain on the islands, with airlines and resorts owned by overseas companies, and most of the food and entertainment imported.

The upshot is that successive generations of policy makers in SIDS have concluded that their states will never be self-sufficient according to a classical understanding of that term but must instead rely on a favourable or permissive external economic and political environment that is attuned to and sympathetic of their unique condition. As a result, much like the climate discussion, SIDS have sought to perform economic vulnerability in the hope that IOs will recognize that they have different development needs to larger states. In return, they hope to gain S&DT for their condition. The main difference between the attempts undertaken by the UNCTAD in the 1970s and today is that: (a) SIDS are more actively involved in contemporary efforts due to their increased participation in multilateral diplomacy (Grote, 2010: 182); and (b) climate change provides both added impetus and international awareness of their condition, and a blueprint for the types of traction collaborative diplomacy can generate in IOs.

The renewed effort to draw attention to the economic condition of SIDS outside the UN system began at the WB. In July 1998 a MGSS delegation, led by then Prime Minister of Barbados Owen Arthur, met with the President of the WB to discuss the SIDS Agenda. This led to the creation of the Commonwealth/World Bank Joint Task Force on Small States which produced an Interim Report on 'Small States: Meeting Challenges in the Global Economy' that was considered and adopted at the global conference on the development agenda for SIDS, in London, UK, in 2000. This report essentially echoed the long-standing position of many Caribbean economists since Demas in describing small state vulnerability as:

[A combination of] factors – remoteness and isolation, volatile economic growth, investor perceptions, high poverty and limited institutional capacity – suggest intuitively that small states would be more vulnerable than their larger developing country counterparts. Vulnerability means exposure to exogenous shocks over which the affected country has little or no control, and relatively low resilience to withstand and recover from these shocks. (Commonwealth Secretariat and the World Bank, 2000)

The Joint Ministerial Committee of the Boards of Governors at the IMF and the WB subsequently approved the Report (Commonwealth Secretariat and the World Bank, 2000), which when combined with the MDGs, generated momentum in the three Bretton Woods institutions to place small states on their agenda. The report led to the WB adopting the Commonwealth definition of a small state. Its Small States Forum has been held every year since 2000 during the Annual Meetings and brought together Finance Ministers and Central Bank Governors from 50 small states. However, acknowledging the need to assist small states did not translate into much action over the subsequent decade because both institutions, along with the WTO, felt they 'had limited role in assisting most small states with their development challenges' (IEG, 2006).

The 1998 joint Commonwealth–World Bank report also had an influence at the WTO which, at the time, was in the midst of deliberating about whether to commence a new round of trade negotiations. When the EU demanded that one set of issues be included on the agenda, and then India and others sought a second tranche, the small states wanted their voice heard too. As a WTO official explained:

'Barbados, leading the SIDS from the UN, said, "We want a work programme on small economies" ... Mike Moore [then Director General of the WTO] ... was basically the one who was Mr Small States. So, he played to Barbados and said, "We'll get you your work programme".' (Interview with WTO official)

The need for consensus assisted their case. They had to be brought on board for the Round to be launched. The nomenclature changed, however, to 'small, vulnerable economies' (SVEs) as did the membership of the group, which:

applies to Members with economies that, in the period 1999 to 2004, had an average share of (a) world merchandise trade of no more than 0.16 per cent or less, and (b) world trade in non-agricultural products of no more than 0.1 per cent and (c) world trade in agricultural products of no more than 0.4 per cent. (TN/AG/W/4/Rev.4/ paragraph 157)

In the WTO the SVEs is an intermediary grouping, but its formation was seen by SVE diplomats as a huge victory nonetheless. As a former SIDS diplomat who later worked at the WTO asserted:

'This meant the small states had a home. They had a place. They had an anchor to WTO discussions because the report of this committee would then go to what is the highest decision-making body in the WTO which is the General Council. So, from an institutional perspective, I mean I think that was really, really important ... Every single WTO decision since then has incorporated and recognized the legitimacy of having a dedicated discussion of small vulnerable economies. So, we've never had to go in there and renegotiate. We've never had to reaffirm the importance of keeping it there. It is something which is now ingrained in the DNA of the WTO.' (Interview with former SIDS diplomat and ICS)

Even though the WTO SVE category encompasses many small states that are not islands, including a number of Latin American countries, there are important affinities between the agenda outlined at the inaugural 1994 UNSIDS conference in Barbados and the articulation of vulnerability in the WTO.

Aside from the category and dedicated work programme, the biggest success of the SVEs has been the negotiation of special treatment under non-agricultural market access (NAMA). They also won export concessions under Article 27.4 despite opposition from countries such as the US, EU, Australia, and Japan. Other successes relate to process: the general council allowed the small islands to use regional bodies to make notifications in the areas of Sanitary and Phytosanitary (SPS) and Technical Barriers to Trade (TBT). This provided a way for OECS and PIFS states, who do not have individual missions in Geneva, to participate by proxy. But despite these successes, in general the feeling among diplomats is that their agenda has stalled. One reason is continued opposition to the idea that they should receive S&DT based on their vulnerabilities, as one Caribbean diplomat explained:

'It's a very, very political issue. It's a systemic issue, because there are some who are very, very sensitive about any categorization – not the small, developing countries, but the large developing countries. They don't want that door opened, because if it's opened from the bottom then – well, if it's opened from the bottom, then it exposes them at the top ... small always gets caught up in age-old solidarity issues of developing countries have to be together, north versus south, us versus them, that sort of rhetoric.'

The point is that SIDS efforts have been challenged by the large developing states, rather than developed economies (Gilbert and Vines, 2000). A second reason is that SIDS have struggled to achieve the same level of collaboration on economic issues as they have on climate change.

Collaboration

To deal with giants a lot of pygmies have to get together because, even if the giants are not bad people, they are so gigantic that they inevitably crush the pygmies. So that, if the pygmies get together, at least the giant would notice them and be very careful not to step on them. (Demas cited in Payne, 2008: 239)

The creation of the WTO SVEs group in particular highlights the ability of SIDS to expand their agenda from the UN to other IOs. It provided the opportunity for small states to work as a bloc, a strategy that was curtailed by the rules of representation in the World Bank Group (WBG) and the IMF (discussed later). During the 2000s, the SVE group, led by active countries like Mauritius, Barbados and Jamaica, were able to build on the momentum to carve out a place within the WTO. Not only did they show that SVEs had a voice and could fight their corner, but they came to be seen as a constructive player in the WTO system, leading to occasions when their representatives were invited to Green Room meetings when their participation assisted in compromises that were thrashed out by key players. Initially, the SVEs grouping worked well with an effective coordinator on issues such as agricultural reforms and liberalization. The group presented its unified concern of rural subsistence economies, for instance, that impressed many member states.

For member states, SVEs provided access to information. Focal points were created, by which individual member states took responsibility to act on behalf of their group colleagues. Countries with a particular interest would take the lead: El Salvador led on NAMA, Dominica on services, Guatemala on fisheries. Although SVEs included about 32 active countries, the central American and Caribbean are slightly larger and better resourced than Pacific countries and thus have more resources on the spot. They were also geographically closer to the centre of action. That is important because there is a cost in leading. First the coordinator spends extensive time providing information and leadership to the group, preparing papers, selling the outcomes; that is in effect cross subsiding the other countries. Several countries, an observer commented acidly, are 'comfortable when other people do the work and you just come and comment'. The second problem is that, as convenor or focal point, the coordinator is trying to find the common ground among participants, not pressing the interests of their own country. The benefit is that the coordinator gains standing in the broader system, invitations to meetings, and better access to the heads of the secretariat and to the delegations of bigger countries.

This initial success appears to echo the climate change story about the benefits of collaboration. Collaboration has also long been touted as a panacea to the economic problems of SIDS. Again, the conventional economic arguments hold sway: by working together and integrating their economies as much as possible SIDS can achieve the economies of scale required to promote their development. Despite the optimism that integration attracts, only rarely has it succeeded. The Eastern Caribbean, which is home to a number of similar economies in close geographic proximity, the majority of whom have a similar history of British colonialism, has achieved a level of economic integration analogous to the EU through the OECS. But elsewhere integration, whether via CARICOM in the Caribbean or Pacific Agreement on Closer Economic Relations (PACER) in the Pacific, has typically achieved less than its proponents hoped (Bishop et al, 2011; Lawson, 2016). A key reason is that while these economies appear similar when compared to large states there are also considerable differences between them, both within and between regions. Given that small and large vulnerable economies differ so greatly in their trade interests and objectives, SVEs were unable to establish its position in all negotiating groups and on all issues (Laurent, 2016).

These differences would soon work to undermine the SVEs agenda at the WTO. Since the late 2000s, the SVEs acted more as a political tool to veto proposals rather than as a group able to present unified positions at various negotiations. One cause is that negotiations on specific issues have become "super-specialized", explained one WTO director. "On a given issue, such as civil aircraft, or state trading enterprises or trade remedies, there were often 25–35 participants. They are the technocrats, understand the issues, not their ambassadors, who went into the greenroom discussion, completely uninformed. I was shocked." Another one added, "Coordinators of some groupings, such as those of ACP or G90, did not know what they were talking about; they were not up to speed; and were absolutely useless." Some diplomats from SVEs agreed:

'[The leadership] changed, and it changed very much because of what I would consider a downgrade in quality of representatives ... individuals count, the support in capitals count. The ability to know that as a small state you are not going to be immediately on the top of the list so you have to manoeuvre, you have to be strategic, and you have to get yourself involved in the processes of being smart about it.'

In addition, the SIDS countries started doubting whether SVEs could represent them and speak on their behalf, given countries from Central America seemed to have taken it over. A chair of a key negotiating committee explained:

'While sharing some features with SIDS, those Central American states after all have long-term potentials that countries like Vanuatu or St Kitts & Nevis would never have – they have got a few million people and land mass – and the interests are not identical. SIDSs were flirting with the idea of setting up a small states group like they had done in UN; then they could have defined their positions more specifically in the WTO. Yet, to get recognized, they would have to be able to agree on their own positions.' (Interview with committee chair).

A veteran former ambassador to the WTO, chairing the Council for Trade in Goods, once commented:

'Trade is an important issue for development and developing countries in general need help in fulfilling their obligations and adapting rules that would help them develop. Developing countries formed various groups to discuss how to move forward and the secretariat tried to help. It has been very difficult to forge common interests – and we often ended up with a situation of Singapore/ South Korea vs LDC vs island states vs Latin America.' (Interview with WTO ambassador)

Another ambassador from a developing country complained, "What are they doing here if they always demand special treatment, exceptions and limitation of trade?" The ambassador from its neighbouring country admitted, "We have a secretariat here to help, but I can tell you it is more difficult to negotiate among ourselves than to negotiate with others" (interviews with ambassadors).

Even within a region, some economies have moved up global supply chains and their views on trade can differ greatly from their neighbouring states. Costa Rica, Trinidad and Tobago, and Fiji would often take positions uncompromising with other SVEs. Representatives from those countries reminded the ambassador of Costa Rica, 'You have Intel in your country, it does not mean you are the king of the mountain'. Some of these countries wanted to torment other SIDS. In response, the ambassador of Costa Rica used to ask in various groupings, 'If you do not want to liberalize trade, why are you here? You know you don't have to be here.'

In general, it is difficult for SVEs to reach an agreement on any negotiation position. For example, the agenda for negotiations on fishing subsidies was set in 2001 at the Doha Ministerial Conference and members were mandated 'to clarify and improve' existing WTO disciplines on fisheries subsidies. The mandate was elaborated in 2005 at the Hong Kong Ministerial Conference, with a call for prohibiting certain forms of fisheries that contribute to overcapacity and overfishing. Fisheries are the main source of natural wealth and proteins in many SIDS. SVEs argued in 2003 that fisheries management issue was not an appropriate subject matter for the WTO and it should be addressed in places such as the FAO, in part because many were not members yet and in part it was not their priority. In the following years, large players dominated the negotiations – Japan and South Korea in Asia, later joined by China and India, and the EU, US, and Brazil. ACP and SVEs in the following years constantly raised issues about of the significance of artisanal and small-scale fishing to developing countries.

Several issues stand out. The problem of illegal, unreported, or unregulated (IUU) fishing for instance, raised several questions: (1) who may determine what is IUU fishing – the subsidizing WTO members, the WTO members in whose waters IUU fishing is carried out by a foreign-flagged vessel, regional fisheries management organizations, or the FAO; (2) what are harmful subsidies – subsidies for fishing, subsidies for vessels construction, or subsidies for trading fish captured; (3) who decides; and (4) who will monitor the implementation of regulating fisheries subsidies – the government of the fishing fleets, of the country where they registered their vessels, or of countries in whose water fishing takes place. Over these and many other detailed issues, small island states have their own internal conflicts (UNEP, 2011; Bahety and Mukiibi, 2017; Tipping, 2020; Van Damme, 2020). Indeed, the scholars working on SIDS foreign policy have long noted that there is often a lack of coordination between foreign affairs and trade domestically, let alone at the regional level (Braveboy-Wagner, 2007; Panke, 2020). The exceptions are when the Prime Minister is also the Foreign Minister.

The 20-year history of SVEs thus clearly shows both its strengths and limitations. SVEs had made some progress; member states at the WTO accepted SVEs as a group; they expect the SVEs to report on the progress of its work programme when the Committee on Trade and Development (CTD) met; and most took its positions seriously. More importantly, as at the WB, member states at the WTO were more amenable to the demands of small island states when they could reach a common position. Another WTO insider explained, "They [SVEs] probably could have got what they had asked for in terms of S&DT in whichever negotiating groups." The reason, he implied, was because their demands were not central to the principal outcomes. He went on: "But here, it remains a big-boy game. When big guys cannot agree, small states are irrelevant." For instance, many small states do not even attend CTD meetings, but "large countries are always there even though they are neither small, not vulnerable. They want to at least stop certain things from being adopted even at this committee." A diplomat from a small state noted that the SVEs were "very useful for swapping information, but at the end of the day when they are being asked to do a deal here, it all comes down to the individual state. Everyone's interest is different. If you [small states] cannot operate here, you won't be able to get what you want."

Active participation

In the previous chapter we alluded to the fact that the SIDS were aided in their activities at the UN by their collective presence in New York. This presence allowed for considerable informal collaboration and created a sense of community, especially among the sub-regions. By contrast, many find the costs of maintaining missions in Geneva too prohibitive. For starters, not all SIDS are members of the WTO. As a result, while the addition of Latin American small states adds to their numbers in the SVEs, they are not able to achieve the same physical presence in WTO forums as they are at the UN. Indeed, as outlined previously, the Eastern Caribbean states are jointly represented by a small OECS mission while most Pacific states have historically been represented by the PIFS who can act as an intermediary and representative at various headquarters. One diplomat reminded us that: "You have to understand many of our members are non-resident in Geneva, and their missions may be in Brussels or in London." While the WTO and its membership recognize that these diplomats speak for a collection of members – a concession that speaks to the need for them to generate throughput legitimacy – the symbolism of their collective presence is diluted.

A similar position is apparent in Washington, as many SIDS, especially from the Pacific, do not have a physical embassy in the US capital. Instead, their small New York mission of 2–4 staff is accredited to both (and the US and often other countries too). SIDS have more contacts and engagement with the WB than the IMF and the WTO even though their interest in the WTO has been growing. This is not only because promoting development is the mandate of the WB, but also because the Bank has a presence in these countries, or at least in their region, whereas the IMF and the WTO do not. With the major organizational reform in the mid-1990s, the WB decentralized its regional and country offices. The country office for the Caribbean region resided in Washington, DC until very recently when it moved to Santo Domingo, Dominican Republic. Eleven Pacific Island countries are members of the WB and have a combined population of about 2.3 million people, scattered across an area equivalent to 15 per cent of the globe's surface. The country office for the Pacific was set in Sydney; as the Bank explains, Sydney was chosen as the hub with relatively equal distance to all member states and for its convenience to commute to Washington, DC.

Running programmes and projects in both regions involved much higher transaction costs and staff flying in and out. Getting extra resources to run programmes and projects in these remote states is necessary. "At the Board meetings," explained one ED, "the regional VPs [vice presidents] could bombard EDs, wanting to scare them off with their proactive demands; this would never happen at the Board meetings of IMF." Indeed, regional VPs spent considerable time with relevant agencies of the donor countries to get assistance and support for their small members. The formal organizational arrangement at the Bank makes it a complex exercise. For instance, as a senior Bank official in the Pacific region noted:

'The Pacific island states belong to several constituencies: many are in the one with Australia–South Korea, I can always go to Australia given its interests in the region. We also have Fiji and Tonga in the Thailand–Indonesia constituency where two-thirds are borrowers. Timor Leste is in the Brazilian constituency that I have taken care of. Of course, we spend a lot of time with the ED office of the Pacific and I also need to make sure sufficient support for other Pacific small countries. When we got trust funds from donors, I told them, that "you are not going to free-ride with us; your commitment would have to be integrated into our programmes". I need to make sure donors' commitment fit our programmes, not theirs. I've got the largest amount of trust funds beside Africa. This is in part because the Europeans have been exiting the region in terms of the presence of their agencies; they are staying engaged by giving us the resources and essentially having us work through things that need to be done. In addition, Australia is a big source of my money for the Pacific.' (Interview with senior WB official)

The key point, however, is that while the Bank has an active presence in small states, and as a result has some first-hand knowledge of their issues, there is little capacity for SIDS to form a global bloc and work collectively to influence the Bank's agenda when their work programmes are regional.

In sum, while SIDS have had some important successes in advancing their agenda in economic IOs, a combination of opposition from larger states to their rhetorical claims about differentiated development and SIDS vulnerability, combined with barriers to collaboration and the absence of many of their number from both Geneva and Washington, has meant that their efforts have produced mixed outcomes. This mixed report card is matched on the IOs side: they have made efforts to include SIDS but the imperatives of 'throughput' legitimacy are at their most acute in relation to absolute poverty, rather than the development challenges of middle-income states.

Throughput legitimacy and the right to development

SIDS have sought to pursue their agenda in economic IOs amid a broader global shift to liberalize trade. For the most part their needs have taken a back seat to this broader agenda in IOs (Heron and Murray-Evans, 2016; Morgan, 2018; Lindsay, 2019), as we saw in relation to the winding up of preferential access under the Lomé Convention. But the right to development remains a key norm of IOs and so as the economic conditions of SIDS have remained stubbornly resistant to many of the benefits of liberalization, and as awareness of how they are being impacted by climate change has risen in recent years, they have started to receive more attention. What remains to be seen is whether groupings like the SVEs, and the increasing attention to the SIDS agenda in IOs like the WB and IMF, is a symbolic consolation prize for countries whose development prospects appear to have stalled, or whether it will beget substantive changes that produce economic gains.

Promoting norms and principles

Development quickly became a key interest for the Bretton Woods institutions after their formation. The idea of development as a group 'right' would later be enshrined in the UN Declaration on the Right to Development, adopted by General Assembly resolution 41/128 of 4 December 1986. For our purposes the key point is that development is firmly on the agenda of IOs and their ability to deliver it for *all* members is central to their legitimacy. This mandate provides a strong motivation for IOs to recognize the unique development challenges of SIDS, as outlined previously, and engage them in their processes and programmes. But the importance of SIDS to this agenda has also meant that they have become embroiled in, and at times have emerged as collateral damage of, debates within these IOs about development principles and priorities. Despite the imperative for IOs to recognize the emerging norm of differentiated development, as captured in the creation of groupings dedicated to small countries, they have also faced strong opposition in these institutions that has typically negated success and ensured that IOs treatment of them has been primarily symbolic rather than substantive.

The opposition that SIDS have faced in economic IOs echoes debates about the impacts of state size on development outcomes discussed previously. Only a handful of SIDS are LDCs; most are middle- or upper middle-income countries. Many are no longer official development assistance (ODA) eligible or are on the threshold of graduation. Of the 34

IMF SIDS, 7 are high-income countries, with GDP per capita of $12,476 or more in 2015, 12 upper middle-income countries, with income level between $4,036 and $12, 475, 14 lower middle-income countries of the level between $1,025 and $4,035 and only one a low-income country (Comoros) in 2015 (IMF, 2018).

The WB's IDA offers concessional loans to those countries that have relative poverty, defined, for the fiscal year (FY) 2021, as gross national income (GNI) per capita of $1,185 and below, or/and countries that lack credibility to borrow on markets terms. Thus, those eligible for IDA funding are considered as 'poor' countries. None of the SIDS had GNI per capita below this level, including Comoros ($1,420). In the past two decades, the IDA has become the lynchpin of the Bank support to small states through its blended lending – that IDA used its lending to leverage normal lending by the WB – and special concessional small economy terms established in 2018 (The World Bank, 2018). In 2020, 20 of the 39 UN SIDs were IDA borrowers and not a single one had GNI/per capita below the IDA cut-off lines.

The point is that in both the IMF and the Bank, SIDS do not fit the mainstream development agenda concerned with poverty, fragility, conflict, and violence. Indeed, most are stable democracies (Corbett and Veenendal, 2018). As a result, they are perceived by many within the development community as requiring less urgent attention than larger LDCs. For example, a recent guideline provided by the IMF to its staff in dealing with small developing economies stated: 'although small states are often poor, poverty is not an issue of scale', and thus is not an issue to be focused on by IMF staff (IMF, 2018).

In light of this, keeping SIDS on the agenda is largely an exercise of re-educating these three institutions and re-engineering their programmes. For instance, high public debt burdens undoubtedly threaten growth and development. That is the reason so much attention has been paid to heavily indebted poor countries (HIPCs) and debt relief since the early 1990s. Yet, many Caribbean island states were not 'eligible for debt relief under the Heavily Indebted Poor Countries or Multilateral Debt Relief Initiatives (HIPC/MDRI)' because of their middle-income status. Neither were the Pacific Island States because of their 'generally moderate' debt levels (IMF, 2018). The IMF and the WB then set up a Debt Sustainability Framework for Low-Income Countries that was expanded in 2018 not only to help small states to identify potential rising debt problems but also provide concessional financing to deal with the problems.

The situation is similar in the WTO where large, rich states have committed themselves rhetorically to their cause, including allowing the establishment of the SVEs, they have not always followed through in practice. When the

Table 5.1: SIDS who are IDA borrowers

Country	GNI/per capita	Country	GNI/per capita
Atlantic, Indian Ocean, and South China Sea (9/4)			
Bahrain	$22,110	**Capo Verde**	**$3,630**
Comoros	**$1,420**	Guinea Bissau	**$820**
Maldives	**$9,650**	Mauritius	**$12,740**
Sao Tome & Principe	**$1,450**	Seychelles	$16,870
Singapore	$59,590		
Caribbean (16/5)			
Antigua & Barbuda	$16,660	Bahamas	$31,780
Barbados	$17,380	Belize	$4,450
Cuba	$7,480	**Dominica**	**$7,691**
Dominican Rep.	$8,090	**Grenada**	**$9,980**
Guyana	**$5,180**	Haiti	$790
Jamaica	$5,250	St Kitts and Nevis	$19,030
St Lucia	**$11,020**	**St Vincent**	**$7,7460**
Suriname	$5,540	Trinidad and Tobago	$16,890
Pacific (12/10)			
Fiji	**$5,860**	**Kiribati**	**$3,350**
Marshall Islands	**$4,860**	**Micronesia**	**$3,400**
Nauru	$14,230	Palau	$17,280
Samoa	**$4,189**	**Solomon Islands**	**$2,050**
Timor Leste	**$1,890**	**Tonga**	**$4,300**
Tuvalu	**$5,620**	**Vanuatu**	**$3,170**

Note: Countries in bold are the IDA borrowers.

Source: Compiled by authors from material on IDA website.

WTO Dispute Settlement ruled in favour of Antigua and Barbuda against the American prohibition of online casinos in 2003 (Bohl, 2009; Cooper, 2009; Jackson, 2012), the case was repeatedly used by some politicians in the US as an example of the WTO out of control, overstepping the sovereignty of the US. The fact that the US won most cases brought to the WTO Dispute Settlement procedures was seldom mentioned in the country to the public. Worse still, 15 years later, when the US government refused to pay $21 million annually as the compensation, an equivalent of a quarter of the annual GDP of the tiny island state, Antigua and Barbuda was a clear victim of its own smallness and thereby its vulnerability. The inability of the

WTO to 'force' the US to comply with the ruling meanwhile undermined its legitimacy in the eyes of many member states.

The SIDS agenda has not been aided by the fact that there are numerous practical difficulties in designing programmes to assist the very smallest: the costs of engaging with and in running programmes and projects are much higher than in other places. Remoteness is a key factor; small size and remoteness means high operating costs. In 2000–05, average costs of WB operations in small states, measured in $ per $1,000 of total commitment, were $86 in comparison with $27 average of all Bank projects and they went up to $308 in Solomon Islands, $191 in Dominica, $160 in Guyana, and $97 in Vanuatu (IEG, 2006).

There are primarily three ways to finance programmes and operations – funding from the IBRD (borrowing from the WB under normal conditions), concessional funding from the IDA, or funding from donor countries entrusted to the WB. Even for those qualified for IBRD loans, their small size means limited borrowing capacity as the first source of funding. IDA concessional lending to small states has always been a contested issue. In 1985, the Executive Board approved an exception to the IDA's eligibility criteria for six small island economies (SIEs) to access IDA concessional funding – five in the Caribbean and one in the Pacific. Their GNI per capita was above the operational cut-off of IDA resources, while they were not yet creditworthy for the Bank lending. The decision was not unanimous with two EDs wishing 'to be recorded as opposed' to the decision because the Bank tried to deal with the problems of small states 'on an exceptional basis, not as a general Bank policy' (Shihata, 2000). The debate became perennial in every following IDA replenishment.

In every replenishment, funding the IDA depended on the willingness of donor countries to compromise and contribute. The IDA started with 15 signatory countries (Australia, Canada, China, Germany, India, Italy, Malaysia, Norway, Pakistan, Sudan, Sweden, Thailand, the UK, the US, and Vietnam); its members expanded quickly to 51 in just eight months and to over 170 states in 2019. Around two dozen are the core donors. IDA replenishment every three years is an exercise primarily conducted between Bank/IDA management and donor countries. Even though the Deputies of the IDA who represent donor countries are not recognized by the Article of Agreements as a distinct group nor do they have formal decision-making power, they must agree on the amount of the contribution and way to distribute it. To get their agreement on S&DT for small remote states was difficult (Shihata, 2000) and consensus was not reached until IDA18 that 'GNI per capita does not fully capture a country's level of development' (World Bank, 2018) and small remote states do qualify for S&DT. SIDS were seen to represent a poor return on limited development assistance spending compared with projects in larger LDCs.

The financing of extra costs of running programmes and projects in small developing states thus depends to a large extent on the willingness of regional donor countries. As the WB acknowledged, 'the high cost of operating in these small, remote countries, and limited resources from IDA constrained the World Bank Group to engage with [the Pacific island countries] at the regional level or through multi-country platforms until 2008' (IEG, 2017) when Australia and New Zealand, in particular, decided to bankroll the WBG's engagement in the region. The decision was made for several reasons. First, in the 1990s, assistance to HIPCs was made a priority at the WB and other institutions (IMF, 1996; Sanford, 2004). Small countries were not only part of the consideration because of their relatively low external debts, but also because of their relatively larger inflow of ODA. On average SIDS received higher ODA per capita from their donor countries in comparison with other developing countries, whether measured against GDP or on a per capita basis. Pacific microstates receive the greatest amount of ODA per capita (Dornan and Pryke, 2017).

When measured on a per capita basis (in constant US dollars) the Pacific states received $278 in 2007–2010, compared to $112 in the Caribbean; they also got more than small states generally within the emerging economies groupings at the IMF ($187 to 'small' states and $258 to 'micro' states) (IMF, 2013: 54).

The large inflow of bilateral aid to the Pacific island states had one immediate impact on their participation and engagement with multilateral institutions: they preferred to go to Wellington or Canberra for assistance than Geneva or Washington. One Antipodean ED representing several SIDS identified the consequence: "I find out more about what small states in this constituency really want from my capital than from themselves" (interview with ED). Another ED added, "We know they care a lot about climate change. Besides this, they show little interest. So, the World Bank programme is something that just happened to a country, rather than something the country took the control over" (interview with ED). Thus, often demands on the WB to do something for SIDS came from the regional donor countries rather than small states themselves.

But IOs must pay attention because development in SIDS has stagnated. In the decade 1996–2005, PSIDS, with the exception of Samoa, all had a weak performance and 'per capita GDP fell steadily' in the Marshall Islands, the Solomon Islands, and Vanuatu (Favaro and Peretz, 2008). When economic performance in PSIDS was identified as a 'strategic' issue in Australia and New Zealand, the two governments decided to help 'create an environment conducive to generating growth and employment opportunities for the Pacific Island countries' (Independent Review Report, 2012) by leveraging the WBG's comparative advantage in providing policy advice and technical assistance with their combined funding. Another driving force behind entrusting financial resources to the WBG was 'the sensitivity of the Australian and New Zealand governments to the perception of neo-colonialism inherent in their relationship with the PSIDS – the combination of high levels of aid, migration, expatriates in executive positions in PSIDS governments, and so on' (Independent Review Report, 2012: 8).

The shift from providing bilateral aid to channelling aid funds from donor governments to be administered by multilateral institutions did not occur in the Pacific alone. 'While trust fund contributions amounted to far less than IDA contribution through the mid-1990s, they surpassed total IDA contribution in the three-year periods of both IDA 13 (fiscal 2003–05) and IDA 14 (fiscal 2006–08)' (IEG, 2011: 13). The increase in trust funds provided organizational benefits for multilateral institutions, but can be controversial too. The Bank welcomed trust funds because they were able to supplement its activities and engagement in small states. It considered itself not only in a position to leverage sources of trust funds to help regional cooperation and regional programmes, but also in a position to act as honest broker in situations where 'small states have to deal with large and very large neighbours,' and 'asymmetry in resources, negotiation skills and bargaining power often work to the disadvantage of the small states' (IEG, 2006: 14).

The other side of this development is that increasing trust funds meant increasing dependence on the cooperation with donor countries in the regions not only to run programmes and projects but also to determine its programmes and projects. The Bank management repeatedly emphasized that detailed strategic objectives of trust funds must work for SIDS and indeed they should be provided as part of country strategies negotiated by the Bank official in cooperation with small states. A regional vice president said,

'I find it a little disingenuous that the same people that are telling us not to increase our regular budget are then coming to us with trust funds, saying "would you do this or that with this money?" I would much prefer the Board sat down as a group to decide what we should do with the increasing resources. Then, both sides can be held accountable and both have a little explanation to do with the strategies and their implementation. This being said, I am grateful with the money I get from donors in this region. With it we can run programmes and projects in some very small and remote island states, which otherwise would not get on the agenda at the Board.' (Interview with a regional vice president)

Integrating trust funds in country strategies was done better in some regions than in others. In general, reports from the Bank's Independent Evaluation Group (IEG) concluded that the 'Bank's trust fund management framework have enhanced controls but focus more on the processes than strategic issues for guiding the continuing uptake of donor funds' (IEG, 2011; IEG, 2016). Indeed studies by the IEG showed similar patterns across WGB programmes and projects. The balance between the two strategic objectives – building economic resilience and encouraging inclusive growth – was determined more by the interests of the donor countries than to suit the needs of SIDS. The Australian Department of Foreign Affairs and Trade (DFAT) could not have made it clearer:

> The first and strongest motivation was to leverage the multilateral development banks' specialist skills and relationships with partner governments to increase Australia's role in shaping recipient government policies. The second major motivation was to improve the World Bank's effectiveness by helping them to overcome institutional constraints, largely in their budgets for administrative costs and technical assistance, and in the rules that govern their budget allocations. The third major motivation was to provide aid that was harmonized with other donors, and thus reduce administrative costs and complexity for recipients. (IEG, 2016: 9)

In addition to trust funds, there is some evidence that the combination of lagging development and the threat of climate change is changing how these IOs approach SIDS. In 2015–16 the WB produced a 'Small States Roadmap'. The impetus came from growing recognition of climate vulnerabilities, as one official relayed:

> 'So you have Rio+20 where we sort of crystallized the idea that no one should be left behind. That every country should be represented, every one of our population should have a place at the table. That's a very new notion that is still trying to make headway. It was decided only, what, five years ago? All the multilateral frameworks that have been decided since have sort of tried to take this to another level. To continue this idea that everyone should be at every forum. But you look at the older institutions, you look at the WTO even, and that's not the case.'

As a result, while these institutions have always had some minor interest in SIDS, they are gaining increased attention in recent years. An official noted:

'[The SIDS focus has] been heavily lifted over the last – or it's been given a much more prominent position within the World Bank corporate agenda because of the IDA18 financing that was considerably increased over the last IDA allocations. So, some small states for example, like Tuvalu, received times three allocations on what they received in IDA17. So, there's been a huge focus on small states through the financing increase, which has been a very, very good positive step for small states.'

Likewise, at the IMF officials noted that:

'IMF adapting the policy such that it covers small states has been relatively new. There's been some new guidance issued to staff about how to operate within a small states environment, what things to think about ... I think that's been quite new. That guidance has been developed, I guess, over time to now be quite explicit.'

The point is that despite the fact that SIDS are not the 'poorest of the poor', the norms that govern IOs mean that they cannot ignore certain types of states altogether. They have to offer something for everyone otherwise their legitimacy as global actors is undermined, as this official succinctly summarizes:

'I mean, you look around at the development agenda and it's important to just keep coming back to these types of issues and realities ... the small states are not the poorest, lowest income clients of the Bank. But that doesn't mean that the development challenges are not persistent and the Bank of course is there to serve all of its clients.' (Interview with ICS)

Upholding rules, conventions, and traditions

The participation and influence of SIDS in economic IOs is also shaped by the organizational structure of these institutions. As we have seen, SVEs have the most opportunity to work as a bloc at the WTO. In theory, SIDS can also work within the other two dozen or more groups in the WTO to advance their agenda. However, the position of the secretariats is vastly different in the degree to which they can assist the under-resourced small member states. An ambassador to the WTO who had served as the ED at the IMF compared his expectations of the secretariats in the two places. It was possible to ask for opinions in the IMF.

'This is definitely not the case here [at the WTO] where each member state is jealously preserving its individual voice and by virtue of the long-standing consensus for the General Council, despite various groupings. Thus, we are not trying to export our constituency from the IMF to the WTO. As a member of the Commonwealth and a traditional major donor, we are always available for friendly advice and provide our assistance through other channels, such as the Commonwealth, but not at the WTO itself.'

He also compared his ambassadorial role with his previous position as an ED in the IMF:

'At the Fund, Executive Directors' accountability and responsibility are to the Fund, not to the member state. We are supposed to act with the best independent judgement and act in the best interests of the institution. This requires me internalise well what my constituent governments thinking and what their perspective might be, exercise my sound judgement and make the voice of my constituencies heard for the benefit of the entire system and to keep that system well-functioning.' (Interview with ICS)

The point is that the member-driven nature of the WTO mandates that it would not 'dispense trade rule-making and liberalization in a "top down" manner but proceed at a deliberate pace to be set and closely monitored by the Members' (Harbinson, 2009: 2). In practice, consensus doesn't help SIDS in the WTO as much as they would like. It is true that the principle of consensus means that every member state holds a veto power, but the principle does not work in practice for various reasons, the most important of which is that the secretariat cannot advocate for them.

The convention at the WTO is that while the secretariat has the expertise on all trade issues, they cannot offer advice to any single member state unless they are asked to do so. "If you do not know anything, it is difficult to ask questions and to seek advice," explained one from a small state. States instead rely on groupings – formal or informal coalitions seeking to speak with one voice using a single spokesperson or negotiating team. There are about 19 recognized and active groupings in the WTO and by and large they are among large trading states. In groups where SIDS are present, such as ACP (including three Pacific island states) or G33 (including seven Caribbean island states), they have to compete with those large ones in the group. In addition, the WTO has only three categories of states: developed, developing, and least developed status. Many SIDS find it difficult to fit anywhere. The creation of the SVEs was an attempt to resolve this. The Development Division at the WTO Secretariat serves the CTD; it designated one person in helping coordinate SVEs. But, that person's freedom to offer opinions was constrained. As one senior WTO director explained:

> 'You cannot do that here at the WTO. We are not the IMF. The minute we do that [advocate for them], we are dead – no one would ever trust us, and we would lose our legitimacy right away. Of course, we can produce papers and analyses when member states ask for, but not our positions.' (Interview with WTO director)

A coordinator of major grouping agreed: "You simply do not ask the secretariat to provide that kind of advice." SIDS are thus in a precarious position in fighting their battles, as a veteran GATT/WTO insider explained:

> 'Small developing states might have their distinct issues related to trade, but they are susceptible to approaches in capital from the big guys – particularly the EU – that would come along telling them, "Oh, we have this economic cooperation agreement or we give you so much in aid. Don't you think you could be a little bit more broad-minded on this particular issue?" When small states do not want to put themselves in this position, they would attach themselves to bigger groupings, like ACP or the G33 or whatever. Then they get – India is very, very fond of saying – and always has been – of saying "on behalf of developing countries, we object". They (small states) sitting there are saying, "Really?" This is a real dilemma for the small countries. They often get taken hostage by these huge developed and developing markets.' (Interview with ICS)

Small states are highly reliant on the SVE coordinator to develop consensus within the group. That is, like chairs of all WTO committees, the chair of the CTD must maintain impartiality. When the person also advocated positions of SVEs, it not only undermined the credibility of the chairperson but also the SVEs as a grouping.

Small states' representation at the WB and the IMF differs from other IOs. There are a limited number of Executive Directors in each IO; some represent individual countries, but the majority represent groupings of countries. Most of the Anglophone Caribbean countries are in a group where Canada provides the ED. The Pacific countries are in a grouping where the ED rotates between Australia, New Zealand, and South Korea. The members of the group take turns in providing representatives to serve in the EDs' office. The EDs insist they represent all the countries in their group.

"I am an Executive Director, not an Ambassador," one insisted (interview with ED). When the Prime Minister of Barbados and leader of the Joint Task Force, Owen Arthur, wanted to present the report at the Bank his appearance was arranged by the (Canadian-led) ED's office as Barbados is a member of the group. At the WB the relationship between the regional vice presidents and country directors and these EDs can make a difference in terms of the type and size of the assistance small states get.

The important point is that the institutional structure of the Bank and IMF militates against small states forming a collaborative bloc in the same way that they have in the UN system or via the SVEs in the WTO. There is, therefore, a tension between the cross-cutting concerns of SIDS and the imperatives of each region: between yesterday's rules and traditions and today's challenges. These organizations are changing and adapting as IOs have sought 'to reinvent the institution so as to hang onto a role once the original purpose had faded away' (Boughton, 2004: 20) While acknowledging the need and demand to assist SIDS in the early 2000s, all three institutions, especially the WBG that is dedicated to development, continued 'to have a limited role in assisting most small states with their unique development challenges' (IEG, 2006: 21). It then took more than another decade for the issue of small states to be accepted. That stake has a potentially large global effect. If small countries lack the ability to attract financial inflows to finance economic stability and development, then the overall health of the world economy will be negatively impacted.[1] Legitimacy required they were involved in the process and not squeezed out by the demands of the bigger states, including larger developing countries.

The renewed emphasis on SIDS in the last decade has generated some of these changes. The key, again, has been climate change, as this WB official relays:

'If you will recall, back in 2016 there was a couple of really important high level meetings including some of the COPs on climate and then there was also financing for development (FfD), which was held in Africa. The small states constituency had a rather large voice, both within the FfD agenda and also within the climate disaster risk and resilience agenda as well. They created a small states coordinator position [and a] Small States Secretariat which is housed within the Operations Policy and Country Services Vice Presidency Unit.' (Interview with ICS)

There was also a three-year work programme to examine the inclusion of vulnerability as a criterion for concessional financing. It builds on the longer-standing institutional adaptation created for SIDS: the annual Small States Forum. Officials described it as a meeting:

> 'which is always on the margins of the spring meetings and annual meetings. There used to just be [a Small States Forum] at the annual meetings but now, because of the demand for a lot of our work, we've been having meetings at the spring meetings as well. We've had a couple of really excellent meetings that we've organized over the last couple of years but that has been going on since 2000; but as I said, and I think mentioned right at the beginning, this has been quite an increased profile in terms of the corporate agenda. So, there's been very high level, lots of prime ministers and ministers of finance and governors of central banks attending and so on. Not only that, the relationship between the bank and other partners, such as the United Nations and OECD, of course, the Commonwealth Secretariat, the African Development Bank, Asian Development Bank; it's been really, really galvanized a lot.' (Interview with ICS)

A similar trend is apparent at the IMF where the board has a small states group so that the directors of the various offices who have small states members get together regularly to develop a small state view rather than their own individual country. Within the Asia and Pacific Department, a decision was taken to reorganize so as to:

> '[Bring] together the work on small states in the Pacific, which had been spread across various divisions into one unit and that unit covered cross country, analytical work and policies issues with respect to the Pacific islands. Because the development of that unit was a success, it was then, about 18 months ago, it was made in to a fully-fledged division.' (Interview with IMF official)

In sum, the institutional structure of each of the economic IOs we consider are not naturally conducive to SIDS influence in the same way as the UN system. The WTO via the SVEs has gone the furthest but it still does not have the status of a full group and the preference for consensus means that it is often more difficult for these countries to act as veto players than it appears. In the Bank and IMF, the regional structure impedes a global grouping. Both of these IOs have sought to create cross-cutting institutional adaptations to better capture the needs of SIDS. Again, climate change and the vulnerabilities it is causing has been a key catalyst. But there remains a tension between rules and traditions established decades ago and today's challenges.

Facilitating mutual assistance and alliances

Despite the impediments, the imperatives of 'throughput' legitimacy demand that IOs show some willing to engage their smallest members and assist them to participate. Regional donors (discussed in the previous sections) are one source of assistance. NGOs have not had the same impact in the economic sphere as they have on climate issues. The reasons are straightforward: most development NGOs focus on the 'poorest of the poor' but most SIDS are not LDCs and those that are represent only a minute proportion of global poverty. As a result, the secretariat is their main source of assistance. But as outlined, while the secretariat does help, concerns about politicization remain.

With the belief that 'harnessing globalisation' and trade and development are the two sides of the same coin, Pascal Lamy took over as the WTO DG in 2005 and immediately took Aid for Trade as 'his pet theme', in the words of one senior director at the WTO. To Lamy:

> The WTO cannot be an ivory tower. The high priests of international trade cannot remain ensconced in the comfort of their beautiful Lake Geneva headquarters. The WTO must integrate its work into the agenda of governments, civil society and other international organisations that are working for growth and development. (Lamy, 2013: viii)

This was exactly what the WTO secretariat did on Aid for Trade. "Lamy obviously genuinely does believe in it and made it", said one senior director.

> 'We did not do development then; the World Bank did it. We believed that was the responsibility of other organizations. Then we started working with the World Bank, FAO, UNDP, WHO and others on the issue. Aid for Trade is sort of capacity building. We had to work with the regional development banks where previously we had no relationship whatsoever. Now, parts of this building are almost entirely dedicated to doing those kinds of activities.'

Another added:

> 'Of course, in the process we also found that these countries were more interested in getting technical assistance rather than doing trade. A few with open economies, such as Costa Rica and Mauritius, often ran into conflicts with many small states that insisted their economies and markets needed protection – the position against the "ethos" of WTO secretariat. That is the reason 10 and 15 years later, small states

still could not hold common positions at WTO trade negotiations.'
(Interview with ICS)

Meanwhile, Aid for Trade, described by an official as "the bridge between
trade and development" and "one extremely important initiative that
improves the ability of developing countries to trade" became a collaborative
programme, initiated by the WTO, in partnership with the OECD, the WB,
regional development banks, and UN agencies, mobilizing resources to assist
small states build their capacity to "produce more and trade better" so that
they would be able to enjoy the benefits of open trade and open economy.

While development and capacity building is largely the purview of the
Bank, the WTO nevertheless undertakes some initiatives of this nature to
assist their small, non-resident members. 'Geneva Week' is an important
occasion for non-resident missions because the WTO pays for a delegation
to attend and be briefed on the operation of the organization and state of
key negotiations. Twenty-two countries were eligible, even if several were
in arrears with fees and not active. For those who could not come, the
WTO invested in a trade academy which ran online courses. The SVEs
coordinator also has one permanent member of staff in the secretariat
dedicated to their work programme. But this staff member must tread
carefully when they are asked to assist members – to be factual rather than
even analytical. For instance, they would tabulate a list of commitments
states made under the Trade in Services Agreement, rather than produce an
analysis of the impacts (positive or negative) on their economies. According
to the chief coordinator of a major grouping, SVEs or ACP would have
to "do our own research and own analysis, take our own positions while
these activities are funded by the European Development Fund or any
single donor country". The Commonwealth had been a key ally of small
states and, as we saw in the previous chapter, in the late 1980s they set up
a dedicated office in New York that provides subsidized accommodation
for resident missions. In 2011 they created a similar Geneva office. Like
New York, the office provides subsidized facilities for small state missions.
It also provides an expert Trade Adviser who can be more partisan in their
views and analysis.

Training and capacity building has been more common at the Bank and
IMF. The IMF set up its very first regional training centre in Fiji for the
Pacific region back in 1993 – the Pacific Financial Technical Assistance
(PETAC). It aims to promote a macro-financial stability in the Pacific
Island countries through a focused programme of technical assistance and
training. Its operation depends on the willingness of donors to bankroll it –
Australia, the EU, South Korea, New Zealand, and the Asian Development
Bank (ADB). As the Evaluation Office of the IMF (IEO) noted, the

degree of engagement with its smaller members depends on several factors, including 'the availability of other sources of advice' and 'the level of trust the authorities may have built with specific Fund advisors' (IEG, 2011: 563). For a long time PETAC had very limited operation until after 2010 when more funding was provided by the donors with only its coordinator being funded by the IMF.

The IMF also runs a programme similar to 'Geneva Week' at the WTO where they bring in delegations from small members to the annual meeting in October. In some instances – like when correspondent banking issues were emerging and becoming more difficult and more acute – they also came to the Spring meeting too. The Fund also has a Special Appointee Programme, which is an initiative aimed at low-income countries to send a staff member on secondment for 12 months. It's aimed at mid-level officials. The scheme highlights that it is also difficult to get their nationals on the staff of these institutions, as one diplomat reflected:

'But I will say that sometimes small states, especially the Caribbean and the Pacific, they're not necessarily always first on the list for that kind of diversity that they're looking for. They're usually more people who are from Africa, people from Asia, people from LDCs. The Pacific and the Caribbean could kind of fall through the cracks.' (Interview with SIDS diplomat)

We previously outlined how the organizational structure of the Fund and Bank made the consolidation of a global SIDS grouping in these IOs difficult. The upside of regional representation is that EDs can play a key role in lobbying on behalf of their group.

This is in part determined by the two responsibilities of the Fund: what an official described as a policing role and a policy advising role and in part shaped by the perception of the EDs. One ED with many small states as constituents explained:

'We need to make sure the balance is right, especially with small states. Some single constituent EDs often drift towards the policing role. We need to make sure our constituencies get assistance in the form of policy advice, technical assistance and training and build their capacities. This is in the interest of the whole system. I am not an ambassador here; I am an ED. I have fiduciary responsibility to the institution, but I am also here to reflect the views and interests of the authorities that are within my constituency and indeed represent the interests of my constituents and those of the Fund too.' (Interview with ED)

Such representation is more prominent in the constituency where Canada has been the ED as it holds more than 60 per cent of the total votes and in the Pacific where Australia/New Zealand, Australia/South Korea provide EDs in rotations. The ED works closely with the alternate and senior advisors in the office to ensure the interests of small island states in the constituency. It is not the case in the constituency where the allocation of voting is relatively equal, such as the Nordic group of eight states that engage in close coordination on all positions and decisions, or in two African constituencies where 'smallness' can hardly compete with other needs and demands. One ED explained how he saw his role representing a constituency that included small Pacific islands:

> 'In our formal discussion on whatever, I often try to take a small states' angle, thinking about what they would need, how the Bank could deliver its assistance, potential difficulties in implementing the Bank's policies and those sorts of issues. On specific small state issues, we would lobby behind the scenes to get the issues we want on the table, talking to OPCS and the Regional VP's office. It does take some lobbying and convincing. Some Regional VPs do not believe the Bank has a small-state problem, but a large state problem, because large borrowers give the Bank business. Among the 25 EDs most do not have small states as constituents. Our small states constituents have no clue of the head and tail of this institution. They may not know exactly what they want and I don't think there is any prima facie reason to think we are pushing the wrong things for them. Doing so, I think I am helpful to the bank management too. After all, we are paid by the Bank and we are all Bank staff in this office. Also the word *World* means something here, it has to have a sense of all its members, including its 50 small states.' (Interview with ED)

The IMF covers four broad work areas: 'policy advice and program design, capacity building, financial support and debt relief, and coordinated international efforts' and more specific work on 'the pursuit of stable macroeconomic conditions and macro-relevant structural reforms, with supporting financial and technical assistance' (Fritz-Krockow and Ramlogan, 2007: 44). They have little relevance to SIDS. Small developing countries tend to have open economies in terms of trade, but they have limited financial integration with the global market. Most are on extended Article IV consultation cycles (24 instead of 12 months), and thus have limited engagement with the IMF in terms of surveillance. 'The Fund operational spending on small (and, especially, micro) states is well below that on larger countries', admitted the IMF. Institutionally, its country teams for small states 'tend to be smaller and more junior' (IMF, 2013). Donors 'speak' on their behalf and act on their behalf not only because of the group representation but also financial resources from which multilateral institutions can draw. In other words, representation by large states is more apparent and prevalent and it is also more coordinated. A former Canadian ED explained:

'We represent 11 small Caribbean states here at the Fund. There is not "a Barbados position" or "a Bahamas position" on over 90 per cent of what is going on here even though both countries have sophisticated finance people in capital. In this office, we always have a senior adviser representing the Caribbean. When issues do pop up that might concern small states, I or the alternate ED would run through the matter with this senior advisor and make sure he is in the room and on side. He would canvas small countries, be in touch with the authorities in capital, and tell them what we are thinking of doing with this or that. If we know there are problems in one of our small states, we would write a buff of two and half pages of the situations stating them; we talk to the IMF staff and go through the buff before they go to the field trip of 2–3 weeks. After they return, we would talk to the staff again and produce a grey report that would include our position before the Board meets.' (Interview with former ED)

EDs representing small states, especially those in the Caribbean and the Pacific, tend to make sure that interests of small states are represented, and their concerns are properly considered, but they also make clear to small states their problems and the way forward from the perspective of the IMF as an institution. Explained one ED:

'When the finance in this country was in trouble, we [this ED office] supported the Fund to have a debt-swap programme in place. That brought down inflation from 18 per cent to 8 per cent. When the Prime Minister brought his newly appointed young finance minister to Washington, DC, I took the two to see Christine Lagarde and David Lipton [first deputy managing director]. We told the Prime Minister and his finance minister that we were unhappy with the implementation of the programme and the country had not made sufficient progress on what it had said it would do. We [the Fund] are the only one that can impose conditions, but we also need to make sure progress has been made.' (Interview with ED)

This representation is important because in general small states do not occupy a lot of attention either at the Board or of the staff. One ED acknowledged the difficulty for the Board to get traction on small states – "to get the Board specifically focus on small states always felt like a distraction for EDs from their subject matter tasks" (interview with ED).

This is in contrast to the WB where EDs could work with regional VPs in response to the collective efforts of SIDS, such as the PIFS or OECS, on specific programmes and projects, if there were any demands. Another ED explained:

'When we talk about issues rather than the size of members that are to be affected, we can approach a small division of the OPCS responsible for sectoral programmes and projects as well as the regional vice president office that decides the allocation of resources (human, financial, and technical) in member states.' (Interview with ED)

Often the difficulty is getting small and remote developing states "to figure out what they want from the Bank and how to get what they need" (interview with ICS).

One way the small states can get their issues in front of the board at the Bank is via their advisers on the EDs staff, as one official explained:

'They each have two-year terms. We rotate through all of the countries in the constituency, but each of the small states get an opportunity to come and represent the whole constituency at the board. It's probably every ten years I guess it is, roughly, just because there's so many countries.' (Interview with ICS)

As these quotes illustrate, the Bank has probably done a lot more for small states than other IOs even though its main focus has always been low-income countries. Until quite recently, most of its senior management – regional and sector vice presidents and the presidents – had climbed up the rank internally and most had some field experience. One accepted view was that the voice of all member states must be taken seriously and indeed, voice, legitimacy, and effectiveness were the integral part of the development. It took some time for the WB to have gradually shifted its attention from HIPCs in the 1990s to the relatively better-off small states with many other disadvantages in the development.

The principles developed behind them were similar – listening to the countries the Bank tried to assist (country-ownership), NGOs, and the very poor. This was indeed what many key frontline operators believed (Mallaby, 2004; Marshall, 2008). The reorganization adopted under the presidency of James Wolfensohn in 1996 further made country directors and country offices in the field 'the consistent interlocutors with government and greatly increased their ability to set priorities for the Bank's program' (Adams, 2015). For SIDS, whose country offices may be in Washington, DC and in Sydney, the decentralization did bring together the demands of small states, the regional donors, and the Bank programmes. "Today there are two major differences", one regional vice president explained:

'One is that we are much more involved in policy and policy means that we have to be working with the government and people who make policies. Two is the investment side: being close to regional donors allows us to raise the necessary resources for the programmes and also to delivering the programmes and projects, the capacity is so much more important and we need to work in the field with the locals and the donors to develop that capacity.'

There was a surge of donors' contributions to the programmes in these small states.

In sum, IOs were encouraged to pursue the interests of small states to balance the scale of the competition for dominant positions among large and powerful countries, especially between the US and Europe as a group (de Vries and Garrison, 1976; James, 1996; Solomon, 1999; Boughton, 2001). This is reflected in attempts by the secretariats to ensure a minimum level of participation. In the Fund and Bank, EDs also play a crucial role. The self-perception of EDs in both can explain their activities in small developing states. Single constituency EDs do represent the interests of their country even though they are paid by the Fund or the Bank. A single-constituency ED explained:

'I always made sure I was completely, on every issue, in line with my government's position because you lose any credibility as a representative if you're perceived to have a different position from the people you represent. This was when I was the ED at both the Fund and the World Bank. When I appealed to treat certain countries (whether being highly indebted or small island states) differently, that was because my government had decided on the issue.' (Interview with ED)

A senior official at the Fund added:

'At the Board, tails do wag the dog and big tails wag the dog more often. Yet, when those multi-constituency EDs are effective and efficient in speaking out on behalf of small states, they often get what they want for these small states. The problem is there is little interest among small developing states, especially SIDS in any of these multilateral institutions.' (Interview with ICS)

Conclusion

SIDS have sought to build on their success in the climate arena by drawing specific attention to their economic vulnerabilities in IOs like the WTO, the WB, and the Fund. They have had some success – all of these IOs now recognize that SIDS have unique development challenges and provide some resources to support their participation. The WTO also created the SVEs. Being seen to be supportive of the SIDS and encouraging their participation is a key means by which they pursue throughput legitimacy. And these changes have had some effect by, for example, at the WTO enabling SVEs to gain entry to key decision-making arenas (that is, the WTO Green Room), the WTO Committee on Trade and Development now annually to reviewing their work programme; and at the WB and the IMF reviewing the way they think about the types of lending they provide and the projects they finance. There is a greater recognition that interventions need to be tailored to the scalar dynamics of development in SIDS and SVEs (whether they are in practice is another matter entirely); and in each some recognition that effective groupings of small states have greater scope, at least nominally, to act as a veto player across IOs.

This success, however, has been tempered by numerous challenges. Some arise from SIDS themselves. Most have a limited presence in the key cities where decisions are taken – Washington and Geneva. This has limited informal coordination and placed a considerable burden on those select few SIDS who have the appetite and capacity to lead the group in Geneva, in particular: Mauritius, Barbados, and Jamaica. This task is made harder by the fact that there is less alignment of interests on key economic issues than there has been on climate change. When combined with the absence of NGOs to compensate for capacity deficits, SIDS have been less capable of representing themselves in these IOs than they have in the UN system on climate change.

The rules of IOs have not helped them either. Since at least 2000, economic IOs have a greater imperative to support all members, but IOs also operate with rules and traditions that were created in a different era. When combined with opposition from larger developing countries to preferential treatment for SIDS, these rules and traditions have hamstrung the efforts of both SIDS diplomats and those sympathetic to their cause. The result is that the story of SIDS at the economic IOs is one of mixed success: they have achieved symbolic gains but have struggled to translate them into material changes in their condition.

6

Expanding the Agenda at the WHO and the WIPO

The climate and economic vulnerabilities of SIDS are now well established and widely accepted by IOs. But the idea that small size creates specific vulnerabilities is not restricted to these policy arenas. Indeed, once the idea that being small is a unique condition is accepted, it is no great leap of imagination to consider how other policy areas might be shaped by state size. In doing so the relevant IOs have the potential to become co-opted to the SIDS agenda. For instance, food quality is one of the main drivers of health outcomes and so small, remote economies are more vulnerable to price fluctuations and availability of supplies. Likewise, economies of scale – the cost of equipment and pharmaceuticals, and the availability of skilled labour – limit medical treatment in small states. But, despite their interests and the fact that individual small states have found the WHO to be receptive to these arguments, SIDS do not have the same profile in that IO as they do in the UNFCCC. Likewise, SIDS may have intellectual property concerns but, like many middle powers with few direct interests, they rarely engage with the WIPO.

In this chapter we explore the absence of small states in these two IOs. This absence is relative: we are not claiming there is no activity but rather that this activity has not generated the same profile and attention for SIDS, as a global group, that it has in the IOs we covered in the previous chapters. Indeed, in the interests of generating 'throughput' legitimacy these IOs are much more interested in finding a way to serve the small states agenda than the small states themselves who have typically been passive members. These cases therefore reinforce our claim that to understand the variation in outcomes across institutions we need to account for both sides of the story: the interaction between IOs and small states.

To underscore this point, we reverse the structure used in the previous two chapters – we start with the IOs and then discuss the SIDS. This reversal reflects that the participation of SIDS and the adoption of the SIDS agenda in these IOs have largely been supply- rather than demand-driven. It has also typically been tokenistic. Echoing the previous chapter, there are a number of reasons for this, including the existing rules and traditions of IOs and the capacity constraints inherent to SIDS diplomacy. Despite both SIDS and IOs having strong interests in developing an agenda that recognizes the unique vulnerabilities of small size in these policy domains, there has been very little progress to date on advancing them in these arenas.

Throughput legitimacy and serving the SIDS

The development agenda has become important for all IOs. The WHO has always had a strong interest in development issues but it has tended to address these via disease or condition – that is, the global fight against malaria or polio – or by state, using the established categories of lower-, middle-, and upper-income countries. They have therefore been less involved in the SIDS discussion. The WIPO, by contrast, has only recently embraced the development agenda. In doing so it has followed the lead of the UN. The problem they have faced is getting developing countries generally but also small states specifically interested in what they can offer them. In the interests of generating throughout legitimacy, both IOs have sought to engage with small states in different regions rather more than SIDS have demanded their attention. The reasons for small states' lack of participation stem from both the mission and structure of the IOs and the well-established capacity constraints that we have documented.

Promoting norms and principles

As we have shown throughout, two norms motivate IOs to engage with their smallest members: the sovereign equality of states and the right to development. As UN agencies, both the WHO and the WIPO have been drawn into this agenda despite the fact that when there isn't a global pandemic both are considered comparatively peripheral and technical organizations, much like the IMO discussed in Chapter 4. The principle of the sovereign equality of all member states permeates all WHO discussions. One example is the WHO work programme (WHO, 2019) that identifies the position of small states. Because the WHO is a UN agency it adopts the UN definition of small state. But it does not have a specific SIDS or SVEs group. Rather, its categories are defined by stages of development and some small states are of course comparatively wealthy, even if still vulnerable to natural hazards, and dependent for their middle income on a limited number of sources of wealth. Small states are thus only invoked implicitly when the WHO talks about how it must serve *all* member states, as DG Tedros outlined when he introduced the work programme. The WHO intended to 'strengthen the capacity of all countries, particularly developing countries' (p 14). 'It would maintain a dialogue with all member states' (p 16). It would 'enhance the quality for leadership at country level to ensure a new generation of high calibre WHO representation' (p 21). It promised to 'deliver services for a limited number of fragile states' (p 15). 'Specific reference to small island states was given when they were offered a case study of the health impacts of climate change' (p 13).

When the WIPO launched its development agenda, one area where it might be expected that some small states would be involved, the initiative was dominated by Brazil, India, and Argentina: big players always on the IO stage. The WIPO is primarily responsive to the work that occurs within a country. Its patent registration scheme reflects activity. It seeks to have a single international regime of IP that is universally accepted. Its development agenda is seeking to identify and increase that activity. It is proactive, rather than responsive.

Being seen as responsive to the development agenda has benefits for both IOs. SIDS may see these IOs as the servants of big industry interests. In the WIPO in particular the secretariat was initially regarded as in thrall to the US IP industry. Its interest is therefore in developing contacts in, and developing the IP coverage of, small states so as to demonstrate that they are a member-driven organization. Insofar as it can increase the areas of IP coverage in these small states, its credibility is enhanced and its standing secured. The level of resources that these IOs dedicate to small states may not he high, but they do see a potential return.

A second way they attempt to embody norms about sovereign equality is via their staffing profile, as this quote by DG of the WHO Tedros, made at one of the daily press conferences held during the COVID-19 crisis, illustrates:

'I will tell you a story. When I appointed my Chief Nursing Officer of the whole, wide world I picked her from a country called Cook Islands. Then people started criticizing me and said, what happened, what is this Cook Islands, is it Thomas Cook the company or what Cook? On one hand it could be arrogance. On the other hand it could be ignorance. Ignorance could be okay; you can correct it. But I was so sad when I saw arrogance in it. The arrogance part is, people didn't want to have a Chief Nursing Officer of the whole, wide world from a small country like Cook Islands, which is only 10,000; a Chief Nursing Officer. But my belief is talent is universal, opportunity is not. You can find the most talented person from a country with a population of 11,000 like Cook Islands, or 10,000. So we work with Cook Islands, 10,000 population; we work with China, 1.4 billion population. We were criticized for the 10,000. Is it because Cook Islands influenced us? Using what? And China, using what? We see everybody equally. We want to see everybody equally. That's what we want, that's what we do because we belong to all member states equally. We don't want to create differences between our member states. We would like to see all of them through a very similar principle; identical. I hope the Cook Islands story will tell you loads and loads. So we respect every nation. We work with every nation. We try to understand the problems with every nation. We try to help them understand the root cause of the challenges and help them. The most important thing is that and we see the whole world equally and I assure you of that.' (Tedros, Director General, the WHO, 2 April 2020)

Tedros wanted to indicate that the WHO had the interests of all member states in mind but suggested that when they did, other member states thought it inappropriate that any attention was given to the smallest. He was criticized for the appointment, not by the larger member states but by those who thought that their nationals should have precedence if senior positions were to be filled. In one form or other, the WHO was open to criticism whether it made decisions that appeared to respond to the smallest or the largest of countries. The issue was, and always is, the balance between the interests of individual states and the requirement to fulfil the mission of the organization to humanity at large.

Yet member states are often demanding that their citizens are appointed to positions in the secretariats. Most IOs keep a register that records how many of their staff are citizens of which countries, and how the nationalities are spread across levels within the organizations. In those instances where there are cases of severe under-representation some applicant fields are restricted to those nationalities. It is of course not meant to matter. ICSs are supposed to be supra national; they sign a pledge that they will treat all member states equally. Yet ambassadors continue to ring DGs suggesting good candidates when there are vacancies and grumble when they are not successful. The WHO (2016) provides three lists of those positions counted for geographical representation: those countries that are over-represented, under-represented, or unrepresented. All the small states in the Caribbean and the Pacific are listed as unrepresented, whereas a range of African member states are listed as over-represented.

The WIPO is similar. The WIPO register of its secretariat's country of origin have long columns of countries who only have one or two members of the secretariat. The most substantial number of staff are citizens of the European countries where the IOs are located, particularly the support staff. In June 2014, the 506 professional staff came from 102 countries, 60 per cent of which provide just one or two people. The smaller Caribbean states, Costa Rica, Grenada, Haiti, Trinidad, Barbados, and Jamaica each have one. There are no members from the other small island states. There are no Pacific member states represented at all (WIPO WO/CC/70/1 annex1). Like the WHO, the WIPO officials fought back against the ambassadors' demands for redressing under-representation, because 'if all the appointments ambassadors requested were made, it would de-professionalise the institution. It is legitimate to ask to be represented, but it should be competitive'. The problems emerged when a failure in that request led to opposition within the organization on other issues out of pique.

Does it matter? Member states will say no, as they nominally have the authority, but the frequency and vigour with which they sometimes lobby suggests they see value in finding positions for their people. Both IOs have a predominant professional ethos: lawyers in the WIPO, doctors in the WHO. Small size implies limited depth in both professions in small and developing states. The WHO, for example, notes acute problems with a brain drain of their medical professionals and the inability to train specialist staff. To become a patent lawyer is a long trek: a degree in science, a PhD, and then patent law qualifications. It can take a decade. Of course, it should be expected that there will be far fewer from those states that have problems in even finding adequate health and IP professionals to support their national administration. Geography is another factor. The prominence of French and Swiss staff in Geneva-based institutions is a function of proximity and convenience. However, the dominance of European and North American professionals, for instance, in the WIPO provides one reason for the suspicion, often voiced, that the secretariat represents the views of the Western IP community. The accusation is disputed within the WIPO. But the belief can assist us in explaining the fervour with which a development agenda was supported.

Upholding rules, conventions, and traditions

As will be clear by now, while the norms and principles that provide the impetus for IOs to engage with small states are essentially familiar across the multilateral system, the way they are interpreted is shaped by the rules and traditions of each institution. The WHO is structured around regional offices: the heads of the six WHO regional offices are elected by the member states in that region; they have an independent authority created by that electoral process. In this sense the WHO is more similar in structure to the Bank than the WTO or the UNGA. Regional directors are in far closer contact with their members than a DG in Geneva could possibly be. Regional offices are semi-independent in that they understand better than Geneva the local conditions and are not there to be ordered around. One, the Pan American Health Organization (PAHO) predated the WHO by 40 years; it acts as a WHO region but takes its unique status seriously.

There are also 120 country offices where WHO staff in the national capitals will be in constant touch with the ministry of health. In the West Pacific region the regional office is in Manila. There is also a substantial sub-regional office in Fiji and country offices in Kiribati, Micronesia, Samoa, Solomon Islands, and Vanuatu. These small offices answer both to a country manager and to the superior office in Fiji. The other countries are allocated to both the Fiji hub and to one of the other country centres; so American Samoa, Niue, and the Cook Islands are combined with Samoa; Palau and the Marshall Islands with Micronesia. In the Caribbean most countries such as Barbados, Jamaica, Costa Rica, Haiti, and Trinidad have their own country office. Timor Leste has an office, but is part of the South Asia region.

The point is that there is a presence either directly or comparatively close by where issues can be raised. This ensures that representation cascades through regions rather than across the SIDS group as a whole. For many WHO professionals the real action for which they joined the organization – the alleviation of health problems – is in the field, whether seeking to manage pandemics or overseeing a smallpox vaccination programme that has effectively eliminated the disease worldwide. In the WHO decisions about levels and types of assistance to the health departments of SIDS are primarily taken at country and regional level rather than coordinated via diplomatic channels and through groupings in New York and Geneva. The interests of SIDS as a group can sometimes be lost within larger blocks – for example, the Western Pacific Region.

WIPO staff, by contrast, are predominantly based in Geneva and all policymaking is concentrated there. Gradually it has expanded its suite of External Offices (EOs). Initially there were offices in Singapore, Japan, and Brazil, but inevitably other countries wanted them too. In the proposed budget of 2014/15, the secretariat suggested five more: in the US, China, Russia, and two in Africa. It had received requests for EOs from 23 countries (WO/PBC/21/INF.1). These country offices are intended as contact points; they are used for the distribution of information. They are not centres of independent authority. The WIPO secretariat provided a paper that sought to develop criteria for the establishment of EOs, always reminding the member states that the actual number was for the members to decide, not the secretariat in a member-driven organization. Lists of criteria are essentially camouflage for decisions made on grounds of political weight. There were no small member states seeking an EO.

These issues are exacerbated by their different financial circumstances. The WIPO raises funds from the services it provides, particularly the Patent Treaty. Consequently, its own income covers about 94 per cent of its expenditure and its reliance on the assessed contributions of member states is marginal. That does not mean the secretariat can do as it chooses. Its budget is approved, line by line, by member states who insist that they will determine what activities will be pursued. But it does mean that the secretariat does not have to wonder whether the funds will be available to meet all its expenses. Said an official: "We can have our own agenda. Of course, we discuss it with member states but we do have a sort of coherent rationale."

The WHO is almost in the opposite position; assessed contributions have wavered around just 22 per cent of its proposed expenditure. It requires additional funds either from member states in grants or from other sources of income, such as the Gates Foundation. Some members will provide the additional funds without ties; that is, they expect the WHO to spend the funds on the programmes approved by the EB or the World Health Assembly (WHA) representing the membership as a whole. Others will tie the grants to particular initiatives: to fund a building programme in a specific country on such terms and conditions as they may demand (even to requiring that consultancy services are all sourced to their own citizens). When a substantial level of income is tied the WHO must still maintain its core programmes as determined by the WHA. Some member states can be strategic in where they ask for funds. Core business such as medical education may be hard to fund from elsewhere. So national health departments will use WHO funds for those purposes while finding it easier to finance pandemic management from tied funds. It is worth remembering the comment that the budget of the WHO is the equivalent of a medium-sized hospital: not a small national health budget, a single institution's budget.

Priorities in the health area are contested, and vigorously so. Every country has its priorities; whether primary health care, medical education and the availability of doctors, control of infectious diseases, non-communicable diseases (NCDs) caused by life styles, a need to eradicate smallpox or TB, support for Roll Back Malaria initiatives, among a range of other programmes. They are not equally affected by all but the WHO is required to provide support for them all, as commissioned by its masters in the WHA and the WHO's EB. These are daily challenges, always apparent in a society and at times of epidemics painfully so. Modern medicine is expensive, expert, and not always accessible. It is always in the public eye. Only recently has the WHO rolled out local programmes to tackle the NCDs that are a constant concern in the Pacific in particular.

There is a contrast with the interest in the WIPO. Even if everyone is affected by IP, they usually do not know it; even if aware, they have little appreciation of the complexities of the law. For a long time IP was seen as a process for protecting the interest of the developed countries in terms of pharmaceuticals and industry. Only gradually was it extended to cover traditional knowledge, fabrics and patterns, traditional medicines, and even the viruses that were used by pharmaceutical companies to develop vaccinations.

Rules for leadership selection also works against SIDS. In the UN special agencies all member states are nominally treated as equal: when DGs are elected everyone in the room has a single vote. Initially both the WIPO and the WHO elected their DGs in executive bodies with a limited rotating membership. The WHO's EB had 32 members; the WIPO's Coordination Committee (CoCo) had 82. The EB forwarded its nomination to the WHA for endorsement; CoCo to the WIPO's General Council. These nominations were always accepted. When the WHO decided that the EB would interview the candidates and reduce the field to three and the WHA would elect the DG from the narrowed field, the dynamics changed too. Even where the EDs were seen to represent groups, a ballot of 32 EDs was a very different story to one where there were around 180 member states.

In both IOs the DGs have come from a limited range of countries; they include neither the great powers nor the small states. In the last 30 years the WHO's DGs were from Japan, Norway, South Korea, Hong Kong, and Ethiopia. In the WIPO, the long-lasting DG, Aped Bosch, who served from 1973 to 1997, was American but his successors have come from the Sudan, Australia, and Singapore; no US candidate has contested either position (although by convention there has always been a US deputy). Nor have any small states nominated any of their citizens as candidates either. In both institutions there are issues of rotation and 'turns' between regions. When at a WHA meeting a Liberian delegate declared that the election of the WHO was a Western conspiracy, it divided the meeting and increased demands for rotation between regions. At the next election an African candidate was elected.

The broader the electoral college, the more the decisions are likely to be made on the basis of blocs than of individuals. Small states can be influential if they can deliver a block of votes. Often, they cannot. One example can be taken from a WHO election for the position of regional director in the Western Pacific region. The regional office was based in the Philippines. The PIFS decided it would back Dr Colin Tukuitonga, a public health expert from Niue who was educated and trained in New Zealand; he had been DG of the Pacific Community, the regional scientific organization, since 2014, and was well known in the region. He had the support of Australia and New

Zealand so his candidature was not exclusively backed by the Pacific Islands. He wanted to change the emphasis of the region, with greater attention to the impact of climate change, and also, more specifically, to non-communicable diseases such as diabetes and heart disease which were prevalent in the islands. However, the PIFS could not hold its members together. As the time for the vote neared, it was evident that the unanimity had fractured in response to energetic campaigning by the Japanese candidate who was able to offer benefits in return for votes, such as an airport extension in the Solomon Islands. PNG and the Solomon Islands had defected quickly and others were expected to follow (Krishnamurthi, 2018). As a WHO official remarked: "Small states became skilful at playing different cards when candidates arrived with 'pots of money' … it's not ethical to make promises to five candidates. But that's politics" (interview with WHO official).

Facilitating mutual assistance and alliances

The WHO and the WIPO are both specialist agencies of the UN with headquarters in Geneva; they work within the continuing arrangements of specialist agencies. They both have around 190 member states. They are membership-based and are, in terms often expressed, member-driven organizations. Both have leaders elected by the member states. For a long time the election was held by members of an inner-management committee: the EB in the WHO and the CoCo in the WIPO. Both had a rolling membership and was the continuing body that oversaw its activities. In the past the recommendation of the EB/CoCo was sent to the WHA or the Ministerial Council for approval; it was never withheld. In 2016 the WHO changed its rules. The EB interviewed candidates and reduced the number to three and sent their names to the WHA for an election.

Leading an organization with 190 members is a challenge for any DG. The members have different interests and views, different strategies and capacities, and different levels of interest. Yet the DGs must cater for all. The WHO's mission declares that 'Health for All' is its target. They must maintain a balance between those with strong voices and those with pressing needs. Health will always be an evocative topic, a matter of life and death in which all of a population has a rather direct stake. When a lethal virus appears, everyone suddenly gets really interested in the way the DG of the WHO has managed resources and international relationships. IP is a more intangible product that only a few cognoscenti really understand in detail. Its significance is often concealed by its complexity, but it is also a subject where member states have a real interest in outcomes and the need for a DG to chart a path remains difficult. Apart from the occasions when DGs must respond to external events such as pandemic – and they can be overwhelming – they will respond to and shape the demands of their member states. It is perhaps inevitable that the big players demand the greatest attention.

The secretariats have staff ranging from around 5,000 (the WIPO) to 8,000 (the WHO). In both IOs there is a dominant discipline. In the WHO, medicine rules; most leading officials are medically trained, with an expertise in public health, epidemiology, and infectious diseases. In the WIPO, lawyers with a specialism in IP dominate the key levels of the organization. The staff of ICSs are generally professional and career appointees and in both cases are treated with suspicion by member states, accused of trying to manipulate them, having their own agenda, or of being under the control of the US, China, developed countries, professional associations, or anyone else who can be used to attack the secretariat. Like the IMO, they are both therefore recognizable as technical IOs with levels of expertise in specific areas with a need to work within the constraints of a diverse membership where the membership *is* the IO.

So the dynamics are different, particularly on formal occasions such as meetings of the WHA and the EB meeting, from the economic IOs discussed in the previous chapter. In its original conception an EB meeting was to constitute 32 members, initially described as experts, nominated by their countries in a personal capacity and not as national 'representatives'. That distinction has long been discarded. So too has the concept of an EB as a small executive committee. Now any member state can attend and speak at an EB meeting. So too can registered representatives of NGOs, whether they are Business Interest NGOs (BINGOs) or Pastoralists Indigenous NGOs (PINGOs). They just cannot vote. An EB can have several hundred registered attendees. They include industry and civil society, medical and patient bodies (the latter sometimes seen as stalking horses for the former). Some NGO representatives would even be seconded as members of a national delegation (discussed later).

Both leaders and secretariats are concerned to ensure that member states can be adequately represented at these key meetings. The WHO pays the costs of all members of the EB to attend, regardless of the country from which they come. It also pays for at least one delegate to attend the WHA from developing states. However, even that support cannot necessarily provide the expertise needed to understand, let alone participate, in the debates. When the additional cleavages are added, between the local delegates who are normally foreign affairs officers, and the health officials who will attend the WHA, the difficulties abound. The members of the local delegation may have done the groundwork for any agreement and might appreciate the diplomatic consequences; the members of national capitals are the subject experts.

Familiarizing new arrivals with the modes of the IO is one continuing practice. The WHO provides mission briefings four to five times a year. The

Country Cooperation Branch provides information on the WHO, and acts as an entry point so the member state officials can make connections with the technical departments. Few of the delegates to the WHO are doctors, or even health attachés. Even a country like Australia, better resourced than many, will send a second secretary to many WIPO meetings. Sections of the WHO argue that they are responsible for helping new delegates find their way through the processes of the organization:

'We try to help negotiate a way ahead, prior to actual negotiations. We're the process police. If members say we want to get here, and Legal say there is a barrier, my job is to find a way to allow member states to get what they want. I'm a facilitator, the good guy. Small states have no idea of process; they need us for different reasons. We take it from the beginning and walk them through the stages. We can provide support in writing resolutions, tell them they need to talk to like-minded states (there is no point going on your own), how to set up negotiations, ways of garnering support.'

A different section of the WHO, the Department of Country Cooperation, also works with the countries to develop the Country Cooperation Strategies. The first lines of contact may be the regional offices, but the HQ branch can act as a backstop.

The WIPO secretariat was well aware of the difficulties of the small states in an area where the benefits were not as obvious as in areas of health. The WIPO, a senior officer explained, had two mandates. The first was the protection and maintenance of the systems of patents devised over 150 years in a series of treaties that had been gathered under the WIPO's auspices. The second, more recent, responsibility was to help developing countries develop their capacities to protect their own trademarks and copyright over areas such as designs, fashions, and reggae. The WIPO had four pillars it sought to build. A senior WIPO executive argued that the member states needed:

'the message that the developing world should use it. Those where … the developing goal is weak or feeble, we help them. In which way? Basically, through four or five pillars or areas. (1) is the so-called national IP study. We tell them – we help them to develop their own [national] strategy put the idea of developing the IP in their national strategy for development. Every country in the world, they have some sort of plan, sometimes, not very often really, it's written but there is a plan there. So the idea is to develop an IP strategy that should be … compatible, coherent … We have around – I have a list with me here.

Around 60 countries with IP strategy. The green ones are we already have a national IP strategy.

So that gives us the possibility to establish a framework to work with them in future for the coming years on their IP. So this is one of the pillars. The second is the office, the national IP office. We make a diagnostic of how the IP office is working in terms of software, in terms of personnel, and this stuff. After that, the diagnostic will help them to improve too. We put money for that. This is usually done with external consultants. The third area is the legal. So we check the current rules on IP. For instance, if 30 years ago, 50 years ago, we had gone to Jamaica. We would have told them "look, you need to establish your national copyright system". So we help them to develop this and to update the rules.

In the fourth area, it's capacity building, basically human capacity building. We train people, we educate people around the world. The most important one is through the academy. We have an academy here in WIPO. We have face-to-face courses and distant-learning courses. Only last year we had almost 60,000 people train through distant-learning courses. Different courses, from basic IP rules and regulations, up to sophisticated ones.'

At times there were more specific courses for regions. The official added:

'but that's our job, to help them to develop those areas. For instance, how we do it, usually we organise the staff of the region or sub-region. Regional [sub-regional] meetings once per year or once every two years with all the people involved from those countries. Let's say for example, the small – the Pacific Islands, that is a sub-region. So they organize every two years, a meeting over there. We pay for that. We bring all the people ... two or three per country. We organize the meeting and I will usually attend the meeting for it changes views, it changes experiences, and we educate them. This is putting aside the regular courses that we are providing through the academy, the distant-learning courses.'

There were other modes of assistance, the WIPO official noted:

'For instance, a couple of weeks – two weeks ago was here, the director of the Samoa office. It was the first time ever that he came to WIPO. He didn't know anything about WIPO. So I was with him for almost the entire afternoon. Telling basic but with more details. Clearly, he will be back now in Samoa, having in the back of his mind that this is important for them. So he will participate. Because before, they didn't participate in this meeting. They were invited but they declined.

So this is the way that we help them. It's not enough, it's not perfect. But we try to do so.'

The WTO TRIPs agreement had established minimum standards for IP, patents, and trademarks. The member states needed to know how they could provide sound rules. Of course, all states could not be treated the same. The WIPO put developing countries into three groups:

- those that understood IP and took action – they were mostly in Latin America;
- those that did not understand IP; and
- those that were unaccustomed to the concept of patents.

The task of the WIPO was to assist the states to develop. The most pressing demands and areas of friction were over the patents and pricing of medicines and the need to persuade the small states of the potential value. Without the WIPO it is likely these areas would remain unexposed. Even with it there are issues because it is essentially an area of soft law. Given the increasing volatility of opinions there is little likelihood of a broad treaty on IP. The narrow range of the treaty for IP on materials to assist the blind was difficult enough to bring to conclusion. Nevertheless, any development agenda demands a series of small steps in areas of broad agreement before progress is made.

It is within this context that we need to understand relations between the IOs and many of the small states. Not all member states are represented in Geneva. So both the WHO and the WIPO have to devise means of keeping their members informed. They provide all papers online, so countries may not have to wait for the weeks it can take to mail. Or they stream their workshops and provide webinars so that all countries can efficiently keep informed. When delegations are sent, the WHO provides staff to explain what happens, to assist in developing tactics, to cost proposals. But in these circumstances the officials in capitals will always be dealing with local and immediate problems rather than more distant and perhaps less obviously pressing demands over which their impact is limited.

Small states, especially when members of the WHO EB or WIPO's CoCo, are typically looking for help in order to navigate a complex and technical process with limited capacity. There are invariably offers aplenty. At the WHO's EB meetings there will be a wide range of representatives registered for interested bodies. One description refers to them as PINGOs and BINGOs. They may speak but not vote and they can move motions as long as a member of the EB or CoCo seconds the proposals. In a number of areas where the delegates have little interest or knowledge, the NGOs will provide statements to be read, motions to be moved. It provides the delegates with a position to present and, as most of the proceedings constitute reading of statements from member states rather than actual debate, their lack of knowledge may not be exposed. As a WIPO officer commented on:

> 'NGOs coming to you and saying: "Here on one page is all you need to know about patent law harmonization. So you don't have to read those three documents or the 60-page documents. That's all you need to read." The [delegates from small member states] are very susceptible, very vulnerable.' (Interview with ICS)

The process is described as serial ventriloquism. It can even be extended to delegates proposing motions provided by members of the secretariat who want to put on the record the need for additional resources and have that need recognized by the EB or CoCo. Such actions tend to be regretted by directors general but defended by those staff who adopt the practice as simply fulfilling their obligations to advance their agenda.

Widespread NGOs involvement may also hogtie the IOs too as the depth of the suspicions between these groups can stymie initiatives. The WHO secretariat wanted to establish a world health forum that would allow both PINGOs and BINGOs to participate in exchanges of views with member states and secretariat staff. The intention was not to pass resolutions or determine policy but to provide informed debate. The delegates from the PINGOs were loathe to support any forum that could legitimize the presence of industry groups, particularly big pharma, in what they thought should be a government arena, even though it would have given them an opportunity to more openly advocate their causes. They preferred to say nothing than let their opponents say anything. The proposal lapsed, to the regret of the secretariat who had developed the proposition.

BINGOs and PINGOs are not the only cause of complexity in these IOs; IOs too can clash where their particular agenda and mission put their priorities and programmes in opposition to those of their confreres in other IOs. In 2013 (updated in 2020) the WHO, the WTO, and the WIPO had collaborated in the production of a joint paper on the development of generic medicines. When it was launched by the three DGs, their emphases were very different. The DG of the WTO stressed the need to abide by trade laws. The head of the WHO emphasized the need to ensure that the medicines were provided at a price that allowed access to all peoples who needed them and the need for that objective to remain a priority. The DG of the WIPO explained how important it was that the IP of patents was protected in order to ensure that companies received a return on their investment, or there would be no research and development to meet future crises. Same topic, same paper, common good intentions, but emphases that were inevitably divergent. Each DG legitimately argued the case of their member states, or rather those organizations and interests within the same member states who were served by the work of the IO. The differences, said a leading WIPO official, were the variation of disciplines and the fact that each IO had its own constituencies who had limited interest the missions of the others. The WHO utilizes innovation; the WIPO seeks to encourage it. The point in relation to SIDS is that while there is an imperative for IOs to help them engage, the complexity of the interaction is a substantial barrier to overcome.

New vulnerabilities and small states

Size-related vulnerabilities in the domain of health and IP are not new. But the idea that small states might take coordinated global action in IOs to serve their agenda is. Indeed, it is so new that by and large IOs have pushed the idea much harder than SIDS themselves. Nevertheless, some policymakers have leapt at the potential for these policy domains to fall within the purview of the SIDS agenda. The remainder of this chapter considers how they have done so and the challenges they have faced along the way.

Rhetorical action

The types of rhetorical action that we have seen employed in relation to climate change are mirrored in the policy areas of health and IP. Take this example from the WHO:

> SIDS face a unique combination of challenges due to their small size, geographical remoteness, and fragile environment and also have less resilience to natural disasters such as cyclones and earthquakes. Climate change poses both economic and existential threats to SIDS. Particularly at risk from rising sea levels are the Maldives, Tuvalu, Marshall Islands and Kiribati where over 95% of land is below five metres above sea level. This may result in population displacement and migration, bringing with it political, social, and health issues. Due to the contained nature of SIDS, the potential impact of infectious disease outbreaks on the population is severe. While numerous SIDS have universities and medical schools, a brain drain of health professionals away from these states exists. Furthermore, smaller states, territories or areas may not be able to produce the diverse variety of medical staff at the level required, and rely on other countries for training specialists. (WHO/CCU/17.08)

Similar rhetoric is apparent in discussions about IP, with the added complication that technical assistance from the WIPO often depends on 'a very specific perception about what intellectual property rights are and what they can achieve' (Forsyth and Farran, 2015: 37) that may be at odds with traditional knowledge, especially in the Pacific.

The point in both cases is that the language of vulnerability is easily transferred from issue to issue. The problem is that the 'competent performance' of this rhetoric is limited by human resource constraints in Geneva and as a result generalist diplomats may struggle to keep up with highly technical policy domains and to understand what the possible options are. On health, they are much more effective when working with regional offices. But in Geneva they are sometimes treated with a resigned tolerance by the delegates of larger countries and even by those officials who are trying to help them. What they get in return are the benefits of not having to work in isolation. If they have the time to absorb it, the IO can provide information, expertise, knowledge of international experiences, a developed health plan, and at times funding for areas like medical education that they cannot otherwise afford. They will also get specialized plans for their areas of priority such as NCDs. They can have officials on call dedicated to their case. At the WIPO they can receive assistance in developing an IP plan, support in creating the infrastructure, and education online. None of these benefits are readily available except through a multilateral organization that can inform small states with a minimum of transaction costs. But they have to be able to access this assistance and shape it to their needs.

Peripheral involvement has led to an innate suspicion among small states of these and other similar IOs whose structures were developed by and for large states. It is not without some justification. Thus, at the WHO the small states thought that an EB of just 32 was too exclusive and pushed for its extension. The result was that under the new rules it became a mini Health Assembly. Anyone was allowed to talk or move a motion as long as the motion was seconded by an EB member. Several hundred observers (and potential participants) were registered for EB meetings, leading to some overwrought occasions when a tearful DG complained that the members did not trust the secretariat, and a South American delegate sang back, 'Don't cry for me, Director General'!

Collaboration

SIDS have a shared interest and presence in New York capable of coordinating action on climate change. In economic IOs they have much more diverse interests and only limited capacity to coordinate their efforts. In relation to health and IP they have considerable common interests, including with wealthier small states, but they rarely have the capacity to pursue them as a group. Part of this stems from the rules and traditions of IOs (discussed previously), and part from the limited presence they have in Geneva. But the important point for our story is that instances of SIDS collaboration in the WHO and the WIPO is the exception not the norm. In the WHO the new DG met with the members of the FOSS which was convened by Singapore, where size, not wealth or development, was the criterion for membership. However, the FOSS has a large membership – more than 100 states with populations of less than 10 million – and has multiple interests not all of which are aligned with the SIDS.

Aside from regional offices, a key reason for the absence of SIDS collaboration relates to the way these IOs use categories. The WHO, for instance, has no unique set of categories or groupings. A WHO official argued: "Who are we to categorize countries. We categorize our operations and our roles. Member states are member states. We let them choose what they want to be: SIDS, LDCs." The WHO works through existing groups whether the FOSS with 100 members or SIDS with half that number. Its staff will meet the groupings before a Health Assembly to provide any assistance, including explaining the way the programme budget worked. The secretariat is there to assist but it is limited. The groupings do provide a means of determining access. When there was a new DG who wanted to meet the small states, it was organized through the FOSS. The WHO has no separate agenda for SIDS.

In the WIPO it is more explicit that there are regional groupings with whom the administration interacts. Briefing a focal point has the benefit of ensuring that a message is duly spread. In the past the DG's chief of staff was responsible for liaising with the groupings who could then inform the members. The development push in the WIPO came from the big developing countries and as a result a development division was created in the IO. The WIPO took on the UN developed and developing country categories and did not differentiate within them. They had a mandate. A WIPO official reflected:

'It was a big political fight, but they succeeded and now we have a committee especially devoted to development. It's called CDIP committee on intellectual property development. Out of this process 45 recommendations, very specific recommendations, came. So now our job is to implement these recommendations. That's part of the regular work of WIPO.'

When they chose pilot schemes they were in larger countries: Egypt, Namibia, Ecuador, and Sri Lanka. The Pacific countries, where the returns from IP are smaller, were at the margins. A WIPO official noted: "I don't think even the people who push for development think about SIDS. SIDS could benefit more than they are in this group" (interview with WIPO official). It was not surprising, when there was so much leeway to make up, that the WIPO and the developing countries first tackled the big places. SIDS here neither had the heft nor the economy to put themselves in the front of the queue. The point in both cases is that where the SIDS fought for and won a distinct category in the UN and the WTO in particular, the constitutive norm has had only a limited impact on these technical IOs where their presence is minimal.

Despite the absence of collaboration in practice, the potential for SIDS to coordinate in these IOs in the same way they have on climate change is there. In recent years the WHO European Regions created a small countries initiative. The eight members of the initiative are: Andorra, Cyprus, Iceland, Luxembourg, Malta, Monaco, Montenegro, and San Marino. All have populations of 1 million or less. Echoing our emphasis on process, the initiative was founded in 2013 at an informal meeting during the 63rd session of the WHO Regional Committee for Europe. San Marino organized a high-level meeting in July 2014. The key to its success has been the ability to combine the rhetoric of vulnerability with procedural mechanisms, as a former Chief Medical Officer articulated:

> 'It was I think a little bit of politics. The regional director was up for her renewal, eight small states is eight votes and she committed to do something specific for the small states. San Marino put up the initial funding.' (Interview with former Chief Medical Officer from a small state)

Attempts to create an African SIDS group are also being discussed. The key caveat here is, of course, that the European group are not SIDS. We nevertheless take this development in the WHO as evidence that the discourse of vulnerability has become so pervasive that even wealthier small states have begun to perform it.

Active participation

A key reason why SIDS have not had the impact on the WHO and the WIPO is that they only have a limited presence in Geneva. And what small capacity they do have is typically dedicated to the WTO, the UNCTAD, and for some, like Maldives, the UNHRC. The WHO and the WIPO are peripheral interests to diplomatic posts that are already peripheral to their main foreign policy priorities in New York and to a lesser extent London and Brussels. This trend to prioritize New York and trade is similar for many states – as a WHO official noted it is difficult to maintain the attention of ambassadors in Geneva, although he added, we got their attention when my DG praised President Mugabe. The problem is magnified for the smallest states because they have limited capacity in the first place. Their missions usually have between two and four staff with responsibilities that go far beyond Geneva. Many are not present in Geneva at all. A very few missions may have an identified health attaché from the health department. There will seldom be an expert on IP; that responsibility will usually be allocated to a generalist diplomat, often a second secretary, who attends meetings but is not in a position to negotiate. For information on IP developments at the WIPO most small states will often rely on focal points within collective groups (that is, CARICOM). Even when there are schemes to assist and subsidize delegations, by means of providing cheap accommodation, as the Commonwealth does in Geneva for small countries, they do not all see a benefit in being there. And while the Commonwealth provides a trade expert to help small states, it does not provide expertise in health or IP.

At the WHO there is merit in free-riding as much of the action happens in the regions anyway. In the Pacific, for instance, NCDs are a primary concern. NCDs include heart and respiratory problems, cancer, and diabetes, often caused by high levels of smoking and poor diet. So the region has a number of specific programmes and priorities. The DG, Tedros, established an Independent Global High Level Commission on NCDs in February 2018, comprising heads of state and ministers. The WHO Regional Committee of the Western Pacific, which was created by the WHO in October 2019, includes ministers and practitioners. It listed as its objectives reducing measles and rubella (after a deadly outbreak of measles in Samoa), tackling HIV, and reducing smoking, and other initiatives included a plan to reduce NCDs with sets of targets. The sub-region also produced a number of manuals (for example, WHO, 2018). The point is that PSIDS were involved in the development of these programmes. But they did so as Pacific Island states not as part of the larger SIDS grouping.

In this respect too there is a contrast between the WIPO and the WHO. The WIPO is about the development of consistent and international rules for the protection of IP. It wants to extend IP to new areas where appropriate, but it still wants the one set of rules. So, its task is in part to introduce new countries to these rules, pointing out how they will benefit. In member states where there is little existing IP protection, there is no natural constituency. The recent development IP agenda may expand the issues and provide visibility; it does not of itself provide a natural or an informed group of interest. Nor is the interest likely to be restricted to any single department. The WHO responds to an inevitable set of demands; everyone has health problems, even if much of the time health neither has the most senior ministers, nor a central role nor the attention of national leaders. When in a crisis it becomes central to government, the years of comparative complacency and neglect may emerge. Apart from its normative role, the WHO responds to the particular conditions faced by its member states. Its programmes include country plans and it will insist on country ownership. It is prepared to take on operational roles, through its regional and country offices, to assist those member states that have limited capacity.

In this sense, both IOs have a common problem. Except at times of high crisis, such as COVID-19, neither policy area is at the fore in national priorities. Health ministries are seldom given to the leading cohort of ministers; they sit in the second rank, specialized, but unlikely to have the clout of finance ministers, defence secretaries, foreign affairs, or, these days, security. Any IO that works with health ministers will not usually have ready access to the top national decision-makers; even if a health minister is persuaded of the need for a programme, that is only the first stage. The WIPO is in an even harder position; IP may have a single office but the practical application of IP is spread, often tenuously, across departments with little central control. A visit from the WIPO has been known to provide the first time that IP practitioners from different departments have met. As a WIPO official noted: "It's common to find that the national IP office is a small department in a very low level in a ministry with no power" (interview with WIPO official). Who then pushes the IP case? DGs may sometimes be able to talk to presidents and prime ministers, but IP needs a continuing champion if it is to retain attention. These problems are not unique to SIDS. But their lack of capacity means that they are even less likely and able to dedicate resources to these more peripheral IOs. The consequence of their absence is that they have almost no influence.

Conclusion

SIDS have health and IP concerns. These concerns are shaped by and exacerbate their size. Both the WHO and the WIPO recognize these vulnerabilities and have an interest in addressing them. But very little has been done in the name of the SIDS as a group – as opposed to individual countries and regions – other than tokenistic statements and pamphlets. We have explained this absence by reference to the interaction between the rules and traditions of IOs on the one hand and the capacity constraints of SIDS on the other. As this book has been at pains to point out, despite their size SIDS can have considerable impact on certain issues and in certain IOs. But to do so they have to prioritize their scarce resources. Both the WHO and the WIPO are peripheral concerns for all states but this means they fall off the radar completely for the very smallest. They are rarely present individually and so have limited capacity to work together collaboratively. Despite the efforts of IOs to engage them, and in doing so increase their 'throughput' legitimacy, neither institution has found a way of getting SIDS to participate in great numbers. And, without the numbers, SIDS have very little weight.

7

Conclusion

This book has sought to explain the interaction between IOs and small states and how it has changed over the last three decades in particular. We used SIDS as a proxy for small states as they represent the smallest of the small; if these states want to be involved, however marginally, in the activities of IOs, then the findings on their strategies should be applicable to other slightly larger states too. Their experience reveals two perpetual dilemmas. SIDS argue they need to participate in IOs to safeguard their sovereignty, extract resources, and promote a permissive liberal order. The problem is that the costs of participation are disproportionately high for the smallest who face acute capacity constraints. The IOs' dilemma is that while the norms of sovereign equality and the right to development impel them to be inclusive of those who have been approved as members, the active participation of an increased membership can increase ineffectiveness due to gridlock and delay. IOs thus attempt to balance inputs and outputs by way of throughputs in order to include states in such a way that it enhances, rather than constrains, their effectiveness.

By competently performing their vulnerability SIDS are able to *both* demonstrate that they are functioning states worthy of system membership and illustrating that they require S&DT to remain viable, especially in the face of climate change. For IOs, the establishment of groupings, and thereby collective participation, represented here by the SIDS category or analogous examples like the SVEs at the WTO, allows them to achieve a level of support from its member states by way of 'throughputs': that is, adopting processes and practices that both include small states, thereby honouring their commitment to sovereign equality, but also sharing responsibilities for outcomes with them. Labels such as SIDS that incorporate otherwise disparate member states are therefore useful to both small member states and IOs even though the constitutive norm they represent – in this case, differentiated development – remains contested by larger and more powerful countries.

The existence of the label SIDS also reveals a number of internal problems. The countries we now call SIDS had a vision for collective action, and have put out their 'tentacles and planted SIDS issues' across the multilateral system, but we find no evidence of a shared grand strategy. Reflecting this ad-hoc emergence, or what Sharman (2017: 571) calls hierarchy 'à la carte', each IO has a different definition of what a small state is and some countries are considered small states on certain issues but not others. We explained this variation by reference to the various rules and traditions of each IO, the availability and support of friends and allies, and the differential capacity of SIDS themselves. So, for example, SIDS have been effective at the UNGA because they are all present in New York, the voting system maximizes their strength in numbers, and there are numerous NGOs willing to bridge capacity deficits, especially on climate change. By contrast, despite the efforts of the secretariat to include them, they are virtually inactive at the WIPO because they have a lessor presence in Geneva, they do not see IP rights as a priority issue, their response to IP initiatives will have a far more limited impact than that of larger countries, and there are few NGOs to support them.

This, in brief, is the explanation that we have presented over the previous chapters. Our account is avowedly interpretive. We started with the views and beliefs of the actors involved, from both SIDS and IOs, and developed our explanation based on their experiences. We focused on dilemmas because they both reveal intersubjective traditions and also allow comparison across countries and IOs (Boswell et al, 2019). We organized the material according to a heuristic that outlined the key features of the competent performance of vulnerability (rhetorical action, collaboration, and active participation) on the one hand and throughput legitimacy (promoting norms and principles, upholding rules, conventions and traditions; and facilitating mutual assistance and alliances) on the other. Our heuristic is an analytic device not a set of necessary and sufficient conditions. It helps us see the patterns across disparate and contingent practices and beliefs. It is not generalizable or predictive in a formal sense. But it nevertheless acts as a useful rule of thumb or intellectual shortcut that can illuminate the topic at hand (Boswell et al, 2019). We conclude by considering why our explanation matters, for scholars of SIDS, IOs, and anyone interested in the future of the LIO.

Does the performance of vulnerability produce real benefits for small states?

We started this book with a vignette that showed the PSIDS initiating and then shaping a debate on climate change and security at the UNSC in

2018. The vignette had two purposes: to introduce the dilemmas but also to demonstrate that the smallest members can make a difference in IOs even when opposed by larger and more powerful states. This latter issue – when, how, and why they can have an influence –has dominated the extant IR literature on small states. There is, however, little agreement on what it means to 'matter', either in IOs or more generally in interstate diplomacy.

Keohane (1969: 295–6) differentiated between: (i) system-determining states; (ii) system-influencing states; (iii) system-affecting states; and (iv) system-ineffectual states (see Long, 2017a, b for further discussion). The early work on the countries we now call SIDS in IOs (for example, Vital, 1967) was pessimistic about their influence because it tried to imagine them as an unaligned state capable of acting unilaterally (that is, a system-determining state) and concluded they could not possibly fulfil that role. There seems little point in our disputing this claim; none of the SIDS we discuss cross that threshold or come close to it. Even in the UNGA, for example, the small states worked in concert with larger states, like Sweden, who championed their cause and helped them overcome capacity deficits. This observation alone is scarcely a surprise because in the world of IOs no state, large or small, can act unilaterally. If consensus is the norm in IOs then every state that seeks to exert an influence must build a coalition. In other words, there are no 'system-determining states' in IOs. The question therefore is: can small states be system-influencing or system-affecting? The book shows that they can (see also Panke, 2013). They might be of greater or lesser importance on certain issues and in particular forums. They might lead on occasion and follow on others. But in either role they matter because without them consensus, and the legitimacy of IOs as global actors who work for *all* members, isn't possible.

So far this position could well align with most neo-realist accounts of the influence of small states. Where our interpretive account differs it that we argue that attempting to determine the consequences of actions creates a second-order problem: different actors have different views on who, when, and how somebody mattered. Relatedly, even if we agree that an actor mattered, the reasons may vary – they may matter because of the state they represent or they may matter because of their personality and the talents and characteristics they bring to the role they occupy – and these interpretations are impossible to untangle empirically even if we can make distinctions analytically (Hay, 2014). A final problem is that virtually all actors believe in their own agency (and were not slow in telling us about it in interviews); all of us need to feel that we mattered to some extent. Of course, when something goes wrong, all of a sudden, their best efforts and most noble intentions did not really matter at all.

We have sought to highlight, rather than supress, this problem in our book because our method assumes that it is unresolvable. For example, in Chapter 4 we saw how the competent performance of vulnerability has produced numerous real, tangible benefits for SIDS, both in process and financial terms. But we also saw that their main goal – loss and damage compensation – remains unrealized. The SIDS story is not over so perhaps they will get there in time. But the key point in relation to this book is that successes and benefits are always relative to the goals and aims of the actors themselves rather than an objective criterion for influence that we impose from outside.

SIDS diplomats debate among themselves whether their record of successes and failures across multiple issues and IOs makes the disproportionate costs of their participation worth it. We can see this in their varying presence in IOs: some free-ride while others participate and lead. We can also see this dilemma played out within countries over time. The example we used was Mauritius, who had taken a prominent leadership role in Geneva but had ultimately come to the conclusion that it had not brought them the benefits that they had hoped and were now opting for a lower profile. They may shift their position again in the future.

The question of when, how, and why SIDS participation has an influence, and whether this brings them real benefits, is further complicated by the fact that a permissive LIO is said to be key to their survival given their lack of military capabilities in particular. As we showed in Chapter 3, sovereign recognition can bring tangible benefits for SIDS because it allows them to develop niche industries in sovereignty sales: philately, economic passports, flags of convenience, and financial services. But this recognition would have less value if it were under persistent threat from larger states or if their membership could be withdrawn unilaterally by IOs. Only a select few SIDS see their participation in IOs as part of a broader strategy of maintaining an order that is permissive to their presence. Still, as we have shown, they think their membership is important even if it produces few other tangible benefits; otherwise, why would they participate?

Ultimately, an interpretive approach can never definitively resolve the 'do they matter' question in such a way that would satisfy realists, in much the same way that simplistic assumptions about power and rationality will never satisfy interpretivists. The question of when a state, or indeed agent, matters is always easier to distinguish in abstract analytical terms than it is to uncover empirically. When we dig into the detail of specific cases, as we have done here, these abstractions melt away amid the complex and contingent nature of everyday practices. Our account thus follows from the interpretive assumption that it is impossible to identify empirically the parameters of the 'action space'; where structure starts and agency stops. Likewise, there are no causal mechanisms in our analysis. Rather, our explanation turns on the interplay between individuals and intersubjective beliefs about what the purpose of IOs is and the role of states within them.

While we avowedly sidestep the question of whether the participation of small states such as SIDS produces real benefits in favour of a more qualified assessment –they matter on some issues in some IOs and they have realized some benefits but have not achieved everything they sought – we can more confidently say how our account of their participation in IOs matters for existing scholarship. There are two main implications from our account for scholars of small states. First, we add to recent scholarship (Sharman, 2015, 2017) on the existence of small states under anarchy by illustrating that their survival is not merely a by-product of an international regime of norms; SIDS are actors in their own right and their participation in the processes of IOs has brought them recognition and benefits from the international system. Again, we are not saying they have achieved either of these things unilaterally. The permissive LIO, which they helped shape (Getachew 2019), is key to explaining why they became states in the first place and continues to facilitate their participation in IOs. But they are also key actors in the maintenance of that order and the constitutive label SIDS and the S&DT it implies is evidence of that. Second, we also add to the literature on the creative diplomacy of small states by showing that the well-documented strategies of European states can also be adapted for SIDS, even if they do not seek the same 'status' (de Carvalho and Neumann, 2015). Being recognized as a distinct group defined by its structural weaknesses has ostensibly entrenched SIDS' lowly status, but it has also brought benefits. Indeed, in the context of climate change (Vaha, 2015), those facing extinction argue that highlighting their vulnerability is key to their survival.

SIDS as norm entrepreneurs

The recognition that the countries we now call SIDS have created a constitutive label to aid their participation in IOs and by extension their development highlights that the material we present also has implications for the study of norms and in particular Towns' (2010, 2012) claim that norm diffusion can occur 'from below'. As outlined, the constitutive label SIDS rests on the norm of differentiated development and the belief that these countries require S&DT due to their unique conditions, including their small population size and island geography. The claim that small islands with developing economies face particular challenges, has been central to their rhetorical action across multiple IOs. It builds on existing norms – sovereign equality and the right to development – while adapting them to their specific needs. In doing so SIDS have sought to increase the perception of their vulnerability. Our emphasis on increased vulnerability is the key to our contribution to the literature on norm diffusion.

Our emphasis on agency highlights the importance of persuasion, which is a mainstay of the norms literature. We use the word *competent* to denote the importance of persuasion. The importance of competence highlights that the case must be embedded in existing processes in order to perceived by others as substantive. The creation of the label would not have occurred if SIDS had not couched their claim to vulnerability as an extension of existing principles – the right to development and the sovereign equality of states. But they also had to choose the right forums and approach within existing rules, and this meant active participation in the processes and practices of IOs. We posit that if their performance of vulnerability had invoked different existing norms, been less coordinated, or was pursued outside multilateral forums, then the label might either not exist or might have an alternate meaning.

Having made this claim, the important caveat is that we are not saying that the other forms of norm diffusion – for example, learning, emulation, and competition (Marsh and Sharman, 2009; Maggetti and Gilardi, 2016) – are not relevant for this case. Clearly individual SIDS and SVEs have learned from their success in the UN (Chapter 4) and attempted to replicate it across other IOs (Chapter 5), even if the results have been mixed (Chapter 6). Our account thus supports recent work on norm diffusion across IOs that highlights the importance of interconnectivity between formal and informal networks of actors (Sommerer and Tallberg, 2019). Likewise, IOs were active in creating an environment in which there was a possibility for a sympathetic hearing. Several IOs have sought to emulate the UN by pursuing a 'development agenda'; not all have proved to be fertile ground. There is always likely to a push and a pull: member states who want their case to be heard and a willing audience among the other member states or the secretariat (or better still, among both). In addition, competition between IOs seeking to remain relevant to a dwindling pool of 'developing' client states could explain their increased interest in SIDS. Some large states have sought to further their own agenda in IOs by supporting smaller ones. The point is, we are not seeking to refute the claim that these other explanations matter. Rather, each has important limitations for explaining this case.

An account, for instance, that privileged the explanatory power of learning would emphasize the contribution of SIDS to the operation of IOs. The rise of SIDS in the last 30 years has generally been accepted even though many within IOs see them as 'irritants', responsible for gridlocks and delays (Lewis, 2009), and that 'differentiated development' undermines the status of larger developing states (that is, the BRICS). But perhaps there is little opposition because the actual impact is limited mostly to areas where their case is unimpeachable – climate change – and is less influential where it is more contested, like trade. Likewise, while emulation offers some insights into the claims to exceptionalism employed by groupings of SIDS, it tells us very little about the variation and evolution of the definition of small state *between* IOs (Wiener, 2008: 63). It also assumes that the strong are the only drivers of norm emergence and diffusion. Finally, competition between IOs can perhaps explain why the strong are interested in assisting SIDS, but it has less empirical purchase when seeking to account for why some states are interested in being classified as small in some IOs, but not others.

Our emphasis on persuasion echoes our interpretive approach (Schwartz-Shea and Yanow, 2013; Bevir et al, 2013; Lynch, 2013; Bevir and Rhodes, 2015). Much of the diffusion literature is based on large N quantitative work (Marsh and Sharman, 2009; Maggetti and Gilardi, 2016). One distinguishing feature of an interpretive approach is that it is more open to the value of qualitative, fine-grained, and historicist analysis. Empirically we focused on the interaction between the dilemmas, which themselves arise from decisions taken years ago, including for SIDS to become independent and for the architects of IOs to establish operating procedures that still have binding force on member states, and the practices that shape both routines and expectations in more recent times. We conceived of these intersubjectively held traditions (or norms) as co-constituted by agents in everyday practice: actors are socialized into traditions but also alter them as they interpret and enact them. Agents are thus 'situated' – actions and practices do not take place on a *tabula rasa*. Our claim, that the competent performance of vulnerability in institutional settings can lead to norm emergence and diffusion from below, thus follows a well-worn interpretive logic: that the meanings and beliefs of situated agents, embedded within existing traditions (norms), causes them to act in certain ways. When traditions conflict, they present actors with a dilemma. As actors seek to resolve these dilemmas in practice they alter existing norms. This is an explicitly causal claim based on the principle of 'meaning holism' rather than isolating atomized 'mechanisms' (Bevir and Rhodes, 2015). We thus support the claim that norm diffusion can occur 'from below' while also showing that it can be achieved by moving down hierarchies in a permissive order. But this recognition is only possible if we adopt the view of agency that we have used here.

Do throughputs increase the legitimacy of IOs?

The UNSC vignette clearly illustrates the dilemma that the participation of SIDS, as a proxy for a rapidly expanding and active membership, creates for IOs. The UNSC is an institutional manifestation of the 'old club model' because it provides disproportionate power to a select few large states (or at least states that were large when the UN was created in the aftermath of the Second World War). And yet, the PSIDS (a subset of a subset) have successfully put the nexus between climate change and security on the UNSC agenda on three occasions – 2008, 2011, and 2018 – despite the fact that there is no prospect of their achieving a binding resolution due to opposition from China in particular. Moreover, the preference for consensus and a desire to be inclusive of the entire membership led to the G77 being silenced by the veto of the PSIDS. For those who want to see institutions like the UN take decisive decisions and actions, this example illustrates that small states can indeed be an unwanted distraction on the precious time of larger states and at worst an irritant responsible for gridlock and delay. They could stop action but not generate it in the UNSC (but they have generated it in the realm of Oceans, for example). The problem, as we have outlined, is that the exclusionary nature of the old club model came to be increasingly seen as illegitimate. IOs had to become more inclusive as their expanding membership made demands for real participation. The result is an inherent tension between input legitimacy (through member involvement) on the one hand and output legitimacy (effective actions) on the other.

Building on the work of scholars such Schmidt, we have sought to show that IOs have sought to balance inputs and outputs by way of 'throughputs'. Our use of the term throughput is different to Schmidt and others working on the EU because we are primarily interested in the inclusion of member states, not citizens. But our emphasis on the uses of processes and practices of inclusion has affinities with that body of work. The advantage is that it allows us to show that rather than resolve their inherent dilemma in favour of either 'inputs' or 'outputs' (Agné et al, 2015; Tallberg and Zürn, 2019), IOs seek to devise ways to balance these imperatives. They still rely primarily on a few large and rich states for resources (only the WHO depends on extensive philanthropic donations to survive). At the same time, for multilateral cooperation to function effectively, IOs have to accommodate assertive emerging powers and more active participation by a large number of small states. The creation of the SIDS category is emblematic of this attempt at balancing. By formalizing the SIDS as a grouping IOs are able to include them while also streamlining their participation to reduce the impact on their effectiveness.

This account can explain why and how IOs are paying greater attention to the whole range of member states and why they often work through a multiplicity of groupings. Some are regional, some economic, some commodity-based. All must be serviced. SIDS is emblematic of the process; they are members whose voice must be given a time and whose demands are considered regardless of their economic or political power. The more organized the grouping, the more relevant its concerns, the more pressing the needs, the more it may be heard.

If, as we have asserted, that the practices and processes of IOs need to be regarded as proper and appropriate by those member states who work within its systems, then it is the prerequisite to any effective action. It will not be an end in itself but a means to allow an IO to pursue its mission. Secretariats are invariably regarded with greater or lesser suspicion by member states. Some, particularly those at the WTO, are given no scope for initiative; others, at the IMF, have their independent expertise more frequently acknowledged. The members of the secretariat will work with all members ("it's our job" said one senior WIPO official when asked why they did it when there was little response). The internal legitimacy created through open and accepted practices can provide a more effective and less suspicious working environment. That is the point. It is not likely to mitigate against the broader complaints that challenge the very existence of IOs themselves; criticisms that posit a democratic deficit are of a different nature. They ask should IOs exist; here our concern has been how they work.

Time will tell whether IOs can safeguard and increase their legitimacy as global actors. In the interim, our conceptualization of throughput legitimacy and how it is used to facilitate the participation of SIDS adds to the literature on IOs which emphasizes that they are institutions (not arenas) whose processes are shaped by a host of actors (for example, Finnemore, 1996; Martin and Simmons, 1998). Thus far this literature has focused on the influence of the big countries, the secretariat, and NGOs. We add the smallest members of the multilateral system, using SIDS as our proxy. In doing so we show how the influence of both the secretariat and NGOs has facilitated their involvement by reducing SIDS capacity deficits. Our account therefore provides a more rounded picture of the plural nature of influence in IOs and how this has increased over recent decades.

Canaries in the global governance coal mine

The significance of SIDS for IOs shows that even the smallest states can tell us something important about the international system because they are a proxy for active membership or the 'strength of the weak' (Katzenstein, 1985). Our book thus serves as a direct challenge to Waltz's (1979) dictum that the discipline of IR should focus on a 'few big and important things'. It is precisely because SIDS are small that the attention they attract in IOs matters. A LIO is premised on the principle that all people and states are equal and have the right to development. Clearly it does not deliver on that promise. But it has to have a story of about how those principles and values might be achieved if it is to maintain the pretence that it is 'rules based'. Most SIDS do not have canaries, coal, or mines (Connell, 2013: 1). Yet this inconvenient truth has not stopped them being used as a metaphoric gauge of impending climate catastrophe. The same can be said for the system of multilateral global governance. Small states are emblematic of how permissive the LIO is. If small states start to be ignored by IOs, then it heralds the return of a more transactional, self-help, system.

We conclude therefore by suggesting IR and IO scholars should moderate their fetish for great powers. Dismissing small states flouts the general social science approach to selecting cases – representativeness and variation – by focusing on exceptional cases (large states) (Veenendaal and Corbett, 2015). Scholarship that proceeds on this basis can only ever tell part of the story. A full account must include the views and experiences of big and small, strong and weak, developed and developing. This book adds to the effort to rebalance the scales. IR has had many turns – sociological, linguistic, cultural, and historical – but has not adequately considered the differential impact and experience of state size. Where it tries to do so it is hopelessly Eurocentric (Acharya, 2014). The story of small states in IOs can help address both gaps. Our aim is to mainstream the study of hitherto neglected people and places (Baldacchino, 2018). By studying the participation of SIDS in IOs we learn something about the LIO too.

Notes

Chapter 1

[1] Sweden (president); the Netherlands, Kazakhstan, the UK, Peru, the US, France, Russia, Bolivia, Ethiopia, China, Cote d'Ivoire, Equatorial Guinea, Poland, Kuwait, Nauru, Maldives, Trinidad and Tobago, Sudan.

[2] See Rezvani (2014) on non-sovereign territories.

[3] The officials came from: AOSIS, ComSec, FAO, IMF, IMO, OECS, PIDF, PIFS, UNDP, WB, WHO, WTO, and WIPO. In many cases we interviewed far more than one official from each IO.

[4] The small states were: Antigua and Barbuda, Bahamas, Barbados, Brunei, Botswana, Cape Verde, Costa Rica, Cyprus, Estonia, El Salvador, FSM, Fiji, Guatemala, Guyana, Haiti, Iceland, Jamaica, Kiribati, Maldives, Malta, Malawi, Mauritius, Nauru, Palau Samoa, Seychelles, Solomon Islands, St Kitts and Nevis, St Vincent and the Grenadines, Tuvalu, Tanzania, and Vanuatu. In many cases we interviewed more than one diplomat from each small state.

[5] For example, the UK, Australia, Switzerland, Sweden, Norway, Canada, and New Zealand.

[6] This case-based approach to political judgement is often referred to as casuistry or casuistical analysis (see Jonsen and Toulmin, 1988).

Chapter 2

[1] Just a few examples: IMF, 'Asia and Pacific Small States; Raising Potential Growth and Enhance Resilience to Shocks', 20 February 2013; IMF, 'The Role of the IMF in Supporting the Implementation of the Post-2015 Development Agenda', 17 August 2015; IMF, '2017 Staff Guidance Note on the Fund's Engagement with Small Developing States', January 2018.

Chapter 3

[1] See the Republic of the Marshall Islands Budget book 2016–21, p 13. Available from: http://rmi-mof.com/wp-content/uploads/2017/02/MTBIF-RMI-2016-2021-2.pdf.

[2] Australia, Cook Islands, Micronesia, Kiribati, Nauru, New Zealand, Niue, Palau, Papua New Guinea, Marshall Islands, Samoa, Solomon Islands, Tonga, Tuvalu, and Vanuatu.

[3] Morocco was hosting COP22, and it was a period where it was more 'receptive' to these submissions (interview with an academic aware of the events).

[4] The three-step approach is one according to which, before taking any measures on GHG reduction, there would be a need to: (1) collect data regarding emissions from shipping; (2) analyse the data collected; then (3) the data collected will form the base for policy decisions. It was adopted at MEPC68.

5   The objectives contained in this second document are much more detailed and less ambitious; the long-term pathway proposed is: (1) to maintain international shipping's annual CO_2 emissions below 2008 levels; (2) to reduce CO_2 emissions per tonne-km, as an average across international shipping, by at least 90 per cent by 2050, compared with 2008; and (3) to reduce international shipping's annual CO_2 emissions by at least 70 per cent, pursuing efforts for 100 per cent reduction by 2050 compared with 2008, as a point on a continuing linear trajectory of CO_2 emissions reduction.

6   See, for instance, resolutions MEPC 64/2/18, MEPC 67/2/13, MEPC 67/4/9.

Chapter 5

1   This was acknowledged during the debate over IDA18 replenishment and confirmed in IDA19 under the overarching theme of 'Ten Years to 2030: Growth, People, and Resilience', finalized in December 2019. See the documents under IDA18 and IDA19 at https://ida.worldbank.org/replenishments/ida19.

References

Abbott, A.D. (2004) *Methods of Discovery Heuristics for the Social Sciences*, New York: W.W. Norton and Company.

Abbott, K. and Snidal, D. (1998) 'Why states act through formal international organizations', *Journal of Conflict Resolution*, 42(1): 3–32.

Acharya, A. (2014) 'Global International Relations (IR) and regional worlds: a new agenda for International Studies', *International Studies Quarterly*, 58(4): 647–59.

Adams, J. (2015) 'Reform at the World Bank', in P. Weller and Y.-C. Xu (eds) *The Politics of International Organisations: Views from Insiders*, New York: Routledge, pp 58–81.

Adams, T. (2006) 'The IMF: back to basics', in E.M. Truman (ed) *Reforming the IMF for the 21st Century*, Washington, DC: Peterson Institute for International Economies, pp 133–40.

Agné, H., Dellmuth, L.M., and Tallberg, J. (2015) 'Does stakeholder involvement foster democratic legitimacy in international organizations? An empirical assessment of a normative theory', *The Review of International Organizations*, 10(4): 465–88.

Aldrich, R. and Connell, J. (1998) *The Last Colonies*, New York: Cambridge University Press.

Alesina, A. and Spolaore, E. (2005) *The Size of Nations*, Boston, MA: MIT Press.

Apostolopoulos, Y. and Gayle, D.J. (2002) 'From MIRAB to TOURAB? Searching for sustainable development in the Maritime Caribbean, Pacific, and Mediterranean', in Y. Apostolopoulos and D.J. Gayle (eds) *Island Tourism and Sustainable Development: Caribbean, Pacific, and Mediterranean Experiences*, London: Praeger, pp 3–13.

Aquorau, T. (2019) *Fishing for Success: Lessons in Pacific Regionalism*, Canberra: Department of Public Affairs, Australian National University.

Armstrong, C. and Corbett, J. (2021) 'Climate change, sea level rise and maritime baselines: responding to the plight of low-lying Atoll states', *Global Environmental Politics*, 21(1): 89–107.

Armstrong, H.W. and Read, R. (2003) 'The determinants of economic growth in small states', *The Round Table*, 92(368): 99–124.

Arter, D. (2000) 'Small state influence within the EU: the case of Finland's "Northern Dimension Initiative"', *JCMS: Journal of Common Market Studies*, 38(5): 677–97.

Ashe, J.W., Van Lierop, R., and Cherian, A. (1999) 'The role of the alliance of small island states (AOSIS) in the negotiation of the United Nations framework convention on climate change (UNFCCC)', *Natural Resources Forum*, 23(3), Oxford: Blackwell Publishing.

Avant, D.D., Finnemore, M., and Sell, S.K. (2010) *Who Governs the Globe?* Cambridge: Cambridge University Press.

Bahety, S. and Mukiibi, J. (2017) 'WTO fisheries subsidies negotiations: main issues and interests of least developed countries', Geneva: CUTS International.

Bailes, A.J.K. and Thorhallsson, B. (2013) 'Instrumentalizing the European Union in small state strategies', *Journal of European Integration*, 35(2): 99–115.

Baldacchino, G. (2006) 'Managing the hinterland beyond: two ideal-type strategies of economic development for small island territories', *Asia Pacific Viewpoint*, 47(1): 45–60.

Baldacchino, G. (2009) 'Thucydides or Kissinger? A critical review of smaller state diplomacy', in A.F. Cooper and T.M. Shaw (eds) *The Diplomacies of Small States*, Basingstoke: Palgrave Macmillan, pp 21–40.

Baldacchino, G. (2010) *Island Enclaves: Offshoring Strategies, Creative Governance, and Subnational Island Jurisdictions*, Quebec: McGill-Queen's Press-MQUP.

Baldacchino, G. (2011) 'Surfers of the ocean waves: change management, intersectoral migration and the economic development of small island states', *Asia Pacific Viewpoint*, 52(3): 236–46.

Baldacchino, G. (2014) 'Small island states: vulnerable, resilient, doggedly perseverant or cleverly opportunistic?', *Études caribéennes*, 27–8. Available from: https://journals.openedition.org/etudescaribeennes/6984

Baldacchino, G. (2018) 'Mainstreaming the study of small states and territories', *Small States and Territories Journal*, 1(1): 3–16.

Baldacchino, G. and Bertram, G. (2009) 'The beak of the finch: insights into the economic development of small economies', *The Round Table*, 98(401):141–60.

Baldacchino, G. and Wivel, A. (2020) 'Small states: concepts and theories', in G. Baldacchino and A. Wivel (eds) *Handbook on the Politics of Small States*, Massachusetts: Edward Elgar, pp 2–19.

Baresic, D., Rehmatulla, N., and Smith, T. (2015) 'MEPC 68 Agenda item 5, reduction of GHG emissions from ships, an analysis of the plenary session', University Maritime Advice Service [online]. Available from: https://www.imo.org/en/MediaCentre/HotTopics/Pages/Reducing-greenhouse-gas-emissions-from-ships.aspx.

Barnett, M. and Finnemore, M. (2004) *Rules for the World*, Ithaca: Cornell University Press.

Baxter, P., Jordan, J., and Rubin, L. (2018) 'How small states acquire status: a social network analysis', *International Area Studies Review*, 21(3): 191–213.

Beetham, D. (1991) *The Legitimation of Power*, Hampshire: Palgrave Macmillan.

Benedict, B. (ed) (1967) *Problems of Smaller Territories*, London: Athlone Press.

Benwell, R. (2011) 'The canaries in the coalmine: small states as climate change champions', *The Round Table*, 100(413): 199–211.

Bertram, G. (2006) 'Introduction: the MIRAB model in the twenty-first century', *Asia Pacific Viewpoint*, 47(1): 1–13.

Bertram, I.G. and Watters, R.F. (1985) 'The MIRAB economy in South Pacific microstates', *Pacific Viewpoint*, 26(3): 497–519.

Betzold, C. (2010) '"Borrowing" power to influence international negotiations: AOSIS in the climate change regime, 1990–1997', *Politics*, 30(3): 131–48.

Betzold, C., Castro, P., and Weiler, F. (2012) 'AOSIS in the UNFCCC negotiations: from unity to fragmentation?', *Climate Policy*, 12(5): 591–613.

Bevir, M. and Hall, I. (2020) 'The English school and the classical approach: between modernism and interpretivism', *Journal of International Political Theory*, 16(2): 153–70.

Bevir, M. and Rhodes, R.A.W. (2010) *The State as Cultural Practice*, Oxford: Oxford University Press.

Bevir, M. and Rhodes, R.A.W. (eds) (2015) *Routledge Handbook of Interpretive Political Science*, London: Routledge.

Bevir, M., Daddow, O., and Hall, I. (2013) 'Introduction: interpreting British foreign policy', *The British Journal of Politics and International Relations*, 15(2): 163–74.

Bexell, M., Tallberg, J., and Uhlin, A. (2010) 'Democracy in global governance: the promises and pitfalls of transnational actors', *Global Governance: A Review of Multilateralism and International Organizations*, 16(1): 81–101.

Biermann, F. and Siebenhüner, B. (eds) (2009) *Managers of Global Change: The Influence of International Environmental Bureaucracies*, Cambridge: MIT Press.

Bishop, M.L. (2012) 'The political economy of small states: enduring vulnerability?', *Review of International Political Economy*, 19(5): 942–60.

Bishop, M.L. (2013) *The Political Economy of Caribbean Development*, Hampshire: Palgrave Macmillan.

Bishop, M.L. and Payne, A. (2012) 'Climate change and the future of Caribbean development', *The Journal of Development Studies*, 48(10): 1536–53.

Bishop, M.L., Girvan, N., Shaw, T.M., et al (2011) 'Caribbean regional integration', *Report by the UWI Institute of International Relations (IRR)*, UK Aid, Department for International Development (DFID), St Augustine, Trinidad and Tobago.

Bishop, M.L., Heron, T., and Payne, A. (2013) 'Caribbean development alternatives and the CARIFORUM–European Union economic partnership agreement', *Journal of International Relations and Development*, 16(1): 82–110.

Blokker, N.M. and Wessel, R.A. (2005) 'Editorial: updating international organizations', *International Organizations Law Review*, 2: 1–8.

Bohl, K. (2009) 'Problems of developing country access to WTO dispute settlement', *Chicago-Kent Journal of International and Comparative Law*, 9(1): 1–71.

Boswell, J. and Corbett, J. (2017) 'Why and how to compare deliberative systems', *European Journal of Political Research*, 56(4): 801–19.

Boswell, J., Corbett, J., and Rhodes, R.A.W. (2019) *The Art and Craft of Comparison*, New York: Cambridge University Press.

Boughton, J.M. (2001) *Silent Revolution: The International Monetary Fund, 1979–1989*, Washington: IMF.

Boughton, J.M. (2004) 'The IMF and the force of history: ten events and ten ideas that have shaped the institution', IMF Working Paper, WP/04/75, May.

Bowman, C. (2005) 'The Pacific Island nations: towards shared representation', in P. Gallagher, P. Low, and A.L. Stoler (eds) *Managing the Challenges of WTO Participation: 45 Case Studies*, Cambridge: Cambridge University Press, pp 450–8.

Bradford, C.I. and Linn, J. (eds) (2007) *Global Governance Reform*, Washington, DC: The Brookings Institution Press.

Braveboy-Wagner, J. (2007) *Small States in Global Affairs: The Foreign Policies of the Caribbean Community (CARICOM)*, New York: Palgrave Macmillan.

Brazys, S. and Panke, D. (2017) 'Why do states change positions in the United Nations General Assembly?', *International Political Science Review*, 38(1): 70–84.

Briguglio, L. (1995) 'Small island developing states and their economic vulnerabilities', *World Development*, 23(9):1615–32.

Briguglio, L., Cordina, G., Farrugia, N., and Vella, S. (2009) 'Economic vulnerability and resilience: concepts and measurements', *Oxford Development Studies*, 37(3): 229–47.

Brisk, W.J. (1969) *The Dilemma of a Ministate: Anguilla*, Columbia: Institute of International Studies, University of South Carolina.

Browning, C.S. (2006) 'Small, smart and salient? Rethinking identity in the small states literature', *Cambridge Review of International Affairs*, 19(4): 669–84.

Buchanan, A. and Keohane, R.O. (2006) 'The legitimacy of global governance institutions', *Ethics & International Affairs*, 20(4): 405–37.

Bueger, C. and Wivel, A. (2018) 'How do small island states maximise influence?', *Journal of the Indian Ocean Region*, 14(92): 170–88.

Burci, G.L. (2005) 'Institutional adaptation without reform: WHO and the challenges of globalization', *International Organizations Law Review*, 2(2): 437–43.

Burci, G.L. and Vignes, C-H. (2004) *World Health Organization*, The Hague: Kluwer Law International.

Byron, J. (1999) 'Microstates in a macro-world: federalism, governance and viability in the Eastern Caribbean', *Social and Economic Studies* 48(4): 251–86.

Calliari, E. (2016) 'Loss and damage: a critical discourse analysis of parties' positions in climate change negotiations', *Journal of Risk Research*, 21(6): 725–47.

Camdessus, M. (2000) *The IMF and Human Development: A Dialogue with Civil Society*, Washington, DC: International Monetary Fund.

Campling, L. and Rosalie, M. (2006) 'Sustaining social development in a small island developing state? The case of Seychelles', *Sustainable Development*, 14(2): 115–25.

Carter, G. (2015) 'Establishing a Pacific voice in the climate change negotiations', in G. Fry and S. Tarte (eds) *The New Pacific Diplomacy*, Acton, ACT: ANU Press, pp 205–22.

Carter, G. (2020a) 'Small islands states' diplomatic strategic partnerships in climate negotiations', *New Zealand International Review*, 45(4): 21–5.

Carter, G. (2020b) 'Pacific Island states and 30 years of global climate change negotiations', in C. Klöck et al (eds) *Coalitions in the Climate Change Negotiations*, Routledge, pp 74–90.

Chan, N. (2018) '"Large ocean states": sovereignty, small islands, and marine protected areas in global oceans governance', *Global Governance: A Review of Multilateralism and International Organizations*, 24(4): 537–55.

Chasek, P.S. (2005) 'Margins of power: coalition building and coalition maintenance of the South Pacific Island States and the Alliance of Small Island States', *Review of European, Comparative & International Environmental Law*, 14(2): 125–37.

Chong, A. and Maass, M. (2010) 'Introduction: the foreign policy power of small states', *Cambridge Review of International Affairs*, 23(3): 381–2.

Chorev, N. (2012) *The World Health Organization between North and South*, Ithaca: Cornell University Press.

Chowdhury, I. A. (2012) 'Small states in UN system: constraints, concerns, and contributions', Institute of South Asian Studies (ISAS) Working Paper No 160.

Claude, I.L. (1956) *Swords into Ploughshares: The Problems and Progress of International Organization*, New York: Random House.

Commonwealth Advisory Group (1997) *A Future for Small States: Overcoming Vulnerability*, London: Commonwealth Secretariat.

Commonwealth Consultative Group (1985), *Vulnerability: Small States in the Global Society*, London: Commonwealth Secretariat.

Commonwealth Secretariat and World Bank (2000) *Small States: Meeting Challenges in the Global Economy*, Washington, DC: World Bank.

Connell, J. (2013) *Islands at Risk?: Environments, Economies and Contemporary Change*, Cheltenham: Edward Elgar.

Cooper, A.F. (2009) 'Confronting vulnerability through resilient diplomacy', in A.F. Cooper and T.M. Shaw (eds) *The Diplomacies of Small States*, London: Palgrave Macmillan, pp 207–18.

Cooper, A.F. and Shaw, T.M. (eds) (2009) *Diplomacies of Small States*, London: Palgrave Macmillan.

Corbett, J. (2015) *Being Political Leadership and Democracy in the Pacific Islands*, Hawaii: University of Hawaii Press.

Corbett, J. and Connell, J. (2015) 'All the world is a stage: global governance, human resources, and the "problem" of smallness', *The Pacific Review*, 28(3): 435–59.

Corbett, J. and Veenendaal, W. (2018) *Democracy in Small States*, Oxford: Oxford University Press.

Corbett, J., Xu, Y.-C., and Weller, P. (2018) 'Climate change and the active participation of small states in international organisations', *The Round Table*, 107(1): 103–5.

Corbett, J., Xu, Y.-C., and Weller, P. (2018) 'Small states and the throughput legitimacy of international organizations', *Cambridge Journal of International Affairs*, 31(2): 183–202.

Corbett, J., Xu, Y.-C., and Weller, P. (2019) 'Norm entrepreneurship and diffusion "from below" in international organisations: how the competent performance of vulnerability generates benefits for small states', *Review of International Studies*, 45(4): 647–68.

Corbett, J., Ruwet, M., Xu, Y.C., and Weller, P. (2020) 'Climate governance, policy entrepreneurs and small states: explaining policy change at the International Maritime Organisation', *Environmental Politics*, 29(5): 825–44.

Cox-Alomar, R. (2003) 'Britain's withdrawal from the Eastern Caribbean 1965–67: a reappraisal', *The Journal of Imperial and Commonwealth History*, 31(3): 74–106.

Crandall, M. and Sulg, M.-L. (2020) 'Small states "thinking big" in a multiplex world: Estonia's foreign policy', *Small States & Territories*, 3(2): 397–412.

Dahl, R. (1999) 'Can international organizations be democratic? A skeptic's view', in I. Shapiro and C. Hacker-Cordon (eds) *Democracy's Edges*, Cambridge: Cambridge University Press, pp 19–36.

de Águeda Corneloup, I. and Mol, A.P.J. (2014) 'Small island developing states and international climate change negotiations: the power of moral "leadership"', *International Environmental Agreements: Politics, Law and Economics*, 14(3): 281–97.

de Brum, T. (2014) 'Climate diplomacy: a perspective from the Marshall Islands' [online]. Available from: https://www.climate-diplomacy.org/news/climate-diplomacy-%E2%80%93-perspective-marshall-islands.

de Carvalho, B. and I. Neumann, B. (eds) (2015), *Small States and Status Seeking: Norway's Quest for International Standing*, New York: Routledge.

de Rato, R. (2006) 'The IMF view on IMF reform', in E.M. Truman (ed) *Reforming the IMF for the 21st Century*, Washington, DC: Institute for International Economies, pp 127–32.

de Vries, M.G. (1976) *The International Monetary Fund, 1966–71: The System under Stress*, Washington, DC: IMF.

de Vries, M.G. (1985) *The International Monetary Fund, 1972–1978: Cooperation on Trial*, Washington, DC: IMF.

Deitelhoff, N. and Wallbott, L. (2012) 'Beyond soft balancing: small states and coalition-building in the ICC and climate negotiations', *Cambridge Review of International Affairs*, 25(3): 345–66.

Demas, W.G. (1965) *The Economics of Development in Small Countries: With Special Reference to the Caribbean*, Montreal: McGill-Queen's Press-MQUP.

Dommen, E. and Hein, P. (eds) (1985) *States, Microstates, and Islands*, London: Routledge.

Doner, R.F. and Schneider, B.R. (2016) 'The middle-income trap: more politics than economics', *World Politics*, 68(4): 608–44.

Dornan, M. and Pryke, J. (2017) 'Foreign aid to the pacific: trends and developments in the twenty-first century', *Asia & the Pacific Policy Studies*, 4(3): 386–404.

Doumenge, F. (1983) 'Viability of small island states' [online], TB/B/950, UNCTAD. Available from: https://documents-dds-ny.un.org/doc/UNDOC/GEN/GL9/913/32/PDF/GL991332.pdf?OpenElement

Drezner, D.W. (2008) *All Politics is Global: Explaining International Regulatory Regimes*, Princeton, NJ: Princeton University Press.

Dugal, M. (2020) 'Special and differential treatment in fisheries subsidies negotiations: priorities for Pacific SIDS', *The Commonwealth Trade Hot Topics*, 158: 1–10.

Eagleton-Pierce, M. (2013) *Symbolic Power in the World Trade Organisation*, Oxford: Oxford University Press.

Easterly, W. and Kraay, A. (2000) 'Small states, small problems? Income, growth, and volatility in small states', *World Development*, 28(11): 2013–27.

Easton, D. (1965) *A Systems Analysis of Political Life*, New York: John Wiley.

Eckstein, H. (1975) 'Case studies and theory in political science', in F.I. Greenstein and N.W. Polsby (eds) *Handbook of Political Science, Vol 7 of Political Science: Scope and Theory*, Reading, MA: Addison-Wesley, pp 79–138.

FAO (2020) *World Fisheries and Aquaculture: Sustainability in Action*, Rome: FAO.

Farrell, T. (1980) 'Arthur Lewis and the case for Caribbean industrialisation', *Social and Economic Studies*, 29(4): 52–75.

Favaro, E.M. and Peretz, D. (2008) 'Overview of studies of economic growth', in E.M. Favaro (ed) *Small States, Smart Solutions: Improving Connectivity and Increasing the Effectiveness of Public Services*, Washington, DC: The World Bank, pp 265–80.

Finnemore, M. (1996) 'Norms, culture, and world politics: insights from sociology's institutionalism', *International Organization*, 50(2): 325–47.

Finnemore, M. and Sikkink, K. (1998) 'International norm dynamics and political change', *International Organization*, 52(4): 887–917.

Forsyth, M. and Farran, S. (2015) *Weaving Intellectual Property Rights into Small Developing Island States*, Cambridge: Intersentia.

Fox, A.B. (1959) *The Power of Small States: Diplomacy in World War II*, Chicago: University of Chicago Press.

Fritz-Krockow, B. and Ramlogan, P. (eds) (2007) *International Monetary Fund Handbook: Its Functions, Policies and Operations*, Washington, DC: IMF.

Fry, G. (2019) *Framing the Islands: Power and Diplomatic Agency in Pacific Regionalism*, Acton, ACT: ANU Press.

Fry, G. and Tarte, S. (2015) *The New Pacific Diplomacy*, Acton, ACT: ANU Press.

Fry, I. (2005) 'Small island developing states: becalmed in a sea of soft law', *Review of European, Comparative & International Environmental Law*, 14(2): 89–99.

Fry, I. (2016) 'The Paris Agreement: an insider's perspective – the role of Small Island Developing States', *Environmental Policy and Law*, 46(2): 105–8.

Gay, D. (2005) 'Vanuatu's suspended accession bid: second thoughts?', in P. Gallagher, P. Low, and A.L. Stoler (eds) *Managing the Challenges of WTO Participation: 45 Case Studies*, Cambridge: Cambridge University Press, pp 590–606.

Gayoom, M.A. (1987) President of the Republic of the Maldives, Maumoon Abdul Gayoom, 'Address to the 42nd session of the UN General Assembly on the issues of environment and development', New York, 19 October.

Gelpi, C. (2010) *The Power of Legitimacy: Assessing the Role of Norms in Crisis Bargaining*, Princeton, NJ: Princeton University Press.

Gerring, J. (2012) 'Mere description', *British Journal of Political Science*, 42(4): 721–46.

Getachew, A. (2019) *Worldmaking After Empire: The Rise and Fall of Self-Determination*, Princeton, NJ: Princeton University Press.

Gibbs, M. (2017) 'The tax-free shipping company that took control of a country's UN mission', Climate Change News [online]. Available from: https://www.climatechangenews.com/2017/07/06/tax-free-shipping-company-took-control-countrys-un-mission/

Gilbert, C.L. and Vines, D. (eds) (2000) *The World Bank: Structure and Policies*, Cambridge: Cambridge University Press.

Gill, I.S. and Pugatch, T. (2005) *At the Frontlines of Development: Reflections from the World Bank*, Washington, DC: The World Bank.

Goldin, I. (2013) *Divided Nations: Why Global Governance is Failing, and What We Can Do About It*, Oxford: Oxford University Press.

Goodhart, M. (2007) 'Europe's democratic deficits through the looking glass: the European Union as a challenge for democracy', *Perspectives on Politics*, 5(3): 567–84.

Goodhart, M. and Taninchev, S.B. (2011) 'The new sovereigntist challenge for global governance: democracy without sovereignty', *International Studies Quarterly*, 55(4): 1047–68.

Goulding, N. (2015) 'Marshalling a Pacific response to climate change', in G. Fry and S. Tarte (eds) *The New Pacific Diplomacy*, Acton, ACT: ANU Press, pp 191–204.

Green, J.F. (2018) 'Transnational delegation in global environmental governance: when do non-state actors govern?', *Regulation and Governance*, 12(2): 263–76.

Greenpeace (2015) 'Why do the Marshall Islands serve the oil companies who drown us?', Greenpeace [online]. Available from: https://www. greenpeace.org.au/blog/marshall-island-oil-companies

Grøn, C.H. and Wivel, A. (2011) 'Maximizing influence in the European Union after the Lisbon Treaty: from small state policy to smart state strategy', *Journal of European Integration*, 33(5): 523–39.

Gronau, J. and Schmidtke, H. (2016) 'The quest for legitimacy in world politics: international institutions' legitimation strategies', *Review of International Studies*, 42(3): 535.

Grote, J. (2010) 'The changing tides of small island states discourse: a historical overview of the appearance of small island states in the international arena', *Verfassung und Recht in Übersee/Law and Politics in Africa, Asia and Latin America*, 43(2): 164–91.

Grynberg, R. and Joy, R.M. (2006) 'The accession of Vanuatu to the WTO: lessons for the multilateral trading system', in R. Grynberg (ed) *WTO at the Margins: Small States and the Multilateral Trading System*, Cambridge: Cambridge University Press, pp 693–714.

Gurry, F. (2013) 'Challenges for international organizations and multilateralism: Lakshman Kadirgamar memorial oration 2013' [online]. Available from: https://www.wipo.int/about-wipo/en/dg_gurry/speeches/dg_colombo_2013.html

Guthunz, U. and von Krosigk, F. (1996) 'Tourism development in small island states: from MIRAB to TouRAB?', in L. Briguglio, B. Archer, J. Jafari, and G. Wall (eds) *Sustainable Tourism in Islands and Small States: Issues and Policies*, London: Pinter, pp 18–35.

Guzman, A. (2013) 'International organisations and the Frankenstein problem', *The European Journal of International Law*, 24(4): 999–1025.

Hampton, M.P. and Christensen, J. (2002) 'Offshore pariahs? Small island economies, tax havens, and the re-configuration of global finance', *World Development*, 30(9): 1657–73.

Harbinson, S. (2009) 'The Doha round: "death-defying agenda" or "don't do it again"', ECIPE Working Paper, No 10/2009.

Harbinson, S. (2015) 'The World Trade Organisation as an institution', in P. Weller and Y.-C. Xu (eds), *The Politics of International Organizations*, New York: Routledge, pp 17–47.

Hawkins, D.G, Lake, D.A., Nielson, D.L., and Tierney, M.J. (eds) (2006) *Delegation and Agency in International Organisations*, Cambridge: Cambridge University Press.

Hay, C. (2014) 'Neither real nor fictitious but "as if real"? A political ontology of the state', *The British Journal of Sociology*, 65(3): 459–80.

Hayer, S. (2016) *Decision-Making Processes of ICAO and IMO in Respect of Environmental Regulations*, Brussels: European Parliament.

Heron, T. and Murray-Evans, P. (2016) 'Limits to market power: strategic discourse and institutional path dependence in the EU–ACP economic partnership agreements', *European Journal of International Relations*, 3(2): 341–64.

Hey, J.A.K. (ed) (2003) *Small States in World Politics: Explaining Foreign Policy Behavior*, Boulder: Lynne Reimer.

Houel, F.C. (2017) 'Promoting universality of human rights in Geneva: participation of LDCs/SIDS in the work of the Human Rights Council', Universal Rights Group [online]. Available from: http://www.universal-rights.org/blog/promoting- universality-human-rights-geneva-participation-ldcssids-work-human-rights-council/

Hurd, I. (2008) *After Anarchy: Legitimacy and Power in the United Nations Security Council*, Princeton, NJ: Princeton University Press.

IEG World Bank (2006), *Small States: Making the Most of Development. A Synthesis of World Bank Evaluation Findings*, Washington, DC: The World Bank.

IEG World Bank (2011) *Trust Fund Support for Development: An Evaluation of the World Bank's Trust Fund Portfolio*, Washington, DC: The World Bank.

IEG World Bank (2016) *World Bank Group Engagement in Small States: Taking Stock*. Operations Policy and Country Services, September 8, Washington, DC: The World Bank.

IEG World Bank (2017) 'Completion and learning reviews for the Pacific Island countries' [online]. Available from: https://ieg.worldbankgroup.org/sites/default/files/Data/reports/clr_pacificislands_03102017.pdf

Ikenberry, J.G. (2003) 'Is American multilateralism in decline?', *Perspectives on Politics*, 1(3): 533–50.

IMF (1996) 'Annual report of the executive board for the financial year ended April 30, 1996', September, Washington, DC.

IMF (2013) 'Macroeconomic issues in small states and implications for fund management', Policy Papers, 20 February.

IMF (2018) '2017 staff guidance note on the Fund's engagement with small developing states', 26 January.

IMO (2015) *Report of the Marine Environment Protection Committee on its Sixty-eighth Session*, London: IMO.

IMO (2017) *Financial Statements*, London: IMO.

IMO (2018) 'Marine Environment Protection Committee (MEPC), 72nd session, 9–13 April 2018' [online]. Available from: https://imo.org/en/MediaCentre/MeetingSummaries/Pages/MEPC-72nd-session.aspx

Ince, B. (1976) 'The administration of foreign affairs in a very small developing country: the case of Trinidad and Tobago', in V.A. Lewis (ed) *Size, Self-determination and International Relations: The Caribbean*, Mona, Jamaica: Institute for Social and Economic Research, University of the West Indies, pp 310–34.

Independent Review Report (2012) 'The Pacific Facility III Trust Fund (PF3)' [online]. Available from: https://www.dfat.gov.au/sites/default/files/pacific-facility-iii-trust-fund-independent-review.pdf

Influence Map (2017) 'Corporate capture of the International Maritime Organisation' [online]. Available from: https://influencemap.org/site/data/000/302/Shipping_Report_October_2017.pdf

Ingebritsen, C. (2002) 'Norm entrepreneurs: Scandinavia's role in world politics', *Cooperation and Conflict*, 37(1): 11–23.

ISWG-GHG (2017) *Development of Draft Text for Inclusion in the Initial IMO GHG Strategy: Text Proposed for a Vision and Level of Ambition. ISWG-GHG 2/3*, London: IMO.

Iusmen, I. and Boswell, J. (2017) 'The dilemmas of pursuing "throughput legitimacy" through participatory mechanisms', *West European Politics*, 40(2): 459–78.

Jackson, R.H. (1993) *Quasi-states: Sovereignty, International Relations and the Third World* (Vol 12), Cambridge: Cambridge University Press.

Jackson, S. (2012) 'Small states and compliance bargaining in the WTO: an analysis of the Antigua–US Gambling Services Case', *Cambridge Review of International Affairs*, 25(3): 367–85.

James, H. (1996) *International Monetary Cooperation Since Bretton Woods*, Oxford: Oxford University Press.

Jaschik, K. (2014) 'Small states and international politics: climate change, the Maldives and Tuvalu', *International Politics*, 51(2): 272–93.

Jonah, J.O.C and Hill, A.S. (2018) 'The secretariat: independence and reform', in T.G. Weiss and S. Daws (eds) *The Oxford Handbook on the United Nations* (2nd edn), Oxford: Oxford University Press, pp 212–28.

Jonsen, A.R. and Toulmin, S. (1988) *The Abuse of Casuistry: A History of Moral Reasoning*, Berkeley: University of California Press.

Jourde, C. (2007) 'The international relations of small neoauthoritarian states: Islamism, warlordism, and the framing of stability', *International Studies Quarterly*, 51(2): 481–503.

Kahler, M. (2006) 'Internal governance and IMF performance', in E. Truman (ed) *Reforming the IMF for the 21st Century*, Washington, DC: Institute for International Economics, pp 257–70.

Kahler, M. (2008) 'Aid and state building', workshop on economic aid policy and state building, CUNY, Graduate Centre.

Karim, M.S. (2015) *Prevention of Pollution of the Marine Environment from Vessels: The Potential and Limits of the International Maritime Organisation*, New York: Springer.

Katzenstein, P.J. (1985) *Small States in World Markets: Industrial Policy in Europe*, Ithaca: Cornell University Press.

Kelman, I. (2020) 'Islands of vulnerability and resilience: manufactured stereotypes?', *Area*, 52(1): 6–13.

Keohane, R.O. (1969) 'Lilliputians' dilemmas', *International Organisation*, 23(2): 291–310.

Keohane, R.O. (1971) 'The big influence of small states', *Foreign Policy*, 2: 161–82.

Keohane, R.O. and Nye, J.S. (2001) 'The club model of multilateral cooperation and problems of democratic legitimacy', in R. Porter, P. Sauve, A. Subramanian, and A.B. Zampetti (eds) *Efficiency, Equity and Legitimacy*, Washington, DC: Brookings Institute Press, pp 264–94.

King, D. and Tennant, D. (eds) (2014) *Debt and Development in Small Island Developing States*, New York: Palgrave Macmillan.

King, E. (2016) 'Paris "High Ambition Coalition" to tackle unfinished business: Climate Home News' [online]. Available from: http://www.climatechangenews.com/2016/07/22/paris-high-ambition-coalition-to-tackle-unfinished-business/

Kingdon, J. and Thurber, J. (1984) *Agendas, Alternatives, and Public Policies*, Boston: Little, Brown.

Kleine, M. (2013) 'Trading control: national fiefdoms in international organisations', *International Theory*, 5(3): 321–46.

Koppell, J.G.S. (2008) 'Global governance organizations: legitimacy and authority in conflict', *Journal of Public Administration Research and Theory*, 18(2): 177–203.

Kott, S. and Droux, J. (2013) *Globalising Social Rights*, London: Palgrave Macmillan.

Krasner, S.D. (ed) (1983) *International Regimes*, Ithaca: Cornell University Press.

Krasner S.D. (1985) *Structural Conflict*, Berkeley: University of California Press.

Krasner, S.D. (1999) *Sovereignty: Organized Hypocrisy*, Princeton, NJ: Princeton University Press.

Krishnamurthi, S. (2018) 'Tukuitonga goes into battle on behalf of Pacific for WHO position' [online]. Available from: https://asiapacificreport.nz/2018/10/08/tukuitonga-goes-into-battle-on-behalf-of-pacific-for-who-position/

Kronsell, A. (2002) 'Can small states influence EU norms?: insights from Sweden's participation in the field of environmental politics', *Scandinavian Studies*, 74(3): 287–304.

Kuyper, J.W. (2014) 'Global democratization and international regime complexity', *European Journal of International Relations*, 20(3): 620–46.

Lake, D. and O'Mahony, A. (2004) 'The incredible shrinking state: explaining change in the territorial size of countries', *Journal of Conflict Resolution*, 48(5): 699–722.

Lake, D.A., Martin, L., and Risse, T. (2021) 'Challenges to the liberal order: reflections on international organization', *International Organization*, 75(2): 225–7.

Laker, J.A. (2014) *African Participation in the World Trade Organization*, Leiden: Martinus Nijhoff.

Lamy, P. (2013) *The Geneva Consensus: Making Trade Work for All*, Cambridge: Cambridge University Press.

Larmour, P. (2005) *Foreign Flowers: Institutional Transfer and Good Governance in the Pacific Islands*, Honolulu: University of Hawaii.

Laurent, E. (2011) 'Priorities for small states in global trade governance', in C. Deere Birkbeck (ed) *Making Global Trade Governance Work for Development*, Cambridge: Cambridge University Press, pp 204–30.

Laurent, E. (2016) 'Harnessing the Caribbean's external trade partnerships: opportunities and challenges' [online]. Available from: https://www.oecd-ilibrary.org/content/paper/4a01dfb8-en

Lawson, S. (2016) 'Regionalism, sub-regionalism and the politics of identity in Oceania', *The Pacific Review*, 29(3): 387–409.

Lee, D. (2013) 'African agency in global trade governance', in W. Brown and S. Harman (eds) *African Agency in International Politics*, London: Routledge, pp 34–48.

Lenz, T. and Viola, L.A. (2017) 'Legitimacy and institutional change in international organisations: a cognitive approach', *Review of International Studies*, 43(5): 939–61.

Lewis, P. (2002) *Surviving Small Size: Regional Integration in Caribbean Ministates*, Kingston: University of West Indies Press.

Lewis, P., Gilbert-Roberts, T.A., and Byron, J. (eds) (2017) *Pan-Caribbean Integration: Beyond CARICOM*, New York: Routledge.

Lewis, V. (2009) 'Studying small states over the 20th and 21st centuries', in A.F. Cooper and T.M. Shaw (eds) *The Diplomacy of Small States*, Hampshire: Palgrave Macmillan, pp vii–xv.

Lewis, W.A. (1950) 'The industrialisation of the British West Indies', *Caribbean Economic Review*, 2(1): 1–61.

Lindsay, C. (2019) 'Norm rejection: why small states fail to secure special treatment in global trade politics', *Small States & Territories*, 2(1): 105–24.

Linn, J. (2018) 'Recent threat to multilateralism', *Global Journal of Emerging Market Economies*, 9(1–3): 86–113.

Long, T. (2017a) 'Small states, great power', *International Studies Review*, 19(2): 185–205.

Long, T. (2017b) 'It's not the size, it's the relationship', *International Politics*, 54(2): 144–60.

Long, T. (2022) *A Small State's Guide to Influence in World Politics* (forthcoming).

Lowndes, V. and Roberts, M. (2013) *Why Institutions Matter: The New Institutionalism in Political Science*, London: Macmillan International Higher Education.

Lupel, A. and Malksoo, L. (2019) 'A necessary voice: small states, international law and the UN Security Council', International Peace Institute, April.

Lynch, C. (2013) *Interpreting International Politics*, New York: Routledge.

Lyne, M.M., Nielson, D.L., and Tierney, M.J. (2009) 'Controlling coalitions: social lending at the multilateral development banks', *The Review of International Organizations*, 4(4): 407–33.

Maass, M. (2009) 'The elusive definition of the small state', *International Politics*, 46(1): 65–83.

Maass, M. (2017) *Small States in World Politics*, Manchester: Manchester University Press.

Maggetti, M. and Gilardi, F. (2016) 'Problems (and solutions) in the measurement of policy diffusion mechanisms', *Journal of Public Policy* 36(1): 87–107.

Mallaby, S. (2004) *The World's Banker*, New York: Penguin Books.

Manoa, F. (2015) 'The new Pacific diplomacy at the United Nations: the rise of the PSIDS', *The New Pacific Diplomacy*, 89–98.

Mansfield, E.D. and Pevehouse, J.C. (2006) 'Democratization and international organizations', *International Organization*, 60(1): 137–67.

Marke, G.V. (2015) 'Marshall Islands berates "shameful" IMO as it ignores climate change threat', *The Loadstar* [online]. Available from: https://theloadstar.co.uk/marshall-islands-berates-shameful-imo-as-it-ignores-climate-change-threat/

Marsh, D. and Sharman, J.C. (2009) 'Policy diffusion and policy transfer', *Policy Studies*, 30(3): 269–88.

Marshall, K. (2008) *The World Bank: from Reconstruction to Development to Equity*, London: Routledge.

Martin, L.L. and Simmons, B.A. (1998) 'Theories and empirical studies of international institutions', *International Organization*, 52(3): 729–57.

Mathiesen, K. (2015) 'Marshall Islands may stop registering oil rigs, says foreign minister', *The Guardian* [online]. Available from: https://www.theguardian.com/environment/2015/may/13/marshall-islands-may-stop-registering-oil-rigs-in-future-says-foreign-minister

Mawby, S. (2012) *Ordering Independence: The End of Empire in the Anglophone Caribbean, 1947–69*, Hampshire: Palgrave Macmillan.

McElroy, J.L. (2006) 'Small island tourist economies across the life cycle', *Asia Pacific Viewpoint*, 47(1): 61–77.

McElroy, J.L. and Morris, L. (2002) 'African island development experiences: a cluster of models', *Bank of Valletta Review*, 26: 38–57.

McElroy, J.L. and Parry, C.E. (2010) 'The characteristics of small island tourist economies', *Tourism and Hospitality Research*, 10(4): 315–28.

MEPC (2015) 'Reduction of GHG emissions from ships: setting a reduction target and agreeing associated measures for international shipping', MEPC 68/5/1, London: IMO.

Mohamed, A.N. (2002) 'The diplomacy of micro-states', *Discussion Papers in Diplomacy*, Den Haag: Netherlands Institute of International Relations.

Moore, A. (2010) 'Climate changing small islands: considering social science and the production of island vulnerability and opportunity', *Environment and Society*, 1(1): 116–31.

Moore, M.K. (2003) *A World Without Walls: Freedom, Development, Free Trade and Global Governance*, Cambridge: Cambridge University Press.

Morgan, W. (2018) 'Much lost, little gained? Contemporary trade agreements in the Pacific Islands', *The Journal of Pacific History*, 53(3): 268–86.

Morse, J.C. and Keohane, R.O. (2014) 'Contested multilateralism', *Review of International Organisations*, 9: 385–412.

Mountford, A. (2008) 'The formal governance structure of the International Monetary Fund', IEO Background Paper (BP/08/01), Washington, DC: Independent Evaluation Office of the International Monetary Fund, (IEO).

Mountz, A. (2011) 'The enforcement archipelago: detention, haunting, and asylum on islands', *Political Geography*, 30(3): 118–28.

Neumann, I.B. and Gstöhl, S. (2006) 'Introduction: Lilliputians in Gulliver's world', in J. Beyer, I. Neumann, and S. Gstohl (eds) *Small States in International Relations*, Seattle, WA: Washington University Press, pp 3–36.

Newman, A.L. (2010) 'International organisation control under conditions of dual delegation', in D.D. Avant, M. Finnemore, and S.K. Sell (eds), *Who Governs the Globe?*, Cambridge: Cambridge University Press, pp 131–52.

Niezen, R. and Sapignoli, M. (2017) 'Introduction', in R. Niezen and M. Sapignoli (eds) *Palace of Hope*, Cambridge: Cambridge University Press, pp 1–30.

Oates, J.G. (2017) 'The fourth face of legitimacy: constituent power and the constitutional legitimacy of international institutions', *Review of International Studies*, 43(2): 199–220.

Oberst, A. and McElroy, J.L. (2007) 'Contrasting socio-economic and demographic profiles of two, small island, economic species: MIRAB versus PROFIT/SITE', *Island Studies Journal*, 2(2): 163–76.

Odell, J.S. (2010) 'Negotiating from weakness in international trade', *Journal of World Trade*, 44(3): 545–66.

Olson, M. and Zeckhauser, R. (1966) 'An economic theory of alliances', *The Review of Economics and Statistics*, 48(3): 266–79.

Ourbak, T. and Magnan, A.K. (2018) 'The Paris Agreement and climate change negotiations: small islands, big players', *Regional Environmental Change*, 18(8): 2201–7.

Pacific Institute of Public Policy (2011) 'Joining the world's economic parliament: Vanuatu's accession package explained', Port Villa, Vanuatu.

Pacific Islands Forum Secretariat (2013), 'Forty-fourth pacific islands forum: forum communiqué', Majuro: Republic of the Marshall Islands.

Panke, D. (2010) *Small States in the European Union: Coping with Structural Disadvantages*, Surrey: Ashgate.

Panke, D. (2012a) 'Dwarfs in international negotiations: how small states make their voices heard', *Cambridge Review of International Affairs*, 25(3): 313–28.

Panke, D. (2012b) 'Small states in multilateral negotiations: what have we learned?', *Cambridge Review of International Affairs*, 25(3): 387–98.

Panke, D. (2013) *Unequal Actors in Equalising Institutions: Negotiations in the United Nations General Assembly*, New York: Springer.

Panke, D. (2017) 'Studying small states in international security affairs: a quantitative analysis', *Cambridge Review of International Affairs*, 30(2–3): 235–55.

Panke, D. (2020) 'Regional cooperation through the lenses of states: why do states nurture regional integration?', *The Review of International Organizations*, 15(2): 475–504.

Parboni, R. (1981) *The Dollar & its Rivals*, London: Verso Books.

Paus, E. (2012) 'Confronting the middle-income trap: insights from small latecomers', *Studies in Comparative International Development*, 47(2): 115–38.

Payne, A. (2008) *The Political History of CARICOM*, Kingston: Ian Randle.

Petzold, J. and Magnan, A.K. (2019) 'Climate change: thinking small islands beyond Small Island Developing States (SIDS)', *Climatic Change*, 152(1): 145–65.

PIDF (2015) 'Suva declaration on climate change', Suva, Fiji [online]. Available from: http://pacificidf.org/wp-content/uploads/2016/02/ecopy-Declaration.pdf

PIDF (2016) 'Consultation on shipping emissions paper for submission to MEPC 69', Briefing to Pacific Small Islands States Delegations, 1.

Poirine, B. (1998) 'Should we hate or love MIRAB?', *The Contemporary Pacific*, 10(1): 65–105.

Porter, R.B, Sauvé, P., Subramanian, A., and Zampetti, A.B. (eds) (2001) *Efficiency, Equity and Legitimacy: The Multilateral Trading System at the Millennium*, Washington, DC: Brookings Institute Press.

Pouliot, V. (2010) *International Security in Practice: The Politics of NATO-Russia Diplomacy*, Cambridge: Cambridge University Press.

Pouliot, V. (2014) 'Practice tracing', in A. Bennett, and J.T. Checkel (eds) *Process Tracing: From Analytic Metaphor to Best Practices*, Cambridge: Cambridge University Press, pp 237–59.

Razvani, D.A. (2014) *Surpassing the Sovereign State: The Wealth, Self-rule, and Security Advantages of Partially Independent Territories*, Oxford: Oxford University Press.

Reid, G.L. (1974) *The Impact of Very Small Size on International Relations Behavior of Microstates*, London: Sage.

Rhodes, R.A.W. (2011) *Everyday Life in British Government*, Oxford: Oxford University Press.

Sanford, J.E. (2004) 'IDA grants and HIPC debt cancellation', *World Development*, 32(9): 1579–607.

Schields, C. (2018) 'Intimacy and integration', in S. Chauvin, P. Clegg, and B. Cousin (eds) *Euro-Caribbean Societies in the 21st Century: Offshore finance, Local Élites and Contentious Politics*, New York: Routledge, pp 176–89.

Schimmelfennig, F. (2001) 'The community trap: liberal norms, rhetorical action, and the eastern enlargement of the European Union', *International Organization*, 55(1): 47–80.

Schmidt, V.A. (2006) *Democracy in Europe: The EU and National Polities*, Oxford: Oxford University Press.

Schmidt, V.A. (2013) 'Democracy and legitimacy in the European Union revisited: input, output and "throughput"', *Political Studies*, 61(1): 2–22.

Schuhbauer, A., Chuenpagdee, R., Cheung, W., Greer, K., and Sumaila, R.U. (2017) 'How subsidies affect economic viability of small-scale fisheries', *Marine Policy*, 82: 114–21.

Schwartz-Shea, P. and Yanow, D. (2013) *Interpretive Research Design: Concepts and Processes*, New York: Routledge.

Secretary of the Pacific Regional Environment Programme (SPREP) (2012) 'Marshall islands calls on other nations to break "you go first" deadlock at UN climate talks' [online]. Available from: https://www.sprep.org/news/marshall-islands-calls-other-nations-break-you-go-first-deadlock-un-climate-talks

Shakow, A. (2009) 'The role of the International Monetary and Financial Committee in IMF governance', *Background Paper* IOE of IMF, BP/08/03.

Sharman, J.C. (2015) 'War, selection, and micro-states: economic and sociological perspectives on the international system', *European Journal of International Relations*, 21(1): 194–214.

Sharman, J.C. (2017) 'Sovereignty at the extremes: micro-states in world politics', *Political Studies*, 65(3): 559–75.

Shihata, I.F.I. (2000) *The World Bank Legal Papers*, The Hague: Martinus Nijhoff.

SIDS Action Platform (2014) 'SIDS accelerated modalities of action [S.A.M.O.A.] pathway' [online]. Available from: http://www.sids2014.org/index.php?menu=1537

Smed, U.T. and Wivel, A. (2017) 'How do small states influence international counterpiracy policy?' [online]. Available from: http://piracy-studies.org/how-do-small-states-influence-international-counterpiracy-policy/

Smith, T.W., Jalkanen, J.-P., Anderson, B., Corbett, J.J., et al (2015) *Third IMO Greenhouse Gas Study 2014*, London: IMO.

Solomon, R. (1999) *Money on the Move: The Revolution in International Finance since 1980*, Princeton, NJ: Princeton University Press.

Sommerer, T. and Tallberg, J. (2019) 'Diffusion across international organizations: connectivity and convergence', *International Organization*, 73(2): 399–433.

Standing, G. (2010) 'International Labour Organization', *New Political Economy*, 15(2): 307–18.

Súilleabháin, A.Ó. (2014) *Small States at the United Nations: Diverse Perspectives, Shared Opportunities*, New York: International Peace Institute.

Sutton, P. (2011) 'The concept of small states in the international political economy', *The Round Table*, 100(413): 141–53.

Tallberg, J. and Zürn, M. (2019) 'The legitimacy and legitimation of international organizations: introduction and framework', *The Review of International Organizations*, 14: 581–606.

Tallberg, J., Sommerer, T., Squatrito, T., and Jonsson, C. (eds) (2013) *The Opening up of International Organizations*, Cambridge: Cambridge University Press.

The Bretton Woods Committee (2019) *Revitalising the Spirit of Bretton Woods* [online]. Available from: https://www.brettonwoods.org/BW75/compendium-release

Theys, S. and Rietig, K. (2020) 'The influence of small states: how Bhutan succeeds in influencing global sustainability governance', *International Affairs*, 96(6): 1603–22.

Thorhallsson, B. (2000) *The Role of Small States in the European Union*, New York: Routledge.

Thorhallsson, B. (2010) 'The corporatist model and its value in understanding small European states in the neo-liberal world of the twenty-first century: the case of Iceland', *European Political Science*, 9(3): 375–86.

Thorhallsson, B. (2011) 'Domestic buffer versus external shelter: viability of small states in the new globalised economy', *European Political Science*, 10(3): 324–36.

Thorhallsson, B. (2012) 'Small states in the UN security council: means of influence?', *The Hague Journal of Diplomacy*, 7(2): 135–60.

Thorhallsson, B. (ed) (2018a) *Small States and Shelter Theory: Iceland's External Affairs*, New York: Routledge.

Thorhallsson, B. (2018b) 'Studying small states: a review', *Small States & Territories*, 1(1): 17–34.

Thorhallsson, B. and Wivel, A. (2006) 'Small states in the European Union: what do we know and what would we like to know?', *Cambridge Review of International Affairs*, 19(4) : 651–68.

Tipping, A. (2020) 'Addressing the development dimension of an overcapacity and overfishing subsidy discipline in the WTO fisheries subsidies negotiations', International Institute for Sustainable Development (IIISD) and Global Subsidies Initiative [January].

Towns, A.E. (2010) *Women and States: Norms and Hierarchies in International Society*, Cambridge: Cambridge University Press.

Towns, A.E. (2012) 'Norms and social hierarchies: understanding international policy diffusion from below', *International Organization*, 66(2): 179–209.

Tyler, T.R. (2001) 'A psychological perspective on the legitimacy', in J.T. Jost and B. Major (eds) *The Psychology of Legitimacy: Emerging Perspectives on Ideology, Justice, and Intergroup Relations*, Cambridge: Cambridge University Press, pp 416–36.

Uhlin, A. (2010) 'Democratic legitimacy of transnational actors: mapping out the conceptual terrain', in E. Erman and A. Uhlin (eds) *Legitimacy Beyond the State?*, London: Palgrave Macmillan, pp 16–37.

UMAS (2016) 'An analysis of the MEPC 69 debate on reduction of shipping GHG emissions' [online]. Available from: https://u-mas.co.uk/Latest/Post/325/An-analysis-of-the-MEPC-69-debate-on-reduction-of-shipping-GHG-emissions

UNCED (1992) *Agenda 21: Programme of Action for Sustainable Development, Rio Declaration on Environment and Development*, New York: United Nations.

UNEP (2005) *Reflecting Sustainable Development and Special and Differential Treatment Provisions for Developing Countries in the Context of New WTO Fisheries Subsidies Rules*, Geneva: UNEP.

UNEP (2011) *Fisheries Subsidies, Sustainable Development and the WTO*, Geneva: UNEP.

Uvin, P. (1994) *The International Organisation of Hunger*, London: Kegan Paul.

Vaha, M.E. (2015) 'Drowning under: small island states and the right to exist', *Journal of International Political Theory*, 11(2): 206–23.

van Damme, I. (2020) 'Reflections on the WTO negotiations on prohibiting IUU fishing subsidies', IISD [February].

van Fossen, A. (2007) 'Citizenship for sale: passports of convenience from Pacific island tax havens', *Commonwealth & Comparative Politics*, 45(2): 138–63.

vanGrasstek, C. (2013) *The History and Future of the World Trade Organisation*, Geneva: WTO.

van Houtven, L. (2001) *Governance of the IMF: Decision Making, Institutional Oversight, Transparency, and Accountability*, Washington, DC: IMF.

van Marle, G.(2015) 'Marshall Islands berates "shameful" IMO as it ignores climate change threat', The Loadstar [online]. Available from: https://theloadstar.co.uk/marshall-islands-berates-shameful-imo-as-it-ignores-climate-change-threat/

Vanhala, L. and Hestbaek, C. (2016) 'Framing climate change loss and damage in UNFCCC negotiations', *Global Environmental Politics*, 16(4): 111–29.

Veenendaal, W.P. (2017) 'Analyzing the foreign policy of microstates: the relevance of the international patron-client model', *Foreign Policy Analysis*, 13(3): 561–77.

Veenendaal, W.P. and Corbett, J. (2015) 'Why small states offer important answers to large questions', *Comparative Political Studies*, 48(4): 527–49.

Vital, D. (1967) *The Inequality of States*, Oxford: Clarendon Press.

Vital, D. (1971) *The Survival of Small States: Studies in Small Power/Great Power Conflict*, Oxford: Oxford University Press.

Vleck, W. (2008) *Offshore Finance and Small States*, London: Palgrave Macmillan.

Wagenaar, H. (2011) *Meaning in Action: Interpretation and Dialogue in Policy Analysis*, Armonk: ME Sharpe.

Wallis, J. (2010). '"Friendly islands" in an unfriendly system', *Asia Pacific Viewpoint*, 51(3): 262–77.

Waltz, K.N. (1979) *Theory of International Politics*, Long Grove: Waveland Press.

Weber, M. (2012 [1904]) 'The "objectivity" of knowledge', in H.H. Bruun and S. Whimster (eds), *Max Weber: Collected Methodological Writings*, London: Routledge, pp 100–38.

Weitz, C.H. (1997) *Who Speaks for the Hungry?*, Uppsala: Dag Hammarskjold Foundation.

Wendt, A. (2004) 'The state as person in international theory', *Review of International Studies*, 30(2): 289–316.

Wiener, A. (2008) *The Invisible Constitution of Politics*, Cambridge: Cambridge University Press.

Wiener, A. (2014) *A Theory of Contestation*, New York: Springer.

Wildavsky, A. (1978) *Speaking Truth to Power*, Boston: Little, Brown.

Winham, G.R. (1989) 'The prenegotiation phase of the Uruguay round', *International Journal*, 44(2): 280–303.

Wivel, A. and Crandall, M. (2019) 'Punching above their weight, but why? Explaining Denmark and Estonia in the transatlantic relationship', *Journal of Transatlantic Studies*, 17(3): 392–419.

Wivel, A. and Oest, K.J.N. (2010) 'Security, profit or shadow of the past? Explaining the security strategies of microstates', *Cambridge Review of International Affairs*, 23(3): 429–53.

Wolf, M. (2019) 'Today and tomorrow', *Finance and Development*, 5(2): 5–8.

World Bank (2000) 'Small states: meeting challenges in the global economy', *Report of the Commonwealth Secretariat/World Bank Joint Task Force on Small States* [April].

World Bank (2005) *Evaluation of World Bank Assistance to Pacific Member Countries, 1992–2002*, Washington, DC: The World Bank.

World Bank (2017) *The Sunken Millions Revisited*, Washington, DC: The World Bank.

World Bank (2018) 'Small states: vulnerability and concessional finance', *Operations Policy and Country Services (OPCS)* [online]. Available from: http://pubdocs.worldbank.org/en/339601536162647490/Small-States-Vulnerability-and-Concessional-Finance.pdf

World Health Organization (2016) *Global Strategy on Human Resources for Health: Workforce 2030*, WHO Document Production Services, Geneva: Switzerland.

World Health Organization (2018) 'Noncommunicable disease education manual: a primer for policy-makers and health-care professionals', Manila: WHO Regional Office for the Western Pacific.

World Health Organisation (2019) *Draft General Program of Work 2018–2023: Provide Health, Keep the World Safe, Secure the Vulnerable* [online]. Available from: https://apps.who.int/iris/bitstream/handle/10665/324775/WHO-PRP-18.1-eng.pdf

Wulff, H. (2002) 'Yo-yo field work', *Anthropological Journal of European Cultures*, 11: 117–36.

Xu, Y.-C. and Weller, P. (2004) *The Governance of World Trade*, Cheltenham: Edward Elgar.

Xu, Y.-C. and Weller, P. (2009) *Inside the World Bank*, New York: Palgrave Macmillan.

Xu, Y.-C. and Weller, P. (2018) *The Working World of International Organisations*, Oxford: Oxford University Press.

Yeo, S. (2015) 'The carbon brief interview: Tony de Brum. The carbon brief' [online]. Available from: https://www.carbonbrief.org/the-carbon-brief-interview-tony-de-brum

Zhu, M. (2013) 'Making the most of what you've got: small states in the spotlight', deputy managing director of IMF [1 April].

Zürn, M. (2018) *A Theory of Global Governance: Authority, Legitimacy, and Contestation*, Oxford: Oxford University Press.

Index

References to tables appear in *italic* type.
References to endnotes show both the
page number and the note number (231n3).

members *20–1*, 117–18
and NGOs 54, 55, *56*, 157–8
performance of vulnerability 72, 73, 75
secretariats 49, 50, 132–4

staffing profiles 154

Z
Zhu, M. 43